Critical Theory and the Digital

ABOUT THE SERIES

Critical Theory and Contemporary Society explores the relationship between contemporary society as a complex and highly differentiated phenomenon, on the one hand, and Critical Theory as a correspondingly sophisticated methodology for studying and understanding social and political relations today, on the other. Each volume highlights in distinctive ways why (1) Critical Theory offers the most appropriate concepts for under-standing political movements, socioeconomic conflicts and state institutions in an increasingly global world and (2) why Critical Theory nonetheless needs updating in order to keep pace with the realities of the twenty-first century. The books in the series look at global warming, financial crisis, post–nation state legitimacy, international relations, cinema, terrorism and other issues, applying an interdisciplinary approach, in order to help students and citizens understand the specificity and uniqueness of the current situation.

Series Editor
Darrow Schecter
Reader in the School of History, Art History
and Humanities, University of Sussex, UK

BOOKS IN THE SERIES

Critical Theory and Film: Fabio Vighi, Reader and Co-director of the Žižek Centre for Ideology Critique at Cardiff University, UK

Critical Theory and Contemporary Europe: William Outhwaite, Chair and Professor of Sociology at Newcastle University, UK

Critical Theory, Legal Theory, and the Evolution of Contemporary Society: Hauke Brunkhorst, Professor of Sociology and Head of the Institute of Sociology at the University of Flensburg, Germany

Critical Theory in the Twenty-First Century: Darrow Schecter, Reader in the School of History, Art History and Humanities, University of Sussex, UK

Critical Theory and the Digital: David Berry, Reader in the School of Media, Film and Music, University of Sussex, UK.

Critical Theory and the Contemporary Crisis of Capital: Heiko Feldner, Co-director of the Centre for Ideology Critique and Žižek Studies at Cardiff University, UK

Critical Theory and the Digital

DAVID M. BERRY

Bloomsbury Academic
An imprint of Bloomsbury Publishing Plc

B L O O M S B U R Y
NEW YORK • LONDON • NEW DELHI • SYDNEY

Bloomsbury Academic

An imprint of Bloomsbury Publishing Inc

1385 Broadway	50 Bedford Square
New York	London
NY 10018	WC1B 3DP
USA	UK

www.bloomsbury.com

Bloomsbury is a registered trade mark of Bloomsbury Publishing Plc

First published 2014
Paperback edition first published 2015

ISBN: HB: 978-1-4411-6639-5
PB: 978-1-5013-1096-6
ePDF: 978-1-4411-1830-1
ePUB: 978-1-4411-7360-7

Library of Congress Cataloging-in-Publication Data
Berry, David M. (David Michael)
Critical theory and the digital/David M. Berry.
pages cm – (Critical theory and contemporary society)
Includes bibliographical references and index.
ISBN 978-1-4411-6639-5 (hardback)
1. Information society. 2. Information technology–Social aspects.
3. Digital media–Social aspects. 4. Critical theory. I. Title.
HM851.B474 2014
302.23'1–dc23
2013041512

Typeset by Deanta Global Publishing Services, Chennai, India

Til min familie: Trine, Helene, Henrik Isak og Hedda Emilie

Contents

Acknowledgements

This book has been written in a number of places, and even between places – in a plethora of planes, trains, cafes, airports, offices and libraries. Indeed, it has been created in the very frantic disorientation of computational society that this book argues that critical theory must address today. My appreciation of charging points, free Wi-Fi, 3G/4G networks and access to good coffee has also been suitably heightened. Although I note that Java Café, in St Hanshaugan, Oslo, which shuns all these contrivances for the luxury of singularly great coffee, has been a welcome retreat for providing a space disconnected from the always-on digital world.

I have been helped by friends who have always remained kind and supporting even when difficulties arose. I would like to thank everyone for continued encouragement. I am very grateful to *Forskningsrådet* (the Research Council of Norway) for the *Yggdrasil* Fellowship ref: 211106 which funded my sabbatical in Oslo in 2012, and particularly Stig Jarle Hansen and Mohamed Husein Gaas. I would also like to thank Anders Fagerjord, Knut Lundby and Espen Ytreberg and members of *Institutt for medier og kommunikasjon* (IMK), University of Oslo, for making me feel welcome and included in their research activities. Additionally I would like to thank Yngvil Beyer, Ina Blom and the *Nasjonalbiblioteket*, Norway, for the invitation to contribute to the 'Archive in Motion' workshops. Swansea University was kind enough to grant me sabbatical leave during 2012 which greatly facilitated the writing of this book and I would like to thank Chris Williams and all the staff working in RIAH for their continued support.

This book grew out of an earlier conversation with Darrow Schecter and I remain indebted to him for his kind invitation to explore the subject in a book for the Critical Theory and Contemporary Society series. I would also like to express my gratitude to my editor, Marie-Claire Antoine, formerly at Continuum, for her professionalism and support through the writing process, and Matthew Kopel at Bloomsbury, for patience through the final phases of editing. Additionally I would like to thank my PhD students Dr Faustin Chongombe, Dr Leighton Evans, Mostyn Jones, Sian Rees, Emily Stacey and the students on the MA Digital Media programme for providing stimulating conversation and discussion.

I am grateful to have had the opportunity to present earlier versions of the chapters and ideas in this book to: the PhiSci seminar series, organized by Rani Lill Anjum CauSci (Causation in Science) and the UMB School of Economics and Business; *Institutt for medier og kommunikasjon* (IMK) seminar series, invited by Espen Ytreberg, University of Oslo; Unlike Us conference #2, organized by Geert Lovink, Amsterdam University; Digital Humanities Workshop, organized by Caroline Bassett, University of Sussex; the Archive in Motion workshop, *Nasjonalbiblioteket* organized by Ina Blom, University of Oslo; the University of Bergen and the Digital Culture Research Group organized by Jill Walker Rettberg and Scott Rettberg; Sean Roberts at Rackspace for an enlightening insight into cloud computing; New Aesthetic symposium at the Hirshhorn Museum and Sculpture Garden, Smithsonian, Washington D.C. organized by Melanie Bühler; SETUP, Utrecht, The Netherlands, organized by Daniëlle de Jonge; *Universitat Autònoma de Barcelona*, Barcelona, Spain, organized by Òscar Coromina; Digital Expertise Workshop, organized by Caroline Bassett, Lefteris Zenerian and Aristea Fotopoulou, University of Sussex; Digital Transformations Moot, AHRC, Kings College, University of London invited by Andrew Prescott; *Institutt for Samfunnsforskning*, Oslo, Norway, invited by Kari Steen-Johnsen and Bernard Enjolras; COSTECH laboratory, *Université de Technologie de Compiègne*, Paris, France, invited by Jean-Christophe Plantin; HighWire DTC, Lancaster University, invited by Gordon Blair; Digital Humanities research seminar at Kings College, University of London, invited by the Department of Digital Humanities and Andrew Prescott; The Digital Methods Initiative at the University of Amsterdam, and particularly Richard Rogers, Michael Dieter, Anne Helmond, Caroline Gerlitz and Bernhard Rieder; Centre for Digital Cultures, Leuphana University, Germany, especially, Armin Beverungen, Ned Rossiter and Mercedes Bunz; The Centre for Interdisciplinary Methodologies, University of Warwick, invited by Nathaniel Tkacz; and finally, The Digital Humanities Summer School in Berne, University of Berne, and particularly Enrico Natale.

Finally, I would also like to thank my family, Trine Bjørkmann Berry, and my children Helene, Henrik Isak and Hedda Emilie for continuing to (over) fill my life with non-stop excitement and love.

David Berry
Oslo, July 2013

LONG ago, the mice had a general council to consider what measures they could take to outwit their common enemy, the Cat. Some said this, and some said that; but at last a young mouse got up and said he had a proposal to make, which he thought would meet the case. "You will all agree," said he, "that our chief danger consists in the sly and treacherous manner in which the enemy approaches us. Now, if we could receive some signal of her approach, we could easily escape from her. I venture, therefore, to propose that a small bell be procured, and attached by a ribbon round the neck of the Cat. By this means we should always know when she was about, and could easily retire while she was in the neighbourhood."

This proposal met with general applause, until an old mouse got up and said: "That is all very well, but who is to bell the Cat?" The mice looked at one another and nobody spoke. Then the old mouse said:

"IT IS EASY TO PROPOSE IMPOSSIBLE REMEDIES."

Æsop, (Sixth century B.C.), *Fables*.

1

Introduction

This book is primarily concerned with thinking about the relationship between critical theory and the digital. In particular, I attempt to engage with critical theory to directly address the challenge of computation. As such, the aim is to understand how we can think about computation as part of the social totality and also to provide the means to develop an immanent critique in relation to it. There is still much work to be done in humanities and social sciences to understand and critique the computational, and it is a social phenomenon that is accelerating in its growth and ubiquity, adding to the complexity of theorizing the digital adequately. This book is, therefore, a contribution to *questioning* the digital or what we might call the *computal*, and creating the possibility of thinking in an age when thinking is increasingly being delegated into the machines. As our societies are increasingly becoming computational, and with it the attendant tendency of computational systems to reify all aspects of everyday life, it is crucial that we attend to the mechanization of reification and the dangers presented when these processes crystallize into systems, institutions and consciousness itself. This reified world is 'smart', digital and is increasingly colonized by computationally enhanced networks, objects and subjects.

Indeed, the world is transitioning from analogue, structured in most part by the physicality of destination, to the digital. A new *industrial internet* is emerging, a computational, real-time streaming ecology that is reconfigured in terms of digital flows, fluidities and movement. In the new industrial internet the paradigmatic metaphor I want to use is real-time streaming technologies and the data flows, processual stream-based engines and the computal interfaces that embody them. This is to stop thinking about the digital as something static and object-like and instead consider its 'trajectories'. Here I am thinking about the way in which scripts function to create loops and branches, albeit of a highly complex form, and create a stable 'representation', which we often think of as a digital 'object'. Under the screen surface, however, there is a constant stream of processing, a movement and trajectory, a series of lines that are being followed and computed. Twitter suggests the kind of real-time experiential technology that I am thinking about and the difficulty we have in studying something unfolding in this manner, let alone archiving or researching, without an eye on its processual nature.[1]

This change calls for a critique of computational knowledge and as such a critique of the society producing that knowledge. In other words, the critique of knowledge calls for us to again question the movement of instrumental reason into all aspects of social life. As Schecter argues in relation to the original research questions that drove the Frankfurt School,

> Max Weber's analysis of instrumental reason suggests that the objectively revolutionary aspects of modernity and industrialization is the real possibility of human emancipation from economic scarcity as well as from mythology and irrational belief systems. Yet this revolutionary potential is accompanied by the simultaneous risk of the rise of an increasingly one-dimensional society governed by a form of narrowly strategic reason . . . such reason would be unable to address questions of ethics or aesthetics, and would be empowered, at the same time, to undermine the authority of political decision-making bodies to regulate economic processes. (Schecter 2007: 71)

This growth in instrumental reason, as rationalization, facilitates the reduction of thinking to a form of reason wedded to economic necessity, and as the Frankfurt School would argue, the domination of nature. The move towards an informationalization of society, particularly in the over-developed economies in the twenty-first century, has intensified this process, with the growth of a computational world overlaying the physical world, and which, to a greater extent, has been delegated with the logic of rationalization and instrumental reason. This also signals a move away from a previous 'digital' era that was tangential to the capitalist economy, but nonetheless facilitated many economic growth regimes associated with it, such as ICT, finance-led and so forth. Instead we are entering a post-digital world in which the digital has become completely bound up with and constitutive of everyday life and the so-called digital economy.

Nonetheless, people have become accustomed to living in the previous 'historical', digital world that was, actually, only partially computational, and in many ways wasn't computational at all. A result of this is that the older notion of the 'digital' deeply influences the way people understand and think about the computational itself – for example, representational forms of pixels, bitmapped images and low-resolution 'digital' graphics. In hindsight, for example, it is possible to see that CDs and DVDs were actually the first step on the road to a truly computational media world. Capturing bits and disconnecting them from wider networks and constellations of computational systems, placing them on plastic discs and stacking them in shops for us to go, visit and buy seem bizarrely pedestrian today. Yet, people tend to think in terms of these categories of 'digital' as 'printed/encoded' on to packaged and boxed discrete objects, not only for born-digital content, but also for those that have been relatively easily transformed into digital forms, such as film and television.

This shift also includes the move from relatively static desktop computers to mobile computers and to tablet-based devices. Indeed, according to the International Telecommunications Union (ITU 2012: 1), in 2012 there were 6 billion mobile devices (up from 2.7 billion in 2006), with YouTube alone streaming video media of 200 terrabytes per day. Indeed, by the end of 2011, 2.3 billion people (i.e. one in three) were using the internet (ITU 2012: 3), creating 1.8 zettabytes of data and expected to grow to 7.9 zettabytes by 2015 (Kalakota 2011). To put this in perspective, a zettabyte is equal to 1 billion terabytes or information storage capacity equal to 10^{21} bytes or 1,000 exabytes or 1 billion terrabytes – clearly at these scales the storage sizes become increasingly difficult for humans to comprehend. In comparison, a DVD-R can hold about 4.7 GB and a dual-layered Blu-ray disc can hold about 50 GB. A zettabyte is therefore roughly equal in size to 43 billion Blu-ray discs or 250 billion DVDs.[2] Combining this explosion in data creation and usage with the increased embedding of microprocessors in all sorts of everyday devices, from washing machines to coffee-makers, highlights the extent to which we rely on computational systems and software. All of these chips need software to run, without which they would essentially be plastic, metal and glass bricks, and they all produce streams of data which are increasingly networked and stored. As Andreessen argues,

> Six decades into the computer revolution, four decades since the invention of the microprocessor, and two decades into the rise of the modern Internet, all of the technology required to transform industries through software finally works and can be widely delivered at global scale. . . . Over two billion people now use the broadband Internet, up from perhaps 50 million a decade ago. . . . In the next 10 years, I expect at least five billion people worldwide to own smartphones, giving every individual with such a phone instant access to the full power of the Internet, every moment of every day. (Andreessen 2011)

The previous *destination model* – a static, object-oriented model of the digital – draws heavily from a world that was constructed in major part due to material constraints on the delivery of things, but also due to social and historical habits that we took for granted – walking to the shops, waiting for a release date to queue up to buy something, sitting in lectures and seminars, or even visiting friends on quite trivial social matters. This model was clearly constrained by physical limitations, but there was also an element of corporate planning that built release windows, geographical regions and so on into our everyday experience of goods and services. The same applied to non-networked computers and phones which were built and supplied through the same distribution systems of their pre-digital contemporaries. This destination model also justified readings of the computational claiming that the 'digital' had changed very little at all in the status *quo* – the digital was seen as being a process of back-office rationalization, often disconnected with the everyday experience and use of products and services, with newspapers being the exemplar of an industry that failed to recognize the challenges of the digital world. With hindsight, though, it is becoming increasingly clear that the computational is shifting the way in which certain forms of knowledge are created, used, disseminated and consumed across the global economy – including the emergence of the internet-of-things and 3D printing technologies, such as 3D printed guns, prosthesis and so forth. Cheaper, faster and more reliable hardware is combining with new computer languages, frameworks and programming practices to open new spaces of possibility for the 'digital' and this transforms both our understanding and knowledge.

Computation is fundamentally changing the way in which knowledge is created, used, shared and understood, and in doing so it is changing the relationship between knowledge and freedom. We are starting to see changes in the way we understand knowledge, and therefore think about it. It encourages us to ask questions about philosophy in a computational age and its relationship to the mode of production that acts as a condition of possibility for it. Indeed, following Foucault (1982) the 'task of philosophy as a critical analysis of our world is something which is more and more important. Maybe the most certain of all philosophical problems is the problem of the present time, and of what we are, in this very moment . . . maybe to refuse what we are' (Dreyfus and Rabinow 1982: 216). Here we might consider Lukács discussion in *History and Class Consciousness* of Kant's distinction between metaphysical and direct knowledge of nature, which Kant holds to be impossible, and our experience of nature which Kant 'insists is mediated by a priori categories of the understanding' (Schecter 2007: 74). Lukács argues that the distinction within this philosophical structure may represent the 'entrenchment of the division of mental and manual labour – something politically conditioned and historically contingent – than any "natural" or eternal limit to cognition' (Schecter 2007: 75). Kant offers a passive role to the senses, and an active role to the categories – unity, plurality, totality, reality, negation, limitation, inherence, causality, reciprocity, possibility, existence and necessity. Lukács argued that Kant had internalized the division of labour in society and had built it into his theory of knowledge. Therefore, it is no surprise that he also supported the economic development of capitalism and political values of liberalism of his time. In a similar fashion today, the computational industries raise the productive powers of the economy to the level at which it is feasible to consider an economy of abundance and therefore the abolition of material necessity as an objective possibility. But it still nonetheless separates the mental and sensual dimensions of production such that people find it increasingly difficult to critically discuss freedom, potential and need.

Computational over-production becomes an end in itself, even to the extent to which it strips the cognitive capacity of labour from production, both material and social – through technologies of anticipatory computing and notions like 'augmented humanity'. It is likely that we should expect to see new philosophies and metaphysics emerge that again entrench, justify and legitimate the values of a particular accumulation regime. This calls for attentiveness to the tendency of philosophers to declaim their situatedness and historical location, and develop critical approaches to what we might call metaphysics of the computational and to the forms of computational ideology that legitimate a new accumulation regime. Which is not to say that the computational has no benefits nor potential contribution to human emancipation, indeed the critical project is to make these possibilities explicit while simultaneously contesting non-democratic and authoritarian trajectories.

Take that most mundane of everyday communicational technologies: the telephone. Using the telephone in everyday life has changed dramatically with the digitalization of the telephone network and the rise in data services for communication – the telephone has become an increasingly 'smart' media device. Here, I am particularly thinking of the contrast between wired, 'electric' switching technology and digital packet-switching services and new data-centric services. While bandwidth was expensive due to physical constraints, the former economic structure of the telecommunication services made a lot of sense, but today, with smart allocation and adaptive use of spectrum being made possible by digital technology, the plunge in price of data bandwidth, and the giant leaps in computational capacity and corresponding reduction in the size of the packages that contain them, the mode of communication shifts towards a real-time streaming digital world (see Berry 2011a). Blockages still exist, such as telecommunication companies reluctant to break with a billing and accounting model that is deeply embedded in their corporate DNA to charge by time (voice) or bandwidth usage (data) even when this distinction starts to make less and less sense, especially for Voice Over Internet Protocol (VOIP) presence-at-a-distance services like Skype and Facetime (see Lash 2002: 59). However, we can already see the contours of a new communicational landscape appearing before us, and which, as computational media, is enticing to use and interact with. Our phones become smart phones, and as such become media devices that can also be used to identify, monitor and control our actions and behaviour through anticipatory computing. While seemingly freeing us from the constraints of the old wired-line world of the immobile telephone, we are also increasingly enclosed within an algorithmic cage that attempts to surround us with contextual advertizing and behavioural nudges (see, for example, Berry 2012d; Roberts et al. 2012; Morozov 2012b).[3] Indeed, as Steiner (2013) argues, a lot of money is now poured into the algorithms that monitor our every move on the social media sites that have become so extraordinarily popular,

[Facebook] built the tools and the algorithms that still monitor the unimaginable amount of data pouring into Facebook every hour of every day. Part of the reason that Facebook has proven so "sticky" and irresistible to Web surfers is because [Facebook] built systems to track people's mouse clicks, where their cursor stray, and what page arrangements hook the largest number of people for the longest amount of time. All of this click, eyeball, and cursor data gets strained, sifted and examined. . . . Having a nearly captive audience of billions makes it all the easier, and lucrative, to sell ads that can be targeted by sex, income, geography, and more. (Steiner 2013: 204–5)

There are other less obvious examples of this surveillance taking place through digital devices, such as sat-nav devices, laptops, tablets and e-books. Companies have varying degrees of openness about the extent to which they collect data about their users, and also varying degrees of transparency and opaqueness in the user controlling it. E-books and tablets are a useful example of the disciplinary monitoring of the reader by the device through software, such as the case of Amazon mass deletion of Orwell's 1984 from people's Kindle reader, but this has not held back the explosion in readers/ users of e-readers. Indeed, the 'number of those who read e-books increased from 16% of all Americans aged 16 and older to 23%. At the same time, the number of those who read printed books in the previous 12 months fell from 72% of the population aged 16 and older to 67%' (see Raine and Duggan 2012). For writers like Carr (2012) this may also signal a change in knowledge and our reading practices at a profound level,

If book readers continue to shift from the page to the screen, as seems likely, the text of books will end up being displayed in a radically different setting from that of the printed or scribal page that has defined the book for the first 2,000 years of its existence. That doesn't mean that readers won't be able to immerse themselves in books anymore. The technology of a book is not rigidly deterministic. The skill of the writer still matters, as does the desire of readers to get lost in stories and arguments. But the importance of the technology in shaping reading habits (and publishing decisions), particularly over the long run, shouldn't be discounted. If the technology of the page provided a screen against the distractions of everyday life, encouraging the focus that is the essence of deep reading, the computer screen does the opposite. It inundates us with distractions, encourages the division of attention. It fights deep reading rather than encouraging it. (Carr 2012)

We will return to this question later in the book but it is a useful signposting of how changes wrought in digital technology are increasingly articulated and amplified in media debates about what we might call cognitive technologies. Additionally, these new digital technologies form path dependencies that can become strengthened and naturalized as platforms, therefore becoming self-reinforcing, creating a circle of technological leaps and accelerations. These new forms of knowledge platforms are built to structure our reading in particular ways, opening the possibility of distracted and fragmentary reading habits in contrast to deep reading, which may make it difficult to develop critical reflection or offer space for contemplation. Indeed, these changes highlight the importance of asking the question of how technologies might be restructured, regulated or rearticulated, together with the socio-economic institutions that control the labour process, in order to enable the digital to contribute to a project of emancipation through the possible abolition of scarcity and the transformation of work into an aesthetic pleasure (Schecter 2007: 81).

The computational device itself, whose contents would previously have been in the bounded medium of the printed book, presents another example of the move to real-time experiences. This has the potential for transforming the private reading experience of books, with the possibility of semi-public and public readings in as much as the text can be located around what is increasingly thought of as a three-screen system. That is that we will use three different-sized reading and watching screens within our everyday life. The ethics of reading are also embedded in this technical system whereby what was previously conceptualized by Xerox Palo Alto research labs as tabs, pads and boards becomes universalized through technical distribution. Hence, the *tab* (phone) is private, *pad* (tablet) is public/semi-public and the *board* (TV) is public. The book is, then, increasingly dissolved into the user experience

(UX) of a three-screen experience, a world of tabs, pads and boards. Reading is potentially no longer located in a single object, but is automatically synced between phone and tablet, such that the 'book' that one is reading is increasingly understood as a causal, real-time streaming media, which may be picked up and put down with no attention to context/container – indeed writing is also possible in a similar way. With the advent of the third screen of the three-screen world, the 'board' (of which the AppleTV and Xbox One are, perhaps, prototype versions), one wonders how reading might be spread over these three devices/screens and what effects that might have, and also the potential for new writing forms – e.g. simultaneous display of different pages, characters, structures, etc. on the three screens while reading. One only has to look at experiments with two screen games (e.g. tablet and TV) to see that, although this is still in its early phases, there are some interesting new forms of reading and writing under development.

Today, we are additionally inundated by an information deluge that can be overwhelming and difficult to manage without computational means and monitoring through web-bugs and 'compactants' (or computational actants) (Berry 2012d: 391).[4] As Sterling (2012) argues, bringing the currently fragmented algorithmic ecology into a tighter coupling heralds an 'industrial internet', thus,

> The full potential of the Industrial Internet will be felt when the three primary digital elements—algorithmic devices, algorithmic systems and algorithmic decision-making—fully merge with physical machines, facilities, fleets and networks. (Sterling 2012b)

Indeed, these noticeable shifts in the mode of production and the modes of communication increasingly challenge our actual understanding of humanity *qua* humanity as reflected in debates over reading skills, neuromarketing, behavioural nudges and so forth. These digital elements are thought to soften the boundaries between human and machine and pose questions for philosophers and theorists about human autonomy and distinctiveness (see Fuller 2011; Stiegler 2010).

To illustrate, in Freestyle Chess the battle lines are no longer drawn between human and computer, but rather between different teams or assemblages of human and non-human actors – inevitably called Chess 2.0. As Kasparov writes about his experience of playing chess as part of a human-chess-computer assemblage,

> Having a computer program available during play was as disturbing as it was exciting. And being able to access a database of a few million games

meant that we didn't have to strain our memories nearly as much in the opening, whose possibilities have been thoroughly catalogued over the years. But since we both had equal access to the same database, the advantage still came down to creating a new idea at some point. . . . Having a computer partner also meant never having to worry about making a tactical blunder. The computer could project the consequences of each move we considered, pointing out possible outcomes and countermoves we might otherwise have missed. With that taken care of for us, we could concentrate on strategic planning instead of spending so much time on calculations. Human creativity was even more paramount under these conditions. (Kasparov 2010)

Literally, the chess players are only 'autonomous' in as much as they might sit in front of the chessboard. Contrary to previous notions of self-contained grandmaster chess players, these players rely on augmented computational analysis and computing firepower to attack their opponents – they become 'chess centaurs' (half human, half machine). In other words, 'one had to enter into a grey area in which it was no longer clear who would be the horse or the rider in the course of a chess game' (Freestyle-Chess 2010). To ensure that pure engines, which are non-human computational assemblages, would not compromise the play (a previous final had been won purely computationally), tournaments in free chess now have regulations that moves have to be made manually on the physical chessboard, that is, that a human is required to be a member of the team.[5] Likened to the thrill of driving a fast car, the use of offloaded calculative abilities of computers to augment the players' skills is no longer an argument for the transcendence of humanity by computers, but, rather, a new abstract machine for human-computer interaction. Again Kasparov argues,

The surprise came at the conclusion of the event. The winner was revealed to be not a grandmaster with a state-of-the-art PC but a pair of amateur American chess players using three computers at the same time. Their skill at manipulating and "coaching" their computers to look very deeply into positions effectively counteracted the superior chess understanding of their grandmaster opponents and the greater computational power of other participants. Weak human + machine + better process was superior to a strong computer alone and, more remarkably, superior to a strong human + machine + inferior process. (Kasparov 2010)

This is a useful reminder that these new digital technologies are not the sole driver of social and political change, but far from it, as will be argued throughout this book. Rather, the key point is that technology offers specific affordances within certain contexts which enable and disable certain forms of social and political interactions. Putting it another way, certain technologies within historical and social contexts serve to accelerate styles and practices of life, and marginalize others. But crucially they are also linked to associational structures of the specific network, organizational form and processes used to achieve a certain 'performance'. To comprehend the digital we must, therefore, know it from the inside, we must know its formative processes. We can therefore think of technologies, and here I am thinking particularly of digital technologies, as being *embedded* in an important sense. The coming political contestations over the future of the digital will no doubt involve attempts to disembed the digital from political debate and forms of democratic control (see Berry 2008) – exemplified by attempts by the International Telecommunications Union (ITU) to exert full control over the internet structures (see Kampfner 2012). However, we have to remain cognizant of the processual, local and situated moments that make computational systems possible. In other words, we have to be careful not to reify computation and lose its 'processual' aspect. Often these processes are inscribed and documented in standards, such as TCP/IP, the key protocol of the internet. However, these standards are not objects; they are layers of text that require a 'reprocessing' within computational systems – and more specifically in computational processes.

Indeed, the digital is in many ways the creation of a constellation of standards, canonical ways of passing around discrete information and data, that creates what we might call *witnesses* to the standard – software enforcing the disciplinary action of these standards, such as application programming interfaces (APIs). Owning and controlling standards can have a political economic advantage in a post-Fordist society, and much jostling by multinational corporations and governments is exactly over the imposition of certain kinds of technical standards on the internet, or what Galloway (2006) calls protocol.

Returning to the political economy of computational technologies, it is notable that digital technologies are often thought of as somehow autonomous, or separated from the political sphere. Indeed, it often suits technologists and technology advocates for it to be seen that way (Berry 2008). This is especially true in situations where painful decisions are being made in lieu of technology being implemented, for example, the replacement of factory workers by computers. Thus, technology itself can serve as an important seemingly neutral 'force of nature' within (and sometimes exogenous) to our societies. Indeed, as technologies move towards a real-time digital mediation of interaction and stream-based activities that are becoming normalized and naturalized into our everyday lives, we are told that this *is* the future. That is, 'real-time streams' are an ongoing project or computational imaginary. However, this is also a moment in which the shape of the real-time digital world is still open and being built around us, and therefore is subject to possible intervention, critique and questioning. A key concept in relation to the exploration of the digital in this book is the concept of *possibility*, the idea that the digital contains possibilities which may be hidden or obscured, but which remains possible nonetheless. In exploring the concept of possibility, constellations of concepts will be outlined that enable us to explore the historical processes stored in the digital, or more concretely in particular digital objects and processes, and hence form the basis of their actuation and limitation.

The key premise of this book is the relatively uncontroversial claim that the digital (especially, software) is an increasingly important aspect of our post-Fordist societies. However, we have not yet found adequate means to provide a critical response to its multifaceted surfaces. The digital world is increasingly creating destabilizing amounts of dis-embedded knowledge, information and processing capabilities that undermine the enlightenment subject – this forms an important background to critical approaches to computation. Indeed, the book takes a synoptic look at the phenomena of the digital and tries to place the digital within a theoretical and historical context. It does this through an engagement with critical theory to understand the profound ways in which the digital is challenging the way in which we run our politics, societies, economies, our media and even our private everyday lives. As Schecter argues,

> In the second half of the twentieth century, capitalist recodification and reterritorialization is confronted by its own limits, according to Deleuze and Guattari. They suggest that capitalism helped produce the bases of its own demise, but not by producing a unified proletariat that seizes control of the means of production. The system has set a dynamic of de-territorialization in motion that will eventually elude its normalising control – it will be unable to produce the subjects it needs to sustain capital-labour whilst [reining] it in and commodifying the desires of the multitude. (Schecter 2007: 200)

In contrast to the predicted emergence of the 'schizophrenic', Deleuze and Guattari's notion of a new destabilizing subject of de-territorialized capital, we are instead beginning to see the augmented human offered by anticipatory computing. Elements of subjectivity, judgement and cognitive capacities are increasingly delegated to algorithms and prescribed to us through our devices, and there is clearly the danger of a lack of critical reflexivity or even critical thought in this new subject. This new augmented subject has the potential to be extremely conservative, passive and consumerist, without the revolutionary potential of the 'schizophrenic'. Indeed, the norms and values of the computational economy can be prescribed quite strongly as a society of control, limiting action, thought and even knowledge. This we might understand as the danger of a transition from a rational juridical epistemology to an *authoritarian-computational* epistemology. We will return to this issue in detail in the later chapters.

Although this book outlines the general contours of critical theory, it is not intended as a comprehensive guide to critical theory itself, or as an introduction to it. Indeed, the reader is directed to the work of others who cover this material extremely competently and offer useful and helpful exploratory readings (see Held 1997; Jarvis 1998; Jay 1973; Schecter 2007, 2010; Thomson 2006; Wiggershaus 1995). The question this book will address is how can critical theory contribute to this critique of the digital, and what can be drawn from the critical project of the twentieth century, notably from the Frankfurt School, in order to orient and inform a critical purchase on the real-time digital world of the twenty-first century.[6]

Critical theory has always had some engagement with the questions raised by technology, and with the speeding up of the technological feedback and feedforward loops offered by real-time systems – as changes in technology accelerate at an increasing pace – it is crucial that the critical literature engages with these new stream-based iterations of digital technology. These rapid changes present real difficulties for critique, both as a practice and as politics, when attempting intervention or seeking to question the direction of travel with such a fast-moving target. Thus the growth of the digital, both as a technical ensemble and as a global disciplinary system, raises important questions for critical thought today, and the way in which critical approaches can make a meaningful contribution to its development and effects. Not that critical theory must chase the latest digital fad or internet meme, of course, but it must engage with the structures and foundations of the digital. These need to be explored both in their materiality and in their ideological affordances, not only to offer critique, but also to develop new concepts and ways of thinking in relation to the new streaming technical world.

The challenge for a critical theory of the digital is to critique what Adorno calls *identity thinking* and a form of thinking that is highly prevalent in computational rationalities and practices. Here, identity thinking is understood as a *style of thought* that aims at the subsumption of all particular objects under general concepts, and as a result the particular is dissolved into the universal. The distance between computational knowledge and reality is entirely closed when we think we have succeeded in framing reality within these computational categories and by means of computational methods. This is a dangerous assumption, as it is a short step towards new forms of control, myth and limited forms of computational rationality. So there is an urgent need for a project exploring in what sense critique and critical thought can address the computational (see Golumbia 2009; Berry 2011). That is, to explore the dangers and the possibilities offered by digital technologies towards the project of human emancipation and how critical theory can contribute through praxis to that project.

Why study the digital and software?

The focus on digital technologies requires approaches that can provide a holistic understanding of the interconnections and relationships that technologies introduce into everyday life and action. Indeed, 'computers provide an unprecedented level of specification and control over every aspect of human society (and the rest of the environment)' (Golumbia 2009: 216). More specifically, the computer, is a symbolic processing device that has had, and will continue to have, important repercussions for society. As Winograd and Flores (1987) argue, this means that at least some of the analysis of the implications of digital technology must lie within the domain of language itself, as code is both a text and a mechanism,[7]

> The computer is a device for creating, manipulating, and transmitting symbolic (hence linguistic) objects. Second, in looking at the impact of the computer, we find ourselves thrown back into questions of language – how practice shapes our language and language in turn generates the space of possibilities for action. (Winograd and Flores 1987: 7)

This includes the development of a way of thinking about and critically examining what Borgmann (1984: 14) called the technological furniture of our age. Arguably our technological furniture is vastly greater in scope and deeper in its penetration of all aspects of everyday life than any previous system. Following Moore's Law, which states that computing power would double every 18 months, we are now at an important juncture, as the surplus computing power is enormous and its application to social life and even social control is growing, such as demonstrated by drone technologies, which is highly reliant on computation, which can monitor and even kill at a distance.

We will therefore also need political praxis, and in some instances that political praxis will be technical practices such as cryptography and encryption, the practices of restricting what one is reading and writing in digital systems. One might think of it as the technical re-implementation of the bourgeois liberal private sphere in code, and indeed, the space to gather one's thoughts, think privately and apply one's reason critically without being observed is a crucial requirement for a healthy democratic society, provided it is balanced with the public use of reason to debate and contest societal questions. As Assange argues,

> the universe, our physical universe, has that property that makes it possible for an individual or a group of individuals to reliably, automatically, even without knowing, encipher something, so that all the resources and all the political will of the strongest superpower on earth may not decipher it. And the paths of encipherment between people can mesh together to create regions free from the coercive force of the outer state. . . . Cryptography is the ultimate form of non-violent direct action . . . a basic emancipatory building block. (Assange 2012: 5–6)

This is an extremely suggestive notion that cryptography as a basic emancipatory building block will be a key site of contestation in a computational society, and may be manifested by cryptocurrencies, such as bitcoin. Indeed, it seems likely that these new forms of crypto-spaces will be hugely important as a new site of counter-politics, and a new subject position that Assange calls cypherpunks who 'advocate for the use of cryptography and similar methods as ways to achieve societal and political change' (Assange 2012).[8] It is clear then that this potential should be fully developed and made available for widespread democratic use and for that it will require political praxis. But while attempts have been made to understand this situation in terms of a liberal moment, that is to defend a space of so-called 'privacy', the reality is that there is no possibility that an individual, even one as ruggedly individualistic as the neo-liberal subject, can singularly resist the collection of 'data exhaust' that we leave as we go about our daily life and the computational means to watch, analyse, predict and control us. Even going 'off the grid' creates data trails as our colleagues, friends and families continue to talk about us, post pictures or these systems even postulate 'data ghosts', computationally created avatars, created by social network analysis that is able to determine the contours of the absent person. We are also complicit in our own handing over of data and which often plays on individualism as a justification through notions such as 'citizen science'. Examples include the recent move towards the analysis of our internal microbiome constitution through companies that offer identification, classification and diagnosis based on our internal bodily microbes, by organizations such as uBiome and American Gut, or our genes through companies such as 23andme.[9] This leads to a focus on a radical 'now', in as much as the mass collection and processing of data creates a shift from historical thinking to a fetishization of the present, as Gelernter argues:

> . . . no moment in technology history has ever been more exciting or dangerous than "now". As we learn more about now, we know less about *then*. The Internet increases the supply of information hugely, but the capacity of the human mind not at all. . . . The effect of nowness resembles the effect of light pollution in large cities, which makes it impossible to see the stars. A flood of information about the present shuts out the past. . . . But—the Internet could be the most powerful device ever invented for understanding the past, and the texture of time. Once we understand the inherent bias in an instrument, we can correct it. The Internet has a large bias in favor of now. Using lifestreams (which arrange information in time instead of space), historians can assemble, argue about and gradually refine timelines of historical fact. Such timelines are not history, but they are the raw material of history. They will be bitterly debated and disputed—but it will be easy to compare two different versions (and the evidence that supports them) side-by-side. Images, videos and text will accumulate around such streams. Eventually they will become shared cultural monuments in the Cybersphere. (Gelernter 2010)

It is here that critical theory can contribute to the understanding of the computal and the information society beyond the usual critiques offered at a macro-level of the general principles underlying knowledge-based societies, or micro-analysis of users and the practices. Indeed, we need to pay attention to the dialectical relationship between the two, while being able to apply critical approaches to the identity thinking implicit within many discussions of digital technology. This identity thinking manifests itself in a number of ways in what I term computationality (Berry 2011a). For example, Morozov (2013) pinpoints what he calls two 'dominant ideologies' in technical circles, 'Internet-centrism' and 'solutionism', namely the idea that the internet provides the model to 'fix' everything or that everything requires a 'solution', even if the solution subverts or is a poor replacement for its analogue. Morozov argues they,

> feed on Enlightenment-era attitudes toward the liberating power of information. More information is always presumed to be better than less; having more ways to analyze the same piece of information is always preferable to having fewer ways. Legal scholar Julie Cohen calls this set of attitudes "the information-processing imperative" and argues that it gives rise to a mind-set that equates information gathering with a "single, inevitable trajectory of forward progress". (Morozov 2013: 86)

Here, Morozov correctly identifies the symptoms and it is an important critique, with the level of analysis focused on what we might call discursive orders of computationality. Indeed I would argue that this analysis is only partially useful as these 'dominant ideologies' are actually identical in as much as they represent articulations of different moments of computationality, that is, they both understand the world through computational categories and classifications. That these moments should appear now is hardly surprising, and that their discourses sound reassuring and convincing is also of no surprise – the computational is now the background to our experiences. These approaches understand the digital as a collection of tools, and as such have an engineering understanding of the world. However, they also seek to remake the world in the image of computational capitalism, whether through digitalization, discretization, object-oriented methods or the rules of transparency and opaqueness appropriate to code. They represent a moment in the kind of identity thinking that I want to critique in this book and to which the oppositional scepticism of Morozov offers only a partial response.[10]

Indeed, it is important that the digital is also explored in relation to the insights of medium theory, and the theoretical richness that can be developed by using such a theoretical orientation. Digital technologies mediate the world, and in doing so offer frames and limitations. Increasingly, it is rare to experience any media that has not been transformed by or passed through a digital system. Today newspapers, even print copies, are softwarized to the extent that the desktop software that is used to create them imposes certain logics, structures and hierarchies of knowledge onto the process and final product. This is also becoming more evident with the advent of digital broadcast systems, smart televisions and real-time streaming media. We could therefore argue that the long-predicted convergence of communications and computers, originally identified as 'compunication' (see Oettinger and Legates 1977; Lawrence 1983), has now fully arrived. As Oettinger and Legates wrote, 'computers and communications have merged not only in terms of hardware components or techniques, but also in terms of services or, more broadly, in terms of functions. Whether we talk about transmission or storage or manipulation of information, we can no longer tell communications functions apart from computer functions' (Oettinger and Legates 1977: 431). While this early work was ahead of its time in thinking about the implications of computation on communications, and communications policy more generally, we now live in a world in which *compunications* is an everyday experience for citizens in softwarized societies, both in communications, the 'information transfer systems', and in computers, the 'information processing systems' (Lawrence 1983: 37).

This process of softwarization is sometimes problematically called 'remediation' in that the old medium (broadcast, print, film, etc.) has become the 'content' of the new one (software) and networked through digital communications systems (Berry 2013). This has two main implications: (1) that the systems upon which the mediums were previously divided between, and which formed the infrastructure and condition of possibility for their existence, is replaced by a new software-based one, and (2) that once digitized, these mediums become the same in as much as they are software-based files that are subject to the same kinds of software control – and can even be transformed into one another, due to the fact that they are all based on a digital format.

We can assume that the broadcast parenthesis, stretching from around 1900 to 2000, will continue to leave a long shadow over the development of new softwarized media. We have a tendency to think in terms of the old mediums when we try to use the content, but older institutions are also organized in ways that reflect this technical bias. For example, many large media corporations still keep TV, radio and film in separate divisions or departments. However, over the next 10 years, the distinctions between them will continue to be eroded and no doubt new distinctions will be created as software continues to change the media landscape (e.g. see the digital first strategies at the BBC, *The New York Times* and the *Guardian*).

It becomes clear then that media and our knowledge of it are changing and that if we are not careful we will make the mistake of allowing our assumption from past mediums to limit our understanding of the new software-based media. We certainly need to be aware of the pressure software is exerting on these old ways of understanding media and in moving to a new paradigm of knowledge, ensure that we take with us the old theories of the media that are still appropriate, while leaving behind that which is too closely wedded to the older broadcast technologies. But more than this, software is widely used for the management of other resources, technologies and even people. Software is, in short, a key site for the investigation of capitalist practices in the information age. It is also useful due to its two-phase structure, as both text and machine, allowing its program to be read from its textual script form, and normative structures and intentionalities explored. We should also be constantly aware that software 'offer us an imaginary relationship to our hardware: they do not represent the motherboard or other electronic devices but rather desktops, files and recycling bins' (Chun 2006: 20) and today increasingly: streams, clouds and apps. We should read software critically, even when reading software through software tools, software's palimpsest-like structure means that the medium of the computational is always multifaceted and multi-layered but crucially it need not be opaque.

Software itself is changing rapidly, due to limitations now being experienced in the capacity of hardware to support old software paradigms. For example, many of our computing systems, and certainly those that we have used in everyday life, have been built around single processor systems that we expected to get faster and faster based on the notion of Moore's Law, that is, that computer speed roughly doubles every 18 months. Physical limitations are now being hit in the design of computer chips, and therefore rather than increasing the speed (measured in Hz, MHz or GHz), chip manufacturers are increasing the number of 'cores' or processors that we have in our machines. This greatly increases the kinds of things that these devices can perform, and also the means by which they do it. For example, mobile devices can now offload processing tasks to huge 'server farms' which can then return the results to the user, greatly augmenting the processing capacity of a single device – indeed, this is how Apple implemented its ground-breaking voice recognition software, Siri.

Software is therefore one of the new focuses of the massive advances in speed and capability in hardware design. However, most programming is still written in a form that assumes fairly simple computer structures and hardware – like a single core to the processor. These practices are reflected in the habitus of programmers and the toolsets they build and use. We are therefore living in a time of a dual transformation of both: (i) a general move to a softwarized media world, but also (ii) that software itself is about to enter a change in paradigm to take account of rapid change in the hardware and communication environment too, which means more stream-based parallel computation.

What is important for this book is that the captialist system is increasingly *softwarized* (or becoming digital) and also that software increasingly becomes a replacement (restructures) the previous mnemono-technologies, like paper and film. Indeed, it can be said that we live in a post-industrial knowledge work society created by the 'management of, and through, media, which leads in turn to the management of management . . . further, by separating content from both form and materiality, post-industrial knowledge work initiated variable standardization: standardization through databases, and variability thorough the different interfaces that draw upon the database' (Hayles 2012: 201). These imply the formatting of social life through the use of computational technologies, influencing both the economy and the lifeworld more generally. As Liu further argues,

Where the author was once presumed to be the originating transmitter of a discourse . . . now the author is in a mediating position as just one among all those other managers looking upstream to previous originating transmitters – database or XML schema designers, software designers, and even clerical information workers (who input data into the database or XML source document). (Hayles 2012: 202)

The digital has become the paradigmatic means of explaining what it means to live and work in the post-industrial democracies – this I call *computational* identity thinking. Indeed, I argue software, computation and code define our contemporary situation, becoming part of the metaphors by which it is even possible to think today (see Chun 2011). However, looking at code and understanding it, let alone decompiling or 'reading' software, is difficult due to its ephemeral nature, technical requirements and the lack of analytical tools. This book will attempt to contribute to this by gesturing towards ways of understanding the 'digital' through a re-articulation of critical theory towards algorithms, code and software pointing towards future strategies and tools that need to be created.

In order to do this, the book examines how critical theory developed and how it can be rethought to critically engage with the challenges of the digital revolution. More particularly, the book seeks to examine the extent to which enlightenment values, which are strongly embedded both within the cultures associated with digital technology and within the materiality of the digital itself, can be understood and used to explain the changes that are taking place across society. Thus, the book seeks to examine the extent to which a dialectic of enlightenment can be discerned within the structures of digital technology (Horkheimer and Adorno 2006; also see Golumbia 2009). The book examines the deep materiality of the digital and how it both crystallizes particular social forms and values, and generates new mentalities, economic forms and social relations.

Throughout the aim is to develop concepts and ideas drawn from the Frankfurt School towards the project of recovering the ability to draw a cognitive map of the present digital world that surrounds us, and in many cases engulfs us. For this book, the key lies in making connections and pathways between critical theory and the digital, but also drawing on the work of the later Heidegger, to create new concepts for thinking the digital, indeed, contributing to a critical theory for the digital. For example, software is increasingly being used in a number of different contexts for forecasting with extremely sophisticated models. Corporations and governments use this software to predict and monitor individuals, groups, organizations or other national states activities (Berry 2012e). The software gives the capability to make decisions and predictions about future activities based on past (archive) and present (real-time) data sources. Within a security setting one of the key aspects is data collection and it comes as no surprise that the United States has been at the forefront of rolling out gigantic data archive systems, with the NSA (National Security Agency) building the country's biggest spy centre at its Utah Data Center (Bamford 2012). This centre has a 'capacity that will soon have to be measured in yottabytes, which is 1 trillion terabytes or a quadrillion gigabytes' (Poitras et al. 2013). Indeed, the revelations from the whistleblower Edward Snowden about the NSA PRISM programme point in the same direction of a future where governments and their security apparatus seek to obtain the maximum amount of data possible, and attempt to achieve real-time streaming access to it (see Greenwald et al. 2013). Bamford writes, the NSA Utah data centre is,

> A project of immense secrecy, it is the final piece in a complex puzzle assembled over the past decade. Its purpose: to intercept, decipher, analyze, and store vast swaths of the world's communications as they zap down from satellites and zip through the underground and undersea cables of international, foreign, and domestic networks. The heavily fortified $2 billion center should be up and running in September 2013. Flowing through its servers and routers and stored in near-bottomless databases will be all forms of communication, including the complete contents of private emails, cell phone calls, and Google searches, as well as all sorts of personal data trails—parking receipts, travel itineraries, bookstore purchases, and other digital "pocket litter". (Bamford 2012)

The current approach is that data collection should be comprehensive and where possible exhaustive, with these data centres sucking data from the internet, mobile phone, data, satellite and landline networks, in fact, from anywhere that can be plugged into the system. This includes collecting data that cannot currently be used, perhaps due to military grade encryption by a foreign power, the thinking being that in a number of years with faster processors, decrypting the data will be easier, and will provide much-needed context on future conflict, diplomacy and even trade. With adequate data collected in the databases and archives, the next stage of normalizing the data and providing it with structure enables it to be built into forecasting models and prediction systems. Indeed, in the United Kingdom there are plans to start comprehensive collection of data with the proposal for GCHQ (the United Kingdom, Government Communications Headquarters) to have access to communications in real time for tackling crime and terrorism (BBC 2012b). Most of these systems rely on 'abductive' processes, which enable them to work with flawed, fuzzy and incomplete data sets to undertake pattern recognition in order to identify important problems or raise possible threats. The use of 'abductive' logics represents a new diagram for the arms of government or the military which has begun to assess danger and risk in terms of patterns which can be algorithmically handled. For example, in the case of drones, which have grown in use by the US military from 167 in 2001 to 5,500 in 2009 and over 7,000 in 2013, their original function for surveillance has been supplemented with drone assassinations, indeed Schwartz (2013: 13) estimates that between 3,000 and 5,000 people have been killed this way in Pakistan, Yemen and Somalia. To do this, the operators of these drone-killing machines sitting in air-conditioned rooms thousands of miles away must assess the target quickly and to do so the notion of 'signature strikes' is used,

> In a signature strike, a person is made a target not because of their identity but because of certain "signatures" . . . [these] signatures are patterns of behavior that are detected through signals intercepts, human sources and aerial surveillance . . . that indicate the presence of an important operative or a plot against US interests. (Schwartz 2013: 13)

In effect the military collects data in large quantities and performs a pattern-matching function upon it to see if such a signature is recognized. This form of reasoning is connected in a strong way with the kind of computational reasoning that is explored throughout this book. This is connected to the notion of the comprehensive collection of data because, 'if you're looking for a needle in the haystack, you need a haystack,' according to Jeremy Bash, the former CIA chief of staff.

> An enormous haystack it turns out – one comprised of the billions of minutes of daily cross-border telephone traffic. Add to that digital streams from high-bandwidth Internet cables that transport data equivalent to that held in Washington's Library of Congress around the world in the course of a few seconds. And then add to that the billions of emails sent to international destinations each day – a world of entirely uncontrolled communication. (Poitras et al 2013)

The scale of the data collection is staggering and will only grow in the future, and according to Davies (2013), for example, GCHQ has placed, 'more than 200 probes on transatlantic cables and is processing 600m "telephone events" a day as well as up to 39m gigabytes of internet traffic. Using a program code-named Tempora, it can store and analyse voice recordings, the content of emails, entries on Facebook, the use of websites as well as the "metadata" which records who has contacted who' (Davies 2013). This industrial scale data collection spread across a number of institutions and corporations is at an unprecedented scale. By collecting such previously ephemeral information as conversations, movement through cities and consumption habits, these organizations collect our everyday memories and lifestreams and harvest them later for policing, control and exploitation. Indeed, our memory (both cultural and personal) and what might be called 'pre-thought' is also becoming a site for commercialization. This crucial half second before forming a decision about what we want to do has become identified as a site for softwarized intervention. In colonizing out thinking processes, corporations are increasingly attempting to influence the function of cognition and memory: personal, experienced and cultural.

Cultural memory is stored in computational technologies such as online photo storage, document storage, etc., and also through the digitalization of culture with large-scale digital repositories of knowledge (such as the 'Newton Project' an online archive).[11] In consequence, we are seeing a realignment of our contemporary culture. From the throw-away consumer experience of disposable objects, through a softwarization of culture and the economy, it appears that we are developing new forms of creativity that link together the potential for human agency and expression, and which are materialized in new technologies as a site of materialized memory and shared politics. This could be the site of a progressive politics that is linked to the importance of education and the attainment of human potential in order to develop the possibilities within each of us, and which clearly draws from the Enlightenment. This could also contribute to developing a new form of progressive economics with a potential for work that is creative, engaging and interesting. It could also reflect a dystopian turn, with real-time streaming systems used to build a panopticon of totally surveilled populations monitored by an all-seeing state, and nudged through the application of a corporate consumerist culture that operates on the level of citizens' pre-thought. Correspondingly, it highlights the importance of current debates over rights to cryptographic software that enables communication to remain opaque to state and corporate interests and the forms of resistance represented by moments like cypherpunks, megaleaks, social media and peer-to-peer networks.

A critical theory needs to address and understand these issues and provide new concepts and theories to be able to take account of these changes. This book is a contribution to the development of such a project. In order to understand, explain and offer a critical response to them, it is increasingly important that we offer a praxis and a politics that is equal to the questions raised by the digital. In the next chapter we will lay the foundations for this move by looking at the early history of the Frankfurt School and some of the key theorists whose work provides inspiration for this book.

2

From culture industry to computational industries

In this chapter I want to introduce some of the basic ideas that were developed by the Frankfurt School and to give a brief history of the Institute for Social Research, before outlining how their main concepts will be discussed in relation to the digital. The aim is to give a brief contextualization for later discussions for those not already familiar with the work of the Frankfurt School. Indeed, for readers already well versed in critical theory, they are welcome to skip the first section. This introduction will therefore paint with relatively broad strokes the main themes of critical theory, thought and praxis.

I begin by outlining a history of critical theory and particularly the concepts and ideas of the Frankfurt School. Here, due to limitations on space, I draw particularly on the work of Max Horkheimer, Theodore Adorno and Herbert Marcuse, while accepting that other members of the Frankfurt School made important contributions that may not agree with these thinkers.[1] Indeed as Outhwaite (2012) cogently explains, the notion of a unitary school or theory is problematic, quoting Habermas's warning,

> The suggestive fiction of a unitary school should not divert too much energy to self-thematisation in the history of ideas. We should do no better to turn to the problems themselves, to see how far one can get with the ruthlessly revisionist exploitation of the stimulative potential of such a diverse tradition of research. (Outhwaite 2012: vi)

Nonetheless, one can note that critical theorists share some commonalities, notably in reacting to Kant's critical philosophy and, therefore, the importance of Kant to the early Frankfurt School. Kant's critical philosophy specifies the *object* of critique, that which critique acts upon. Secondly, it specifies the *subject* of critique, namely the agent that carries out the critique. Lastly, his critical philosophy is reflexive in seeking to understand the rational limitations of rationality itself, thus it is *self-critical*. Although Kant's philosophy was itself a subject of critique from critical theory, the self-reflective critical model remains important in that there is 'never equivalence between thought and its object – that is, the concept of experience still plays a central philosophical role in critical theory' (Rush 2004: 10).

Thus, following Habermas's call and in the spirit of turning to the problems themselves and the time in which one is living, this chapter aims to tackle the questions raised by the digital and the computational by drawing on this diverse set of thinkers. Indeed, today systems built on computational principles that reduce thinking to calculation and instrumental rationality deserve careful study. I argue that critical theory is a unique resource for giving critical purchase on such a 'computational' society, a society which increasingly seeks to mechanize the processes of thinking, a reliance on calculation that Horkheimer had already identified in 1947 in relation to capitalism, such that,

> Concepts have been reduced to summaries of the characteristics that several specimens have in common. By denoting similarity, concepts eliminate the bother of enumerating qualities and thus serve better to organize the material of knowledge. They are thought of as mere abstractions of the items to which they refer. Any use of transcending auxiliary, technical summarization of factual data has been eliminated as a last trace of superstition. Concepts have become "streamlined", rationalized, labour-saving devices . . . thinking itself has been reduced to the level of industrial processes . . . in short, made part and parcel of production. (Horkheimer 2004: 15)

This chapter will, therefore, examine critical theory and seek to begin to articulate a critical theory of the digital in response to this problematic today. One way it does this is by looking into the very structures of the digital itself, through an active critical engagement with digital code and the way in which it is structured and assembled, and drawing from and developing critical concepts and theories from the Frankfurt School and other critical theorists. For example, what problems and solutions surface in computational societies? What political problems are identified as emblematic or requiring engagement and resolution, particularly by the state? Equally, the tendency for solutions to be cast in a technical register with software being the catalyst for change or resolution is also a striking feature in the growing computationalism of our societies.

As Marcuse argues, 'the choice of a technical rather than a political or moral solution to a social problem is politically and morally significant' (Feenberg

2004). The book seeks to demonstrate how the digital itself needs to be understood within a dialectic of potentially democratizing and totalizing technical power, that is, through notions of control and freedom. This follows the work of the critical theorists, whose aim was,

> to lay the foundation for an exploration, in an interdisciplinary research context, of questions concerning the conditions which make possible the reproduction and transformation of society, the meaning of culture, the relation between the individual, society and nature. While there are differences in the way they formulate questions, the critical theorists believe that through an examination of contemporary social and political issues they could contribute to a critique of ideology and to the development of a non-authoritarian and non-bureaucratic politics. (Held 1997: 16)

The chapter will also introduce how we can understand the 'everyday computational' of the digital economy, intended as a critical introduction to the complex field of digital culture and technology. One of these issues will be the move from the mass culture of the 'Culture Industry' to digital culture and the computational, conceptualized as what we might call the 'Computal Industries'.

The key is to recognize and understand the profound changes that have taken place in national economies around the globe, particularly those in the over-developed nations. They have become part of tighter global markets, managed through incredibly fast digital networks that can organize and enable the management of complex processes distributed around the world. There is an increasing reliance on discrete computational logics and capacities to manage the production process. And, of course, these logistics also involve new tools for the management of consumption through the increasing computational tracking and surveillance of customer behaviour which can then be subject to nudges and behavioural manipulation. All of this is facilitated through computational abstraction and management dashboards that enable high-level control over almost all aspects of production, distribution and consumption. There has also been a corresponding growth in the management of risk, giving rise to gigantic computational financial markets together with the compression of time, which enables productive shifts through examples such as just-in-time manufacturing, personalized and highly customizable processes. Not to mention the growth in online trade, both to the customer and business to business, and 3D printing and additive production (see Berry 2011a; Söderberg 2013).

For sociology, political science or other social sciences to develop an approach to the digital would require that in addition to a focus on questions relating to the structure of the industry, ownership and social patterns, one should also connect material questions of intellectual property rights, innovation and commons-based production in the digital code itself. By learning how to read and decode the structures embedded within software, we can develop understanding of the dark arts of computer programmers and hackers, and connect them more clearly to the way in which technology enables particular digital practices. Indeed, without an understanding of the structure of code, many features of our contemporary situation are impossible to explain or understand. We must, therefore, seek to open up the black box of digital technologies to critique.

The original critical theorists recognized the growing importance of culture for understanding capitalism; indeed, they correctly identified the importance of the cultural industry in the manufacture of minds and cultural products for a growing consumption-led economic system. They also attempted to think through the questions raised by monopoly capitalism and its implications for both a theory and praxis related to critical thought. In many ways, their thought is deeply engaged with many of the problems we face today and it is crucial that a re-articulated critical theory is available for thought today.

Critical theory

The Frankfurt School began in Germany in 1923 following a seminar given at Hotel Geraberg near Weimar in Germany (Schecter 2010: 85). It was based at the Institute for Social Research, which was set up with the specific aim of giving support to the workers movement in Germany after World War I. Their aim was to develop interdisciplinary research within a Marxist framework disseminated mainly through their journal, *The Journal of Social Research*. Carl Grünberg was the first director, but after an illness in 1931, he handed over to Max Horkheimer. Grünberg left an important mark on the Institute positioning the institution as opposed to teaching at the expense of research and the production of 'mandarins' who would 'only be capable of serving the existing balance of power and resources' (Held 1997: 30). Thus the institute was founded on the principles of concrete historical studies with theoretical analysis within the context of Marx's insights into political economy which was an important frame of reference (Held 1997: 31). Indeed, Horkheimer incorporated and extended Grünberg's earlier research programme, but he also 'sought to discuss the role of theory and social research in a more radically historical and theoretical mode.' Thus while he 'accepted the significance of the traditional questions of social philosophy such as the relationship between the individual and society, the meaning of culture and the basis of social life, he rejected purely philosophical approach[es] to these issues' (Held 1997: 32).

Horkheimer called for a 'continuous, dialectical penetration and development of philosophical theory and specialized scientific praxis' (Horkheimer 1993). The institute would set up at least on a very small scale, 'planned work in place of the mere juxtaposition of philosophical construction and empirical research in social inquiry' (Horkheimer 1993) and therefore a project of 'organizing inquiries on the basis of current philosophical questions, in which philosophers, sociologists, economists, historians, and psychologists can unite in lasting co-operation' (Wiggershaus 1994: 39). This would then enable truly interdisciplinary knowledge to be mobilized and deployed in order to explore the questions raised by 'the question of the connection between the economic life of society, the psychical development of individuals, and the changes in the realm of culture in the narrower sense (to which belong not only the so-called intellectual elements, such as science, art, and religion, but also law, customs, fashion, public opinion, sports, leisure activities, lifestyle, etc.)' (Horkheimer 1993).

Critical theory was developed in reaction to the Marxism of the Social Democratic movement before World War I. There was immense industrial and technical development of capitalism during the first 30 years of the twentieth century in Germany and Russia – particularly technological and organizational developments. Following the devastation of World War I, the failure of German revolution (1918–20) and a period of unrest, politics and culture were in constant upheaval. This included the Stalinization of the revolution in Russia, the rise of Fascism in Germany and Italy, and the various artistic, cultural and literary responses to these events, including movements like Dada, Surrealism, Expressionism, *Neue Sachlichkeit* (New Objectivity), ProLit Cult and others. Today, we understand these as 'modernism', but at the time they were seen as disparate movements based on different theories of the relationship between art and society. For the critical theorists, the 'crucible of the whole "critical Marxist" or "Western Marxist" or "Hegelian Marxist" enterprise was the failure of the German Revolution (1918–21) and the success of the Russian Revolution (1917)' (Arato and Gebhardt 2005: 4). As no sophisticated theory was available to elaborate the implications of this for the advanced countries of the West, a task of theoretical reconstruction of Marxism was initiated.

The most active time in the institute was marked by the rise of Nazism and Fascism (from 1930–44), and in the 1930s the institute moved first to Switzerland and then to New York. When Hitler came to power, many of the critical theorists had to decide whether to go East, to Russia, or West, to the United States and after the War they had to decide whether to go to East or West Germany, thus being forced to situate their position in relation to Fascism and/or Stalinism. In the 1940s some members of the School were based in California, Marcuse and Fromm stayed in America, but Adorno and Horkheimer returned to Germany and became professors at Frankfurt University.

When Horkheimer became the director of the Institute in 1931, he gave an inaugural lecture, 'The present situation of social philosophy and the tasks of an Institute of Social Research'. In it, he outlined the research agenda of the institute, calling for an interdisciplinary approach to research including juridical, cultural, historical, economic, political, aesthetic and social questions (Schecter 2010: 86). Philosophers, he argued, 'have all too often treated these questions [about individual and society, the meaning of culture, and the basis of social life] in the abstract, divorced from history and social context' (Held 1997: 32). At the same time 'artistic and cultural production could not be written off as spheres of secondary importance to social theory' (Jarvis 1998: 9). Thus researchers should ask what relations existed between particular social groups, in specific times in history, in particular nations, 'between the position of the group in the economy, changes in the psychic structures of its membership and other relevant factors which condition and affect the group's thoughts and practices' (Held 1997: 32). That is, the historical conditions that lead to different forms of culture succeeding each other and the way in which history, social context and the mode of production are linked with historically situated cultural moments.

The concept of different forms of culture succeeding each other in history was drawn from the work of the philosopher G. W. Hegel, who was a major influence on Marx. Marx critiqued Hegel's idealist conceptualization and replaced it with a notion of different historical social forms and their attendant modes of production (Marx had no theory of culture as such). Other theorists later developed Marx's work into 'Marxism' but in doing so created a more deterministic structure. This deterministic reading influenced the development of Marxism of the twentieth century, which designated the economic base as the key active factor in capitalism, and the superstructure as symptomatic or determined by the base. The Frankfurt School theorists disliked this static and mechanistic distinction between the economic base and political and cultural superstructure and worked to rethink this model.

One of the key intellectual founders of critical theory, Lukács, and other Marxists like Karl Korsch, therefore believed that traditional Marxism had become established, passive, deterministic and orthodox. They suggested re-storing the emphasis on praxis and human subjectivity so Marxism could again become a theory of revolution. For them, social analysis revealed that if the revolutionary subject was defeated, or not emerging, then there would need to be constant critique of these new forms of domination: economic, political and cultural (as the cultural had become political). Critical theory had to be resolutely opposed to Marxism as a science. Indeed, Marxism had to subject itself to criticism to prevent it from becoming passive and orthodox. This critical reflexivity is crucial to understanding critical theory, but also its relation to emancipatory reason and its opposition to instrumental rationality. This work fed directly into and greatly influenced the Frankfurt School theorists, as Horkheimer outlined in his three main themes for the work of the Institute,

> The first . . . the necessity of re-specifying "the great philosophical questions" in an interdisciplinary research programme. The second theme, is a call for a rejection of orthodox Marxism and its substitution by a reconstructed understanding of Marx's project. The third emphasizes the necessity for social theory to explicate the set of interconnections (mediations) that make possible the reproduction and transformation of society, economy, culture and consciousness. (Held 1997: 33)

In order to correct orthodox Marxism's determinism, the Frankfurt School reverted to a dynamic distinction between social processes and resultant social forms by taking as a model of culture and ideology, not base/superstructure but Marx's theory of commodity fetishism. Marx explains that commodity fetishism in a capitalist society requires that commodities are produced for a wage. The surplus value is realized, then the product is sold by the employer/entrepreneur for a profit. This is contrasted with a non-capitalist society, where the worker would sell the product of the labour themselves, therefore realizing directly the value incorporated in the product. Thus a commodity (produced under capitalism) has a *use value* (its value in use), its specific qualities like the warmth of a coat, and its *exchange value*, what a commodity is equivalent to as a unit is usually mediated through money. As a result of this separation of use and exchange, people start to think that value inheres in the product itself, rather than it being an expression of social relations and activities between people. As Marx explained,

> a commodity is therefore a mysterious thing, simply because in it the social character of men's labour appears to them as an objective character stamped upon the product of that labour; because the relation of the producers to the sum total of their own labour is presented to them as a social relation, existing not between themselves, but between the products of their labour. This is the reason why the products of labour become commodities, social things whose qualities are at the same time perceptible and imperceptible

by the senses. . . . This I call the Fetishism which attaches itself to the products of labour, so soon as they are produced as commodities, and which is therefore inseparable from the production of commodities. It is only the definite *social relation of people (der Menschen)* itself which here takes on for them the phantasmagoric form of a *relation of things.* (Marx 1990)

Marx called treating something as a relation between things, when in fact it is a set of determinate social relations, a *fetish.* The Frankfurt School believed that real social relations between people are transformed into and misunderstood as relations between things, providing a model of the relationship between social processes, social institutions and consciousness. Rather than the base/superstructure, which reduces institutional and ideological formations to mere epiphenomena or to simple reflections of an economic base; this model provides a sociological explanation for the social determination yet relative autonomy of other social forms, such as culture. Thus such formations can be both socially determined and partially autonomous. Marx is not saying that the illusions that arise from commodity fetishism are wrong, rather that they are necessary and real, and that they nevertheless remain as illusions. Since Lukács, this has been called reification, although this was not used in this way by Marx himself. The Frankfurt School argued that,

We live in a society dominated by the capitalist mode of production . . . a society based on exchange. . . . The particular constellation of social relations which ensures the unity of the capitalist social process also ensures it fetishization and reification. The products of human labour are viewed as independent, "having a life of their own". . . . Capitalism is . . . based on contradictions. Contradictions between socially generated illusions (ideology) and actuality (performance, effects) leads to crisis. . . . A general tendency exists towards capital intensive industries and increased concentration of capital. The free market is progressively replaced by the oligopolistic and monopolistic mass production of standardized goods . . . (Held 1997: 41)

From the beginning the Frankfurt School also opposed phenomenology and existentialism, as they were thought to lack a historical, political and social awareness (and thus tended to focus on the centrality of alienation). Instead, the Frankfurt School used Marx to develop a theory of culture which analysed the changes in the objective features of capitalism. They called attention to the increase in reification – in effect capitalism's ability to transform social labour into a relation between things. Frankfurt School members not only drew on Marx, but also on Weber, Nietzsche and Freud as major critiques of culture and used these insights to understand social and cultural change in the first half of the twentieth century. They also drew upon Nietzsche and Freud to criticize the traditional ideas of the subject or the individual in philosophical idealism and earlier Marxist theory, and they developed a theory of literary production and reception on the basis of Marxism. According to Horkheimer,

> Direct and violent translation of economic domination to political power ("domination" in Gramsci) is only one and not the best source of the stability of a mode of production. To be genuinely effective power must be translated into authority based on (explicit, implicit, or introjected) consent that is mediated by cultural institutions (family, school, religion, workplace, etc.). To use Max Weber's language, power must become legitimate domination (for Gramsci, hegemony). The actual dynamics of society, the rate of social change, cannot therefore be derived from the economy alone, but depends rather on the specificity of cultural institutions and even specific effects of these on personality structure. (Arato and Gebhardt 2005: 7)

Although there were understandable differences between the work of the members of the Institute, they shared common interests in the relationships between domination, myth, nature, the enlightenment and the structure of reason and technique. The two basic concerns of the Frankfurt School were therefore social philosophy and social psychology (Held 1997: 40). Nonetheless, familiar concerns with traditional Marxists' themes are clear in their work, including the notion that we live in a society dominated by the capitalist mode of production and exchange value, together with a concern over the relationship between exchange and abstract labour time. Particularly in relation to both the objective form and the subjective aspect of the production process, and the character of social relations within capitalist society, which are organized into a constellation of interdependencies which ensure the unity and the resultant fetishization and reification of the products of human labour. These issues together with the production of commodities and its ideological form are subject to contradictions which the Frankfurt School argue can result in antagonisms and conflict within society generating a general tendency towards the concentration of capital and the replacement of the 'free market' with oligopolistic and monopolistic practices and the production of standardized mass goods and services. Thus resulting in an increase in the organic composition of capital, such that the amount of fixed capital per worker causes further instabilities in the accumulation process, thus requiring imperialism, expansion and war. As Horkheimer wrote,

> The critical theory of society is, in its totality, the unfolding of a single existential judgment. To put it in broad terms, the theory states that the basic form of the historically given commodity economy on which modern history rests contains in itself the internal and external tensions of the modern era; it generates these tensions over and again in an increasingly heightened form . . . [that] finally hinders further development and drives humanity into a new barbarism. (Horkheimer 1972: 227)

The increased domination of nature and the control produced through science and technology resulted not in human emancipation, but, on the contrary, in greater oppression. The expansion of production has failed to produce greater liberation for humanity from necessity, as orthodox Marxists expected, rather 'the division of control and the execution of tasks, between mental and repetitive mundane labour along with the effects of the culture industry . . . signalled the eclipse of reason' (Held 1997: 156). To address these issues the Frankfurt School developed five elements from Nietzsche's work. First, Nietzsche rejected a philosophy of history based on the Hegelian idea of an ultimate goal of history, a teleology, ideal society or a reconciliation of all contradictions. Rather, he applied contradiction to the optimistic philosophy of history itself, so that the process of historical change might turn into the opposite of all the ideals – what Adorno and Horkheimer call the *Dialectic of Enlightenment* (Horkheimer and Adorno 2006). Secondly, Nietzsche criticized the traditional philosophical idea of the subject; this concept argued that the unity of consciousness is the basis of all reality. The Frankfurt School, on the contrary, argued that social reality could not be reduced to the 'facts of consciousness', thus social reality cannot be reduced to individuals' consciousness of it. But an analysis of social determinations of subjectivity is essential; in other words, subjectivity is a social category. Thirdly, Nietzsche's thought is based on the idea of Will to Power, and the Frankfurt School were interested in analyzing new forms of anonymous and universal political and cultural domination which affects everyone equally and prevents the emergence or formation of class consciousness. Fourthly, Nietzsche launched an attack on the bourgeois culture of his day, which he called bourgeois philistinism, and the Frankfurt School wanted to demonstrate the re-emergence of social contradictions in popular and serious culture, and were critical too of the distinction between high and low culture itself. Lastly, Nietzsche produced an analysis of the Birth of Tragedy in Greek society which was radically sociological but did not idealize these Greek societies. This provided a model for the Frankfurt School's analysis of literary genre, putting their emphasis on literary forms, rather than content.

In order to replace the traditional notion of the subject used in traditional philosophical and Marxism, the Frankfurt School also used Freudian theory to explicate the social formation of subjectivity and its contradictions in advanced capitalist society. They thought Freud's psychoanalytic theories could help explain the connection between economic and political processes and resultant cultural forms. Interestingly, they did not use Freud's more obviously sociological works, like *Civilisation and its Discontents*, rather they relied on Freud's central psychoanalytic concepts. For example, they were interested in the idea that individuality was a formation, an achievement, not an absolute or given, as they wanted to develop a theory of the loss of autonomy in advanced capitalist society which would not idealize what counted as individuality in the first place. They used Freudian theory in the acceptance and reproduction of authority in late capitalist society, in their examination of the success of fascism and in their development of the concept of the culture industry. They also used Freud to understand the influence of mass communications on people's consciousness and unconsciousness, and finally into their general inquiry into the possibility or impossibility of cultural experience in late capitalist society.

One of the most famous individuals associated with the Frankfurt School was Walter Benjamin, although technically not a member of the institute despite being associated with it. Nonetheless, his ideas were very influential and he argued that fascism introduces aesthetics into political life as a way of giving the masses a chance to 'express themselves', instead of a chance to claim the masses' right to change property relations. Benjamin argued that by contrast, communism responds by politicizing art, by demystifying the production, the distribution, the form and the content of art, in an attempt to make art serve the cause of the masses and not vice versa. His writings were very influential on the Frankfurt School, particularly on Adorno. Indeed, he contributed to many of the themes that the Frankfurt School explored, including theories of capitalism, the structure of the state and of the rise of instrumental reason. These further included innovative analyses of science, technology and technique, of individual development, and the susceptibility of people to ideology, as well as consideration of the 'dialectic of enlightenment' and of positivism as a dominant mode of cognition (Held 1997: 38).

Members of the Frankfurt School applied these theorists to the work of contemporary culture (e.g. Jazz, the mass media, Kafka, Mann and Beckett) and capitalism. Many members were artists as well as Marxist theorists and critics: Bloch was a composer, Benjamin wrote short stories, Brecht wrote poems and plays, and Adorno was a composer. Although the members were deeply influenced by Marx, Nietzsche and Freud, they also developed a Marxist aesthetic through polemics against Mann, Beckett and Kafka. The members of the institute believed that they faced the same dilemma as artists as they did as Marxists. They believed that art must 'modernize' itself in the face of colossal change otherwise it would have no importance or relevance. They naturally differed in how this modernization should be achieved, but what is interesting is that they applied their principles of innovation in both theoretical and artistic work. Horkheimer who had undergone psychoanalysis was keen to explore Freud's work in relation to a materialist theory of society, Erich Fromm worked on psychoanalysis to develop its insights in terms of social theory, Herbert Marcuse developed philosophical issues in confrontation with social theory, Leo Löwenthal developed literary-critical studies, while Friedrich Pollock and Henryk Grossman worked on political economy (Jarvis 1998: 9). This was to be an interdisciplinary project to develop a materialism that contributed towards a unification of philosophy and science.

Critical theory is concerned with understanding the particular historical conditions that give rise to the present. In undertaking this analysis, the political project of extending or augmenting the possibilities and space of freedom is a key theme – that is, extending emancipatory reason. As part of this, critical theorists seek to examine human reality as a self-unfolding, self-structured and, importantly, a contradictory whole. Some ways of approaching this include: (i) an examination of the frameworks and constitution of ideas in consciousness and human interaction – what they would call the dialectics of experience; (ii) analysis of the creation, maintenance and change of people's historical, intersubjective concepts; (iii) looking to explicate and identify contradictions; (iv) to leave open the possibility of a critically reflexive understanding of history and tradition.

However, there are clearly no general criteria for critical theory, as it is itself caught within a historical frame which is constantly unfolding. This, of course, leaves critical theory radically open to correction, re-articulation and a mobility of thought. In other words, humans are of a definite historical epoch, as is the rationality and knowledge that is located within them. Nonetheless, many of the members of the Frankfurt School were committed to an abolition of the economic structure which underlays contemporary social change so that a self-fulfilling praxis could emerge. Horkheimer wrote,

Unemployment, economic crises, militarization, terrorist regimes – in a word, the whole condition of the masses – are not due, for example, to limited technological possibilities, as might have been the case in earlier periods, but to the circumstances of production. . . . Production is not geared to the life of the community [to the common interest] while heeding also the claims of individuals; it is geared to the power-backed claims of individuals while being hardly concerned with the life of the community. This is the inevitable result, under the present property order, of the principle that it is sufficient for individuals to look out for themselves. (Horkheimer 1972: 213)

Thus for Horkheimer, the political task of critical theory is to create the possibilities for the individual to be set free, or to free themselves, from these material conditions. The Frankfurt School explore this in relation to research on the changing relations between techniques, the economy and the state in western economies (Held 1997: 52). Thus, as capitalism became integrative colonizing more and more aspects of social life into market relations, the Frankfurt School aimed to critique it. This could be seen in, for examples: (i) central control over individual decision-making, (ii) bureaucratic deliberation over local initiative, (iii) planning of resources instead of the use of market allocation of resources, (iv) technical considerations of general efficiency and rationality over traditional single-minded concern for an individual unit's profitability (from Held 1997: 64). This was understood in relation to the rise of instrumental reason, most notably in rationalization and bureaucratization.

Today, the rise of computational technology in our everyday lives has become a constant theme of modern understandings of our present situation. However, the salient features identified by the Frankfurt School are also reminiscent of another side to the increasing technological mediation of our lives, namely the interpenetration of computer code and algorithms into our private and public relationships with each other; more so when the code is privately or state owned or controlled, without us having access to the contents of these mediating technologies, what I call code-objects or computal objects. These objects contain the logic of behaviour, processing, or merely act as gatekeepers and enforcers of a particular form of rationalization. Similarly, the Frankfurt School sought to map calculative rationalities that emerged in their historical juncture, particularly, instrumental rationality and a tendency towards means-end thinking.

It is, however, important to note that the Frankfurt School members did not think that the rise of instrumental reason of itself was to blame for the 'chaotic, frightening and evil aspects of technological civilisation' (Frankfurt Institute 1972: 94–5). Rather, it is the mode in which the process of rationalization is itself organized that accounts for the 'irrationality of this rationalization'. In advanced capitalist societies, economic anarchy is interwoven with rationalization and technology to create fewer chances for mental and reflective labour. These include the rationalization and standardization of production and consumption; the mechanization of labour; the development of mass transportation and communication; the extension of training; and the dissemination of knowledge about the execution of jobs (Held 1997: 68). This creates the conditions for a decline in critical thinking, and the increase in the susceptibility of a society towards authoritarian politics and extreme or populist movements, such as Nazism. In these societies,

> The individual has to adapt, follow orders, pull levers and "be ready to perform ever different things which are ever the same". The term "reason" becomes synonymous with the process of coordinating means to ends, or else it appears as a meaningless word . . . [Thus] "thinking objectifies itself . . . to become an automatic, self-activating process; an impersonation of the machine that it produces itself so that ultimately the machine can replace it". The values of instrumental reason are accorded a privileged status since they are embodied in the concept of rationality itself. The confounding of calculatory with rational thinking implies that whatever cannot be reduced to number is illusion or metaphysics. (Held 1997: 69)

This also implies an internalization of the logic of capitalism and technological rationality which sustains and reinforces ways of acting that are 'adaptive, passive, and acquiescent' and through the 'mechanisms of social control are strengthened' (Held 1997: 69). With this, we also see the co-option of forces of opposition and means by which it is rendered ineffective with a consequent dilution of their critical function. Nonetheless, behind this process lies 'the domination of men over men. This remains the basic fact' (Adorno 1969: 149). This is a world where capital becomes highly centralized and the economy and political system become increasingly intertwined, leading to a world caught up in administration. Thus, market and bureaucratic practices increasingly become part of everyday life and are targeted by economic and corporate actors who seek to manage and control these activities. Therefore 'as individual consciousness and unconsciousness were encroached upon by agencies which organize free time – for example radio, television . . . – the Frankfurt theorists stressed the urgency of developing a sociology of mass culture' (Held 1997: 77). For Adorno, Horkheimer and Marcuse,

> Sociology and culture are inseparable: to analyse a work of art, or a particular cultural artefact, is to analyse and assess the way in which it is interpreted. This entails an inquiry into its formation and reception. Such an inquiry seeks to understand given works in terms of their social origins, form, content and function – in terms of the social totality. The conditions of labour, production, and distribution must be examined, for society expresses itself through its cultural life and cultural phenomenon contain within themselves reference to the socio-economic whole. . . . It must

explore in detail the internal structure of cultural forms (the way in which the organization of society is crystallised in cultural phenomenon) and the mechanisms which determine their reception. (Held 1997: 77–8)

Thus, we can now turn to connecting these strands drawn from critical theory to the problem raised by the digital, and how critical theory can confront the digital today, particularly when viewed through the lens of software and computer code.

The digital and critical theory

The challenge to critical theory explored throughout this book is the prescient warning given by the cyberneticist Norbert Wiener in 1960:

> It may well be that in principle we cannot make any machine the elements of whose behaviour we cannot comprehend sooner or later. This does not mean in any way that we shall be able to comprehend these elements in substantially less time than the time required for operation of the machine, or even within any given number of years or generations. . . . An intelligent understanding of [a machine's] mode of performance may be delayed until long after the task which [it has] been set has been completed. . . . This means that, though machines are theoretically subject to human criticism, such criticism may be ineffective until long after it is relevant. (Wiener 1960: 1355)

Today we live in a world of technical beings, whose function and operation are becoming increasingly interconnected and critical to supporting the lifeworld that we inhabit. Crucially though, this is combined with an increased invisibility or opaqueness of the underlying technologies, and an inability to understand how these systems work, either individually or in concert. This digital world is one of complex, process-oriented computational systems that take on an increasingly complex cognitive heavy-lifting role in society. Without these technologies in place our postmodern financialized economies would doubtlessly collapse – resulting in a crisis of immense proportions. Indeed, our over-reliance on digital technology to manage, control, monitor and support many of the aspects of society we now take for granted is predicated on avoiding the kinds of systematic failure and breakdown that occur routinely in computer systems.

Our societies are increasingly relying on digital technologies of the form that incorporate computational and therefore calculative and computational rationalities which therefore raise important questions for critical theory. Many of these systems were initially designed to support or aid the judgement of people in undertaking a number of activities, analyses and decisions, but have long since 'surpassed the understanding of their users and become indispensible to them' (Weizenbaum 1984: 236). Here we might think of the iconic place that the mobile phone has grown to occupy in our societies, as notebook, calendar, address book and entertainment system, as well as multiplexed communications device. Indeed, the 'systems of rules and criteria that are embodied in such computer systems become immune to change, because, in the absence of a detailed understanding of the inner workings of a computer system, any substantial modification of it is very likely to render the whole system inoperative and possibly unrestorable. Such computer systems can therefore only grow' (Weizenbaum 1984: 236).Thus our growing reliance on small software applications soon becomes more complex as they are networked and interconnected into larger software platforms and servers. Think of the increasing networked nature of the simple calorie-counting functionality which is now reconciled across multiple devices, timezones, people, projects and technologies.

As our reliance on these technical systems grows the technical groups responsible for these systems grow in importance – such that their rationalities, expressed through particular logics, embedded in the interface and the code become internalized within the user as a particular habitus, or way of doing, appropriate to certain social activities. As Marcuse argued, 'the objective and impersonal character of technological rationality bestows upon the bureaucratic groups the universal dignity of reason' and likewise with its application in computer programming source code. Indeed, the 'rationality embodied of giant enterprises makes it appear as if men, in obeying them, obey the dictum of an objective rationality' (Marcuse 1978: 154). This is true too of algorithms, perhaps even more so. Marcuse further argues that it creates a danger of a 'private bureaucracy [which] fosters a delusive harmony between the special and the common interest. Private power relationships appear not only as relationships between objective things but also as the rule of rationality itself' (Held 1997: 68). This connects again to the question of power, of those who understand and deploy the computer programming techniques, which includes the reading and writing of code, in our societies. Certainly, the norms and values of a society are increasingly crystallized within the structures of algorithms and software, but also a form of rationality that is potentially an instrumentalized rationality and also in many cases a privatized one too.

As Held writes, 'as a result, the conditions are created for a decline in the susceptibility of society to critical thinking' (Held 1997: 68). Critical theory has long been accustomed to questioning where 'thinking objectifies itself', and applying critical approaches to the specific problems raised by instrumental rationality. Combining both close and distant readings of technologies with critical political economy enables the penetration of these technologies into the culture, ecology and even subjectivity of the postmodern actor to be critically appraised and analysed. Indeed, part of this discussion has to be the relationship between instrumental reason and what I want to call computational reason. But, as Held (1997: 69) argues 'the decline of critical thought is also furthered by the incorporation of opposition. Opposition . . . have all too often become mimics of the dominant apparatus'. Hence, the dominant apparatus serves as a means of communication creating and legitimating accepted discursive strategies and rhetorics which are, to some degree, shaped not only by rationalities of computation, but also by the affordances of the medium of software itself – something we will return to later in the book.

Indeed, as Kitchin (2011) argues, software can be extremely amenable to certain forms of governmentality, an invisible web that wraps itself around society in increasingly dense weaves and patterns,

> Over the past two centuries a mode of governmentality has developed in Western society that is heavily reliant on generating and monitoring systematic information about individuals by institutions. Software-enabled technologies qualitatively alter both the depth and the scope of this disciplinary gaze, but also introduce new forms of governance, because they make the systems and apparatus of governance more panoptical in nature. . . . Software creates more effective systems of surveillance and creates new capture systems that actively reshape behaviour by altering the nature of a task . . . there is still much conceptual and empirical work to be done to understand how forms of governance are being transformed and the role played by software, and not simply the broader technologies they enable. (Kitchin 2011: 949)

It is at this point we can begin to materialize the digital and ask about the specific mediations that facilitate these changes. Here, we need to be cognizant of software and digital computers connected through powerful network protocols and technologies. These systems are generally opaque to us, and we rely on them in many cases without questioning their efficacy. Think, for example, of the number of poorly designed website forms that we are increasingly required to fill in, whether for subscriptions, job applications or college classes. These are becoming an obligatory passage point which cannot be avoided, there is no going around these computational gatekeepers, and they are the only way certain systems can even be accessed at all.

They are also built of computational logics which are themselves materializations of assumptions, values and norms, often taken for granted, by the designers and programmers of the systems (e.g. gender, race, class, etc.). We need to develop methods, metaphors, concepts and theories in relation to this software and code to enable us to think through and about these systems, as they will increasingly have important critical and political consequences. That is why being able to read these code-based protocols is an important starting point (Galloway 2006). Indeed, what we might call *protocol teardowns* will be important for seeing the limits of reading code by breaking code, selectively removing selections from a protocol to see if it works and what happens. New metaphors will also be crucial, for example, another way of understanding these digital systems could be through the analogy of law, such as that made popular by Lawrence Lessig (1999) in terms of 'code is law', as Minsky explains:

> The programmer himself state[s] . . . "legal" principles which permit . . . "appeals," he may have only a very incomplete understanding of when and where in the course of the program's operation these procedures will call on each other. And for a particular "court," he has only a sketchy idea of only some of the circumstances that will cause it to be called upon. In short, once past the beginner level . . . programmers write – not "sequences" [of computer code instructions] – but specifications for the individuals of little societies. Try as he may he will often be unable fully to envision in advance all the details of their interactions. For that, after all, is why he needs the computer. (Weizenbaum 1984: 234)

From the founding of the computational 'polities', the interconnections between them are outlined and the interfaces and boundaries between them are detailed and circumscribed in computer code. These systems are then put into the management and oversight of production, distribution and consumption. This automation and control of the production 'value chain' enables dramatic cost reductions and flexibility. In addition, there is a remarkable feedback loop such that these computational management systems are also applied back into computational technology itself. This leads to an acceleration in the shrinkage of hardware but the expansion of raw computing power for these computational systems and platforms.

In the wake of these new digital technologies facilitated by low-cost fabrication and breakthroughs in software and hardware production, the world has seen major changes in the ways in which we store, access and create information and knowledge, not to mention the profound changes in terms of communication, mobile media and instantaneous connection (Berry 2011a).

This has resulted in huge economic wealth for a minority, and a major increase in the penetration of digital technologies into all aspects of our social lives, from banking to education, from washing machines to home entertainment systems. That is, a rapid growth in the computational industries and the colonization by computation of other industries that have sought to compete, or which are easily turned algorithmic. In particular, we might consider the music industry which with the compact disc became a *partially* digital industry. It was only a small step with the digital transformation of the music industry's databanks into a truly computational form, with the compressed file formats, such as MP3, and digital downloads and streaming technologies, such as Spotify, that it became a fully digital industry – even if it has still not fully accepted its new computational structure. Organizationally, the entertainment industry has remained understandably wedded to its industrial entertainment structure and the production of standardized cultural products stamped onto standardized manufactured discs and boxes – but it is a matter of time before these new digital forces of production lead to a restructuring of these industries. Indeed, the university has also experienced the aftershocks of these changes in terms of electronic scholarship, with the rapid growth of digital repositories, Google searches, 'folksonomies', digital humanities, and of course, a tsunami of student plagiarism thanks to the wonders of Wikipedia and cut-and-paste (see Berry 2012b). How these technologies are mediated through social labour will be crucially important to the structure of the organizations in the coming decades.

The internet has had a lot to do with the growth of this computational 'digital' world, as a gigantic network of networks through the TCP/IP protocol. Built onto this foundation was the original notion of the web, which was designed around 'pages' and a client-server architecture by Tim Berners–Lee. The way we have traditionally thought about the internet as pages or websites (and which was always only a subset of internet technologies) is now changing to the newer industrial internet and the concept of 'real-time streams'.

So too in my own daily experience, I now check my Twitter or Facebook stream first thing every morning, as this aggregates the streams of other people and organizations, giving highlighted links, articles and key issues for the day. This is a crucial resource for keeping up with the latest news and scholarly literature, debates and ideas being circulated, and also connects me to people and things that are being discussed in conferences across the world. Then, if I have extra time, as the Twitter stream is often over-filled with material, I will look at other websites to see what is happening in the technology area and the key talking points and issues being raised – although these are increasingly destination front-ends to real-time back-end systems. These sites are updated in real-time by a process of aggregation and curation, both algorithmic and human, which gives them an excellent overview of their respective areas. Finally, I might check into the Guardian and the BBC to check the daily news. It is this reversal from reading the traditional daily newspaper of record, usually print or broadcast type news and information, that epitomizes the changes I want to argue as being paradigmatic in relation to the reconfiguration of everyday life by the digital.

Here, we might also consider the fragility of the infrastructural systems of the internet, sustained as they are by technical practices that enable incredible computational and communicational feats, while nonetheless being subject to possible break-downs and disruptions. This is demonstrated by the case of a lorry crashing into the power supply at Rackspace, a leading cloud computing provider, 'knocking out power to the company's Dallas facility. The Rackspace data center switched over to generator power, but two chillers failed to start back up again, compromising the cooling system and forcing Rackspace to take customer servers offline to protect the equipment' (Miller 2007), widely reported as 'Quick, Plug The Internet Back In: Major Rackspace Outage' (Arrington 2007) and 'Failure Happens: An SLA is just a contract & Data Centers are single points of failure too' (Robbins 2007), it is nonetheless amazing how much of the internet traffic was taken down by this incident, but also how quickly it was brought back up again – in 3 hours in total. These problems of massive failure of systems that support the internet, especially linked to a single point of failure, are an ongoing research area related to recovery-oriented computing, but also business continuity and internet infrastructure engineering (Radlab 2009).

It should be noted at this point that Morozov's claim that the 'internet does not exist' and referring to it using scare quotes as 'internet' is unhelpful (2013: 15, 61–2, 114).[2] Of course, in an epistemological sense the internet is unrealizable; certainly instantiations of it in empirical, concrete moments clearly are deviations from this sociological ideal-type, however, 'concepts [when] given ideal typical status, are held to be "logically coherent", notwithstanding the fact that [ideal types] are unrealisable in practice. Any empirical deviations are held not to call into question their analytical truths' (Holmwood 2013). In the case of the internet, there are certainly certain claims made about its qualities and its force, which may be distinguished from its empirical reality; however, this is not to diminish the importance of the internet as an important signifier and for its conceptual force, as Holmwood further argues in relation to neoliberalism,

The "hegemony" of neo-liberalism . . . is achieved, in part, by its utilisation of a widely accepted epistemology of social science (that of ideal types, etc.). We could instead take the unrealisable nature of the neo-liberal construct of the market as an index of its irrationality (rather than claim it to be rational but unreal). That we do not is because we remain committed to the social sciences it makes possible. (Holmwood 2013)

With the growth of computationalism and the internet as, perhaps, a legitimating epistemological framework, many sectors of society and the economy are increasingly subject to computational processes and the challenge is to use critical theory to help think through the consequences of this. Rejecting the 'internet' as an irrationality as Morovoz aims to do does not help us to think critically about the way in which concepts can 'provide the basis for policy based upon its putative rationality' (Holmwood 2013). This may be played out as an empty signifier and the idealist prescriptions it suggests, but it is also deployed through the proliferation of material black boxes, cables, routers and opaque computational devices, which due to their opacity we are seemingly unable to read or fathom. Indeed, as Weizenbaum warned in 1984:

> most of us have thought enough about the progressively increasing dependence upon computers in commerce and industry to project a picture in which the very functioning of society depends on an orderly and meaningful execution of billions of electronic instructions every second. . . . In mastering the programming and control of computers, we [in the university] especially could play a critical role. It may well be that no other organization is able to play this role as we are, yet no more important role may exist in science and technology today. The importance of the role stems, as has been noted, from the fact that the computer has been incorporating itself, and will surely continue to incorporate itself, into most of the functions that are fundamental to the support, protection, and development of our society. (Weizenbaum 1984: 242)

The unique means of reading and writing in a computational society is clearly a crucial question in relation to these issues. Addressing the specific problems raised by a particular literacy connected to the digital is a pressing issue. How should we read the digital – and to what extent should and can we be expected to write the digital?

One way of thinking about this is through how the digital (or computational) presents us with a number of seemingly theoretical and empirical contradictions which we can understand within this commonly used set of binaries outlined by Liu (2011) and which I want to extend and discuss here: (1) linearity versus hypertextuality; (2) narrative versus database; (3) permanent versus ephemeral; (4) bound versus unbound; (5) individual versus social; (6) deep versus shallow; (7) focused versus distracted; (8) close reading versus distant reading; (9) fixed versus processual; and finally (10) digital (virtual) versus real (physical). Here, I am not interested in critiquing the use of binaries *per se*, and which of course remains an important task, rather I think the binaries are interesting for the indicative light they cast on drawing analytical distinctions between categories and collections related to the digital itself. These binaries can be useful means of thinking through many of the positions and debates that take place within both theoretical and empirical work on mapping the digital and will play out in the discussions throughout this book. Indeed, the collection of binaries can be thought of as part of a mapping of the digital through a form of constellation of concepts, some of which I now outline in more detail,

Linear versus Hypertextuality: The notion of a linear text, usually fixed within a paper form, is one that has often been taken for granted within the humanities. Computational systems, however, have challenged this model of reading linearly due to the ease with which linked data can be incorporated into digital text. This means that experimentation with textual form and the way in which a reader might negotiate a text can be explored. Of course, the primary model for hypertextual systems is today strongly associated with the worldwide web and HTML, although other systems have been developed. There are, of course, examples of non-linear paperbound systems but it is argued that the digital manifests something new and interesting in this regard.

Narrative versus Database: The importance of narrative as an epistemological frame for understanding has been immensely important in the humanities. Whether as a starting point for beginning an analysis or through attempts to undermine or problematize narratives within texts, humanities scholars have usually sought to use narrative as an explanatory means of exploring both the literary and history. Computer technology, however, has offered scholars an alternative way of understanding how knowledge might be structured through the notion of the database (see Manovich 2001). Although as with all these binaries there are clearly a spectrum of normative forms, nonetheless these distinctions are often pointed towards as indicative of digital media (see Bassett 2007).

Permanent versus Ephemeral: One of the hallmarks of much 'traditional' or 'basic' humanities scholarship has been concerned with objects and artefacts that have been understood as relatively stable in relation to digital works. This is especially in disciplines that have internalized the medium specificity of a form, for example, the book in English Literature, which shifts attention to the content of the medium. In contrast, digital works are notoriously ephemeral in their form, both in the materiality of the substrates (e.g. computer memory chips, magnetic tape/disks, plastic disks, etc.) and in the plasticity of the form.

This also bears upon born-digital from which derivative copies are made. Indeed, it could be argued that in the digital world there is only the copy (although recent moves in Cloud computing and digital rights management are partial attempts to re-institute the original through technical means). The ephemerality of the digital must also be thought about by reference to the counterfactual resilience and permanence of some digital objects such as hard disk drives whose contents can sometimes survive extreme conditions such as fire, water and even physical damage.

Bound versus Unbound: A notable feature of digital artefacts is that they tend to be unbound in character. Unlike books, which have clear boundary points marked by the cardboard that makes up the covers, digital objects boundaries are drawn by the file format in which they are encoded. This makes it an extremely permeable border, and one that is made of the same digital code that marks the content. Additionally, digital objects are easily networked and aggregated, processed and transcoded into other forms further problematizing boundary points between them. In terms of reading practices, it can be seen that the permeability of boundaries can radically change the reading experience. To some extent the boundlessness of the digital form has been constrained by digital rights management and related technical protection measures. However, these techniques remain open to hacking techniques and once the locks are broken the digital content is easily distributed, edited and recombined.

Individual versus Social: Traditional humanities has focused strongly on approaches to texts that are broadly individualistic in as much as the reader is understood to undertake certain bodily practices (e.g. sitting in a chair, book on knees, concentration on the linear flow of text). Digital technologies, particularly when networked, open up these practices to a much more social experience of reading, with e-readers like the Amazon Kindle encouraging the sharing of highlighted passages, and Tumblr-type blogs and Twitter enabling social reading and discussion around and within the digital text. There are also new forms of curating and collaborative writing methods mediated by digital tools such as in practices such as 'booksprints' which are highly creative and collaborative modes of writing text (Booksprints 2013). Relatedly new digital media are also multi-modal in terms of trans-media forms and enable new social reading practices.

Deep versus Shallow: Deep reading is the presumed mode of understanding that requires time and attention to develop a hermeneutic reading of a text, this form requires humanistic reading skills to be carefully learnt and applied. In contrast a shallow mode is a skimming or surface reading of a text, more akin to gathering a general overview or précis of the text. This deep form of reading that is closely associated with humanities scholarship and the appreciation of a well-read book, in contrast to the internet trend towards 'tl;dr' or 'too long; didn't read'. Deep reading as a practice requires training over long periods of time which may be challenged by the real-time streaming forms of always-on short-form or micro-form media such as Twitter and email.

Focused versus Distracted: Relatedly, the notion of focused reading is also implicitly understood as an important aspect of humanities scholarship. This is the focus on a particular text, set of texts or canon, and the space and time to give full attention to them. By contrast, in a world of real-time information and multiple windows on computer screens, reading practices are increasingly distracted, partial and fragmented (hyperattention). However, there have been some interesting attempts to allay this problem with either focal technologies which remove clutter and distraction while working at the computer. Additionally augmented or extended cognition tools that offer reconciliation at a higher level have been developed; however, it does appear that digital media as currently constituted under late capitalism tends towards a distracted form of reading ideal for consumption practices.

Close Reading versus Distant Reading: Close reading is the practice associated with the careful, slow, explication and interpretation of textual sources. It is usually associated with a heteronomous collection of practices, but generally they are concentrated on a small number, or just a single text. Distant reading is the application of technologies to enable a great number of texts to be incorporated into an analysis through the ability of computers to process large quantities of text relatively quickly. Moretti (2007) has argued that this approach allows us to see social and cultural forces at work through collective cultural systems. Again, this is related to a notion of extended cognition through the use of digital technologies to précis, rework, summarize or visualize large quantities of data, whether textual or otherwise. This threat to close reading practices is often manifested or linked to a notion of liberal subjectivity and the enlightenment project of modernity. It is considered highly significant for all humanities disciplines.

Fixed versus Processual: The digital medium facilitates new ways of presenting media that are highly computational. This raises new challenges for scholarship in understanding digital media and the methods for approaching these media forms. It also raises questions for older humanities that are increasingly accessing their research object through the mediation of processual computational systems, and more particularly through software and computer code. The issue of processual media, in relation to the fixed or time-based media of the twentieth century, is that they incorporate feedback into their media forms, such as interactivity, but also this could be reading speed, colour preferences, etc. in order to change the way a media is perceived or understood. Digital media are also able to adapt to the reader/viewer in real-time, changing the content, narrative, structure, presentation and so forth on the fly, as a kind of surveillance literature which is reading the reader as she reads.

Real (physical) versus Digital (virtual): This is a common dichotomy that draws some form of dividing line between the so-called real and the so-called digital. Increasingly, with the collapse in our experience of computation from its fixed desktop location, we are using computation in everyday spaces, and which infuses the everyday environment with a computational overlay or layer, such that the computational is not distinct from but deeply embedded in everyday life and hence is post-digital. It is still crucial to historicize the notion of the digital, though, particularly in relation to our changing experience of the digital as previously 'online' and todays 'always online', such that being offline increasingly becomes an experience of only the very rich (as choice) or the very poor (by necessity).

Above, we gestured towards the softwarization of 'close reading' and the changing structure of a 'preferred reader' or subject position, towards one that is increasingly algorithmic (of course, this could be a human or non-human reader). Indeed, it is suggestive that as a result of these moves to digital real-time streams we may see the move from a linear model of narrative, exemplified by print books, to a 'dashboard of a calculation interface' and 'navigational platforms', exemplified by new forms of software platforms. Indeed, these platforms, and here I am thinking of a screenic interface such as the iPad, allow the 'reader' to use the hand-and-eye in haptic interfaces to develop interactive exploratory approaches towards knowledge/information and 'discovery'. This could, of course, still enable humanistic notions of 'close reading' but the preferred reading style would increasingly be 'distant' partially, or completely, mediated through computational code-based devices.

At this point in the book these issues are necessarily abstract. However, these important aspects will be reflected upon in the chapters that follow, and in the particular critical problematics raised by the digital. Indeed, the use of computational systems creates a highly computationally mediated lifeworld which raises challenging questions that Horkheimer envisioned already in 1947 when he talked about the prevalence of science as the arbiter of knowledge and truth:

Justice, equality, happiness, tolerance, all the concepts that. . . . Were in preceding centuries supposed to be inherent in or sanctioned by reason, have lost their intellectual roots. They are still aims and ends, but there is no rational agency authorized to appraise and link them to objective reality. Endorsed by venerable historical documents, they may still enjoy a certain prestige, and some are contained in the supreme law of the greatest countries. Nevertheless, they lack any confirmation by reason in its modern sense. Who can say that any one of these ideals is more closely related to truth than its opposite? According to the philosophy of the average modern intellectual, there is only one authority, namely, science, conceived as the classification of facts and the calculation of possibilities. The statement that justice and freedom are better in themselves than injustice and oppression is scientifically unverifiable and useless. It has come to sound as meaningless in itself as would the statement that red is more beautiful than blue, or that an egg is better than milk. (Horkheimer, quote in Weizenbaum 1984: 252)

This dislocation of important emancipatory concepts from reason raises challenging questions for a world that increasingly encodes similar principles within the computational logics of software and algorithms. While it is clear that not all judgements and decision points can be delegated to code, nonetheless a substantial number can be, and it is not yet clear where that line is. The question of articulation of these emancipatory concepts within code, and the danger this might pose to critical thinking is an important question. As computation becomes increasingly powerful, there is a temptation to allow algorithms and code to 'judge', as indeed currently happens with, for example, some parking ticket systems. So rationality encoded within the limits of computation is a form of instrumental rationality and becomes automated and prescriptive, an issue that needs to be made manifest for democratic societies.

For this book, this includes a critical engagement with digital code (software), and I seek to reveal how the digital is embedded with a particular instrumental rationality, and how by the development of counter-institutions and 'counter-code', new possibilities for praxis are available within the digital. Indeed, the political potential of code signalled by certain civil society groups such as free and open source software, Wikileaks, hackers, cypherpunks and the Electronic Freedom Foundation (EFF), certainly raise intriguing possibilities, provided they are not limited by instrumentalized computational rationality. However, for the researcher or political actor, even just beginning to understand digital code is horrendously difficult due to its opacity. Indeed, it is still relatively rare for a researcher, let alone a political activist, to perform any form of reading of digital code at all. This again raises key questions about the kinds of literacies that are appropriate for active citizenship today.

I therefore argue, following Adorno, that we need to perform a critique of knowledge (*Erkenntniskritik*) in order that we can make a social critique (*Kritik an der Gesellschaft*) of contemporary social formations. In other words, just as theorists have discussed the 'linguistic turn' in social and political theory, here I argue that we need to question the 'computational turn'. For Horkheimer, Adorno and Marcuse, sociology and critique are inseparable, they must explore a cultural artefact's formation and reception. As Held (1997) explains, 'such an inquiry seeks to understand given works in terms of their social origins, form, content and function – in terms of the social totality. . . . But a sociology of culture cannot rest with an analysis of the general relations between types of cultural products. . . . It must also explore in detail the internal structure of cultural forms (the way in which the organization of society is crystallized in cultural phenomenon) and the mechanisms which determine their reception' Held (1997: 77). That is, it should account for the processes of production, reproduction, distribution, exchange and consumption. With software we are presented with a unique location for just this kind of critique.

But, it is also no longer surprising that code is becoming an important source of profit and as such will be a key resource and source of conflict in the twenty-first century. Today, the digital has become the key medium in our societies and it is critical that we develop our critical attention on this little understood but hugely important subject. The situation has changed due to the quantitative shift in digital usage and reach, and as its functions change so does the way in which the digital interacts with our everyday lives. So, in the following chapters, I want to consider the quotidian experience of the digital and where it lies in our everyday relationships with each other and new media technology. I explore how the digital is increasingly mediating our experiences of the world, through computational devices like the smart phone and mobile tablets. I also start drawing links with critical theorists' concern with the notion of instrumental reason and domination – especially considering that a history of the digital is in many cases also a history of a military-industrial complex that has become a key aspect of the entertainment industry.

However, this is not merely a claim that a magnified or excess of instrumental reason is delegated into machines such that the computational and the instrumental become synonymous. Heidegger criticized this as a poor understanding of technology, and it holds equally true for computational technology. As Dreyfus argues,

> In his final analysis of technology, Heidegger was critical of those who, still caught in the subject/object picture, thought that technology was dangerous because it embodied instrumental reason. Modern technology, he insists, is "something completely different and therefore new." The goal of technology Heidegger then tells us, is the more and more flexible and efficient ordering of resources, not as objects to satisfy our desires, but simply for the sake of ordering. (Dreyfus 1997)

This Heideggerian insight needs to be combined with critical theory to provide an understanding of the extent to which we live in a world full of technologies and devices that also serve to make possible the fulfilment of our desires – although usually without giving any indication of how digital technologies mediate this satisfaction. Digital devices have for many people become akin to magic. As David Parnas argued, 'technology is the black magic of our time. Engineers are seen as wizards; their knowledge of arcane rituals and obscure terminology seems to endow them with an understanding not shared by the laity' (Berry 2011: 35–6). Indeed, 'hiddenness is a powerful . . . force of mystification. . . . Marx writes that truly to understand the workings of exchange, one must leave the marketplace and venture "into the hidden abode of production"' (Galloway 2006: 99). The digital is simultaneously technical and social, material and symbolic, but it is also a historically located concept, as are its instantiations in concrete computational devices. This is not a new problem, but it does make the digital challenging to investigate and, I believe, it puts critical theory in a unique position to problematize.

Further, the social dimension of language production and usage is crucially important both to appreciate the way in which the digital is a social practice that aids interpretation, and the extent to which recent innovations in digital technologies like Twitter, Facebook and Google+ lie at the intersection of technology, language and social practice. As Gadamer argues, 'in fact history does not belong to us, but we belong to it. Long before we understand ourselves through the process of self-examination, we understand ourselves in a self-evident way in the family, society and state in which we live' (Winograd and Flores 1987: 29).

Thus, history and the historicity of our experience of the world are critical to our ability to know and understand ourselves. Digital technologies form a greater part of the technical and media ecology of the environment that surrounds us and records our memories and in some cases *is* our memories. So, increasingly, digital media becomes part of our cultural background, and this contributes to our very way of experiencing the world and living and using language.[3] Again, as Gadamer explains:

> To acquire an awareness of a situation is, however, always a task of particular difficulty. The very idea of a situation means that we are not standing outside it and hence are unable to have any objective knowledge of it. We are always within the situation, and to throw light on it is a task that is never entirely completed. This is true also of the hermeneutic situation, i.e., the situation in which we find ourselves with regard to the tradition that we are trying to understand. The illumination of this situation – effective-historical reflection – can never be completely achieved, but this is not due to a lack

in the reflection, but lies in the essence of the historical being which is ours. To exist historically means that knowledge of oneself can never be complete. (Winograd and Flores 1987: 29)

The task, then, is not merely to undertake better 'science' or more empirical work. Rather, this is an affirmation of the particular research programmes exemplified by the humanities disciplines and thus a call to them to explore the challenges raised by the digital, to uncover, not only the 'politics of the database' (Poster 1996: 93) but also the politics of the stream. Knowledge, and humanities knowledge in particular:

Have a greater familiarity with an ambiguous, intractable, sometimes unreachable [moral] world that won't reduce itself to any correspondence with the symbols by means of which one might try to measure it. There is a world that stands apart from all efforts of historians to reduce [it] to the laws of history, a world which defies all efforts of artists to understand its basic laws of beauty. [Man's] practice should involve itself with softer than scientific knowledge . . . that is not a retreat but an advance. (Weizenbaum 1984: 279)

In the next chapter, we turn to the questions raised here, particularly in relation to unpicking the problematic raised by the digital, to carefully think through the implications of a computational society. This, of course, necessitates a more thorough examination of the conditions of possibility of a digital or informational society, through an exploration and thinking through of the code, software and algorithms that act as the crucial infrastructure of the computational.

3

The softwarization of society

If we confront sociology's most important question: what is society? we could say that we can no longer straightforwardly describe society as a thing. This is a crucial step towards understanding society as a process, which means that our societies are in a constant state of re-making, both as societies and as capitalist economies. Just as Adorno regarded modern capitalism as 'progressively self-totalizing', in as much as nothing can be thought of as outside of capitalism, and 'resist commensurability with exchange-value' (Jarvis 1998: 44), today we are increasingly unable to think beyond the limits of the totalizing effects of computationality. Computational categories increasingly define the limits of our knowledge, even to the extent to which computation reshapes capitalism into its computational capitalist form. Thus, in common with Adorno's articulation of his interest in society, we might agree that,

> this resistance of society to rational comprehension should be understood first and foremost as the sign of relationships between men which have grown increasingly independent of them, opaque, now standing of against human beings like some different substance. It ought to be the task of sociology today to comprehend the incomprehensible, the advance of human beings into the inhuman. (Adorno 1969: 147)

Adorno argues that we should not present social relations, which are 'historical and produced', as if they were objects given to us to study. Indeed, social relations have become a 'real illusion', and even though they remain made up of the human individuals that actuate them, they have some form of autonomy. This is magnified by the introduction of computational structures that crystallize certain social forms and perpetuate and prescribe them back onto society and individuals in a multitude of ways. Nonetheless, the critical insight of Adorno remains relevant. These social relations, regardless of whether they are or are not instantiated with computer code and algorithms, have emerged historically and hence can be changed. Thus we might ask,

> Is it possible to speak of sociological "laws"? Adorno repeatedly, and perhaps surprisingly, rejects the neo-Kantian distinction . . . between the "nomothetic" natural sciences, concerned with organizing appearances under laws, and the "idiographic" human sciences, concerned with specifying unique particulars not susceptible to subsumption under laws. . . . As Adorno points out, there is no such thing as an object which is in itself "purely" sociological; all phenomena have non-sociological aspects. (Jarvis 1998: 46–7)

Rather than attempt to ground an approach in a particular 'scientific' status through the idea of methodology, the aim here, following Adorno, is not to renounce philosophy in favour of methodology. That is, avoiding the so-called distinction between fact and value, immensely important to both Durkheim and Weber, Adorno argues that we are not to think,

> that I would like to fall back into a dogmatic hypostasis of some kind of universal anthropological values. This is as far from my position as is the Weberian position on the other side; rather, the Kantian proposition that the critical way alone remains open seems to me to be of greater relevance, even with reference to the so-called problem of values. (Jarvis 1998: 48)

Hence, we must follow a critical path and the aim 'of a critical social theory is to allow the entanglement of fact with value to become visible, by showing up both the way in which tacit valuations are present in all apparently purely factual description, and the way in which apparently pure valuations always presuppose descriptive models' (Jarvis 1998: 48). This is the historicization of philosophical analysis as a necessary move that goes beyond a purely methodological approach. Adorno made this crucial move because philosophy still takes seriously the possibility of there being a difference between appearance and reality or essence. Indeed,

> existing sociological method . . . examined only appearance. "Dialectics", as he calls his own interpretative approach, "will not allow itself to be robbed of the distinction between essence and appearance". In Adorno's theory this means showing how a supposedly given fact – an appearance, be it epistemological, metaphysical, or sociological – is mediated by something that does not appear. To seek the reality behind appearances is, he claims, "to give a name to what secretly holds the machinery together", the machinery of society. (O'Connor 2013: 24)

With this in mind, I now want to turn to thinking through the context of a society that is increasingly reliant upon a machinery that certainly does not 'appear' – that is, software, algorithms and code. This is a crucial move in developing our understanding of contemporary society, political economy and aesthetics, as software mediation has reached a point at which it is at 'saturation' levels. Thus we need to move to a philosophical and historical critical contextualization of computation beyond purely methodological approaches which seek to empirically map or document their research object. These kinds of ahistorical digital methods attempt to deploy raw 'facts' from which they attempt to derive 'laws' from data, taking, as they do, past and present experiences as though they are predictive of future experience. Indeed, critical theory, as a project committed to social change, is irreconcilable with such empiricism. When software has become crucial to the everyday operation of the society, it is clear that something important has shifted, and that we need to develop critical concepts and theories to take account of it. For example, Bernard Stiegler usefully glosses his important contribution to understanding technology, as he explains:

(1) that technical becoming must be thought through the concept of the technical system; (2) that there is no human society which is not constituted by a technical system; (3) that a technical system is traversed by evolutionary tendencies which, when they concretely express themselves, induce a change in the technical system; (4) that such a change necessitates adjustments with the other systems constituting society; (5) that these adjustments constitute a suspension and a re-elaboration of the socio-ethnic programmes which form the unity of the social body; (6) that this re-elaboration is a selection amongst possibilities, effected across retentional systems, themselves constituted by mnemo-techniques or mnemo-technologies, the becoming of which is tied to that of the technical system, and the appropriation of which permits the elaboration of selection criteria constituting a motive, that is, a characteristic stage of psychic and collective individuation. (Stiegler 2011: 166–7, fn 15)

Through the introduction of softwarized technical systems, it is sometimes claimed that we live in an information society (for a discussion see Berry 2008). While numerous definitions exist, we now appreciate that all around us software is running on digital computers in an attempt to make our lives more comfortable, safer, faster and convenient – although this may conversely mean we feel more stressed, depressed or empty of meaning or purpose due to our new softwarized world. Indeed, it seems more accurate to state that we live in a *softwarized* society. From the entertainment systems we use to listen to music and watch television, to the engine systems that allow us to experience unprecedented fuel efficiency and even electric cars, software is doing the heavy lifting that makes the old industrial and consumer experience better, easier and cheaper. We therefore need to develop an approach to this field that uses concepts and methods drawn from philosophy, politics, history, anthropology, sociology, media studies, computer science and the humanities more generally, to try to understand these issues – particularly the way in which software increasingly penetrates our everyday life. Thus, the relatively new field of software studies has a two-fold challenge of having to reorder and construct methods and theories that are appropriate to studying software, together with undertaking the difficult task of uncovering helpful exemplars and examples that can assist in the teaching of the critical understanding of software itself. As Kitchin explains,

> we know very little about the ways in which software is socially created; the nature of software itself; how discourse, practices, and knowledge get translated into algorithms and code; the geographies and political economy of software development; how software is embedded into various social systems; how software applications work with each other to create complex assemblages that work within and across scales; the power wielded through software's "secondary agency"; and how software alternatively modulates the production of space and transforms the nature of governance. (Kitchin 2011: 946)

The speed and iteration of innovation in this area of technology might be incredibly fast and accelerating, but software *can* be materialized so that we may think critically about it. For example, it is important to recognize that software requires a platform upon which to run. Platforms can be either hardware or software based, but they provide the conditions and environment which makes it possible for the software to function correctly. The platform can offer a standpoint from which to study software and code, and hence the digital, but it is not sufficient without taking into account the broader political economic contexts. Indeed, one of the difficulties with studying software is that is requires a complete assemblage of technologies in order to work at all, what we might call its infrastructure. This might be the specific model of computer or processor that is needed to run the software, or it might be a particular operating system, or network. Here we might note that the term software studies hardly seems to cover the wide variety of software, hardware and historical context that need to be included in what we might call the field of *computational media* – but which may be similarly addressed in cognate fields like digital humanities and computational social science (see Berry 2012b).

This software totality necessarily complicates the study of software and needs to be kept in mind when researching code-based systems and software. Nonetheless, it can be analytically useful to draw distinctions between different levels of analysis when thinking about software, in order to try to understand what it can and cannot do, and more importantly, how we might think about understanding it. For example, we might consider as a basic starting point the division of digital devices into three layers, namely (1) hardware platform, (2) software platform and (3) software application/interface layer. The main reason for drawing these distinctions is that it enables us to pay attention to the salient focus of the analysis we wish to undertake, for example, the changes in the relations of production, without losing sight of the importance of the supporting hardware and software, in other words, the forces of production. This form of layering different technologies on top of each other is very common in computer technology and we will see different forms of this structure throughout this discussion.

The most important aspect of this form of initial and simplified layer model is to abstract the hardware from the software, and this is widely used in creating software and hardware systems. This is crucial in enabling software to, in theory, run anywhere, without having to know too much about the specifics of the underlying technologies. Of course, this is an ideal scenario and even today few technologies can make this claim confidently, although technologies like HTML, Java and so forth were explicitly designed for just this reason. It is important to note that these technologies are digital technologies, but merely appreciating that they are made up of so-called digital code (0's and 1's) doesn't get us very far. Instead, we have to take account of the fact that the internal structures that enable things to become softwarized are complex and structured. Indeed, part of this requires an appreciation of the extent to which software transforms everything it touches – and this includes hardware, which is increasingly softwarized, and also software itself. That is, software increasingly acts upon software producing new levels of abstraction and complexity in software systems. This recursive logic of softwarization in the development of computational systems is an important hallmark of computationality. Indeed, we can account for this move from the flux and flow of everyday life into the logics of software with the notion of grammatization, and particularly with the idea that several layers of meaning are placed upon each moment of grammatization. Stiegler explains that:

Grammatization is the process by which all the fluxes or flows [*flux*] through which symbolic (that is, also, existential) acts are linked, can be discretized, formalized and reproduced. The most well-known of these processes is the writing of language. (Stiegler 2011: 172)

We might add that a *softwarized* grammatization always includes further developments in terms of optimizations, efficiencies and re-grammatizations. Sometimes this is at higher layers (see below), such that *softwarized* grammatization is a qualitatively different form of grammatization process.

This is relevant to the problems we have in dealing with code and software, and the multiplicity of levels that are appropriate to the study of software and code. Here, it is useful to introduce the heuristic notion of *laminated system* from the work of Roy Bhaskar et al. (2010) to help us surface the importance of a multidimensional or interdisciplinary approach to the study of code more generally. By *laminated system*, Bhaskar is trying to draw our attention to the problem of the levels of ontology in studying things (his concern is actually complex open systems like the environment, but I think it can be usefully adopted here for thinking through the question concerning software). This approach can help us develop a language for understanding and describing our object(s) of study at an 'appropriate' ontological level. For example, we might draw up the following ontological levels that are appropriate for the study of the computal:

1 **Physical**: Material and transactional level (of the hardware)

2 **Logical**: Logical, network and informational transactional level (level of software as diagram or platform)

3 **Codal**: Textual and coding logics (level of code as text and/or process)

4 **Interactional**: Surface/interface level (between human beings and non-humans mediated through code)

5 **Logistics**: Social and organizational structure (at the level of institutions, economies, culture, etc.)

6 **Individuational**: Stratification of embodied personality (the psychology of actors, the user, etc.)

What is useful about Bhaskar's approach is that the ontological levels work according to both different logics and different mechanisms. That is the mapping of an ontology that serves to 'make sense' at whichever level of analysis we focus upon. These can be mapped within the domain of each ontology, but importantly they also work together and require explanation in terms of how they are articulated. Of course, allied with this ontology we will need epistemology and concepts of knowledge (which may be appropriate to each ontology) but also meta concepts, which we might think as placed at a holistic level of the system of computation itself (which I call computationality [Berry 2011]). Each level has what Bhaskar would call unilateral dependence (on other things within its horizontal ontology), taxonomic irreducibility (namely that we treat each ontological level as distinct and irreducible, allowing for the emergence of particular concepts at a particular ontological level – and hence avoid the temptation to reduce everything down to voltage levels), or some form of causal irreducibility. That is, contra medium theoretic approaches that seek to get 'close to the metal'. This model has certain benefits in relation to thinking through computational society as it includes an implicit understanding of the way in which abstraction layers function within the design, implementation and execution of computational systems more generally, such that software is 'deep'. But also that these layers, each in their own way, are computational and reliant on certain aspects of softwarization to stabilize and provide a foundation for other layers.

By adapting Bhaskar's work in this way we are able to highlight an interdisciplinary approach like software studies, which sometimes have difficulties in developing referential overlap between different levels of analysis. This also allows us to think in terms of the possibility of a research programme that we could map to particular layers to analyse and understand them, for example, as offered while using the Scalar system (Scalar 2013). It would also allow us to consider the possibility of effective epistemic integration between our approaches and shared trans-disciplinary concepts. These strata of 'ontology', then, can be used to critically approach and situate our knowledges in relation to each other and provide some means of orientation in software/code's obvious multidimensional ontology. For clarity, it is helpful to think of these strata as multiple levels of 'ontic strata' in relation to a more fundamental set of computational categories that transcend this ontic structure.

Of course, this is also the notion of a single ontology that is shared throughout the laminated system and which would be constructed around the notion of strata of emergent properties or qualities. This would imply some notion of irreduction, otherwise higher strata could, in theory, be 'better' studied, or explained by lower strata levels. In some ways, this is the issue with some German media theory which problematically seeks to get closer to 'the metal' of computation in order to get at a perceived foundational level. The layered ontic strata model, even if informed by a single ontology, is helpful in enabling the situatedness of a particular level to be investigated at the correct level, rather than a reductionist search for the 'atoms' of computation as such. For the purposes of this book, I am interested in the idea of a shared ontology, computationality, that permeates all levels, that is in a way reminiscent of fractal geometry we see in computational principles that are repeated and generated at different scales through these computational laminated systems.

What would be the structural features of a world of computationality over and above what Heidegger called 'technicity' (Heidegger 1966)? By technicity,

Heidegger means more than just technology itself. He uses the term to 'characterize the manner in which Being manifests itself in the present epoch of the world, according to which man experiences the beings around him as objects that can be submitted to his control. It is as a consequence of this experience that "technology" becomes possible' (Heidegger 1966, fn 23). For Heidegger, electricity was the paradigmatic metaphor for technicity, both in terms of its generation through the challenging forth of nature: through coal, oil, hydropower, etc., and in terms of the switching systems that were required to route production, distribution and consumption of the electricity itself. He saw this switching capacity as a process of ordering by 'ordering beings' where:

> Everywhere everything is ordered to standby, to be immediately on hand, indeed, to stand there just so that it may be on call for a further ordering. (Heidegger 1977)

I want to suggest that technicity isn't sufficient to describe the contemporary mode of production. Indeed, technicity is better understood, as indeed Heidegger concedes, as a time of *modern* technologies, and indeed I would argue, not necessarily applicable to the kinds of *postmodern* real-time data stream technologies, such as the computer, that increasingly permeate our everyday life. Instead I suggest we think in terms of computationality, a specific historical constellation of intelligibility made possible by computational categories and concepts. An exemplar case of the logic of thinking in real-time data streams is DARPA's ARGUS-IS drone aircraft, which contains a record-setting 1.8 gigapixel sensor array, which has 'the ability to scan an entire city for all sorts of "suspicious" activity, not just in real-time but after the fact. It all adds up to around 6 petabytes (6,000 terabytes) worth of 12 frames-per-second video per day' (Kopstein 2013). This huge data stream is transmitted to the ground at 600 gigabits per second, as part of Wide Area Persistent Surveillance technologies that allow the tracking of individuals and activities in a city at a remarkable level of detail. The Atlantic writes that this drone,

> can just hang out at 15,000 feet over a small city-sized area (roughly, half of Manhattan) and provide video surveillance of the whole thing. The other thing to note is that they are running machine vision on the moving objects, which means they are generating structured data out of the video, not just displaying the pictures. (Madrigal 2013)

Thus it is not the data *per se* as a standing reserve that is crucial in this control technology but rather its cybernetic capacity to provide police and state real-time streams of city-wide behaviour as patterns and calculative dashboards – the logistics made possible by the computal. This enables feedback mechanisms to feed directly into policing practices in real time creating a total system of monitoring and control, a huge increase in the reach and depth of surveillance. It also demonstrates the computational turn at play in intelligence work, particularly the 'open source intelligence' of collecting everyday information and data and using it to undertake sophisticated search and pattern-finding algorithms. For example, the Criminal Reduction Utilising Statistical History system of predictive policing used by the police department of Memphis, Tennessee, whereby crime statistics from across the city are compiled and overlaid with other datasets, such as social housing maps, outside temperatures and so forth, is combined using algorithms to 'search for correlations in the data' to guide policing decisions (Hickman 2013). This is the type of system thinking that drives the PRISM (US-984XN) intelligence-monitoring programme undertaken by the NSA in the United States, and the Tempora programme undertaken by GCHQ in the United Kingdom (Davies 2013). Indeed sources for the Guardian claimed, 'Not so long ago, this was all about attaching crocodile clips to copper wires. And it was all about voice. Now, it's about the internet – massive scale – but still using the same law that was devised for crocodile clips. [UK] Ripa [*Regulation of Investigatory Powers Act 2000*] was primarily designed for voice, not for this level of interception. They are going round Ripa. The legislation doesn't exist for this. They are using old legislation and adapting it' (Davies 2013). Although PRISM collects mostly historical data through *The United States Foreign Intelligence Surveillance Act 1978* (FISA) requests, it also does have some real-time capacity, such as collecting real-time notification of an 'email event' (RTN-EDC), such as login or sent message, and real-time notification of a chat login or logout event (RTN-IM). This real-time capability enables the kind of always-on surveillance that even the East German Stasi could only have dreamed of, indeed as Wolfgang Schmidt, a former lieutenant colonel in the communist secret police stated, 'you know, for us [the Stasi], this would have been a dream come true,' adding that his department was limited to tapping 40 phones at a time due to technical restrictions. So if there was a decision to spy on a new victim then an old one had to be dropped. Indeed, he argued 'it is the height of naiveté to think that once collected this information won't be used. . . . This is the nature of secret government organizations' (Schofield 2013). The probable move to real time beyond the 'batch-processing' of historical records is also surely just over the horizon. Indeed, 'the NSA has developed a program for the incoming streams of data called "Boundless Informant". The program is intended to process connection data from all incoming telephone calls in "near real time"' (Poitras et al. 2013).

These challenges help us appreciate that to understand the 'digital' requires the concept of the computational to be unpacked. Computational technologies are increasing in their capabilities at an astonishing pace, while our theoretical, political, social and legal understanding lags far behind. Indeed, Galloway is correct to assert that 'software . . . asks a question to which the political interpretation is the only coherent answer' (Galloway 2012). However, paradoxically computational systems rely on fairly simple operating logics, and their 'fractal' logic means that techniques from different layers can be reassembled to create new layers and platforms. So, for example, one common distinction that is increasingly used today is between applications (or apps) and files (or data). It is usual for them to be combined together in a so-called wrapper that hides this from the user, for example, in many mobile operating systems, but the basic distinction still remains as 'pocket' and 'cloud'. In this case, we might say the 'digital' is the user interface (UI) that is experienced by the user, opening the possibility for a critically informed phenomenology of the digital, of the experience generated at the screenic level by the operation of the logistics of computational technology. The digital is then made and remade by the underlying computational system and which conforms to expected practices of the digital, both in terms of the UI and in terms of the user experience. It is not the '0's and '1's that are in memory chips within the device but the specific modular organization and deployment of the 'digital' – in its both material and ideological moments, which needs to be considered carefully. Apps are, in this rendering of the representative operation of the UI, the logic and control and are often paid for, and the files are the data or informational content which belongs to the user and is often segregated as a user file area.

This notion of performing operations 'upon data' is reminiscent of notions of the will to power, a controlling logic, in this case by the wielding of software tools. Indeed, often a rural or domestic imagery is associated with the files and user data, contrasted with an industrial or mechanistic imagery with the apps and logic. Although these examples are only meant in an introductory sense, we will explore within particular contexts how these metaphors can quickly become generalized within a softwarized society, such that government becomes conceived as 'apps' or 'platforms' and social action is seen in terms of softwarized processes and technical 'interrupts' to the system.

This becomes a convincing narrative as software presents a translucent interface relative to the common 'world' and so enables engagement with this digitally infused 'world', through what we call its interface. It is tempting when trying to understand software/code to provide analysis at the surface/interactional level; however, software also possesses an opaque machinery that mediates engagement that is not experienced directly nor through social mediations. Without an attentiveness to the layers of software beneath this surface interface, we are in danger of 'screen essentialism'. This is crucial to appreciate, as one of the key issues is that the surface can remain relatively stable, while the physical/logical layer(s) can undergo frenetic and disorienting amounts of change (Berry 2012c). This frantic disorientation underneath the surface is therefore insulated from the user, who is provided with an interactional surface which can be familiar, skeuomorphic (from the Greek, *skeuos* – vessel or tool, *morphe* – shape), representational, metonymic, flat, figurative or extremely simplistic and domestic. It is important to note that the surface/interface need not be visual, indeed it may be presented as an API which hides the underlying machinery behind a relatively benign interface or as a touch or haptic surface.

This surface, or interactional layer, of the digital is hugely important for providing the foundations through which we interact with these technologies. Not only are the interfaces responsive to our questioning via queries, searches, navigation and so forth, they are also designed increasingly to be intuitive, intelligent and contextual, in as much as they attempt not only to guess our intentions but also to shape the direction of our minds' travel. The interface itself is not an impermeable system; however, it does require a certain amount of work to look beneath its often extremely compelling surface. Not only is there an ideological aspect to the interface, which needs to be carefully explored and mapped (see Chun 2011), but there is also a layer of mechanical construction that keeps the interface in motion – literally makes the interface in real time (Berry 2011; Galloway 2012). To think beneath the surface is to explore the layer of software that exists in code, and to use critical concepts and methods to understand and explain its functioning and structuring logics. Indeed, it is important to keep in mind the normative aspect in the design of computation systems, both explicit and implicit in the ideological foundations of computationality as a system of thought.

Looking from the perspective of producing code itself, we might also note the 'drudgery' of production, as 'programming' is something that remains largely hand coded. Computational culture is increasingly made up of artefacts and products that are *code objects* or coded in digital technology by coders, users and people more widely. Indeed, it helps if the complexity of production is constantly abstracted away through the clever use of these computer 'layers', with languages such as Ruby and APIs, and also through the use of Integrated Development Environments (IDEs) and other visual programming techniques. Of course, the 'drudgery' of programming is not really equivalent to the drudgery of working in a factory, and it could be argued that machine-assisted programming allows the creativity of the individual in even the most 'boring' jobs. In fact, often even the 'boring' programming jobs are extremely well paid in the West, due to the difficulties of retaining staff (and options are often made to connect these mundane tasks to more exciting programming practices).

However, we should be aware of the growing disciplinary threat of outsourcing which is used to control labour costs in the digital economy. But nonetheless, there is definitely some interesting work to be done in mapping the way in which creativity, programming languages, abstraction layers, culture and so forth play out in people's everyday experience of programming practice. These are also helpful to think of the ways in which the structures of programming code acts as disciplinary mechanisms or prescriptive technologies that aid in governance – the links to neoliberalism are extremely striking in relation to the extent to which human subjectivity can be observed, nudged and managed through certain technologies – indeed, there is a field within computer science called 'persuasive technology' or 'captology' that attempts to develop software in this direction. It is certainly striking that the code produced within the technology industry is often actually more successful at controlling user behaviour than managers are at controlling their own programmers. Indeed, even in 1951, computer programmers were understood to be a peculiar form of employee, with specific practices associated with their labour, such as a revealing letter from Lord Halsbury to Christopher Strachey, one of the great figures in British Computer Science, who on his appointment to National Research Development Corporation noted,

> It is recognized that the quite peculiar nature of the work you will be doing justifies certain concessions in respect to regular attendance in the office in order that you can do it in solitude to your own satisfaction. Needless to say I rely upon your sense of responsibility to see that this does not become a source of dissatisfaction to other members of the staff who are required to keep more regular hours. (Halsbury 1951)

Today, in the management of programming projects, Taylorist approaches are now widely used in the software industry; however, one only needs to look over the relevant literature to see the slow and partial success in this area. Software engineering is still a relatively recent discipline and there is still a reliance on the superhuman efforts of a small cadre of programmers within a project *a la* Ullman's (2011) *The Soul of a New Machine*. The way in which software engineering projects rely on very long hours and young programmers' labour to produce their products has remained a constant feature of the computing industry and particularly Silicon Valley culture. With the rise in profitability of the digital as an input into the productive process, it is no surprise that the digital has sought to be increasingly rationalized by large corporations and government. Thus, the wayward computer hacker has partially been domesticated though various management techniques and to a varying extent this has been successful in standardizing software writing processes.

Nonetheless, the lack of a 'silver bullet' in software programming still eludes the managers, who are therefore reliant on programmers who know far more about the system they are working on than any of the management. While not wanting to be too optimistic or celebratory about this, after all programmers can, and often are, very mercenary in these situations, nonetheless, this is an interesting moment for those interested in studying software, and of course, the potential for radical politics also remains radically open (see Berry 2008). Understanding the code and being able to disassemble it and read the contents to understand the code objects that perform certain kinds of governmentality on human bodies certainly raise the promise of developing critical approaches to neoliberalism, for example. Here, the links with the concerns of critical theory and the notion of instrumental means of control and rationalization are clear, particularly in terms of a system of identity thinking that attempts to foreclose any alternative or critical voices to be heard. Indeed, as Marx argued,

> Technology reveals the active relation of man to nature, the direct process of the production of his life, and thereby it also lays bare the process of production of the social relations of his life, and of the mental conceptions that flow from these conceptions. (Marx 1990: 493, fn 4)

Critical analysis of neoliberalism through close reading of code and distant reading practices is possible through their application to code and software systems – especially its tendency to code things with a view to markets, efficiency and instrumental rationality. In a similar vein, for Foucault, neoliberal governmentality is a particular form of post-welfare state politics, in which the state essentially outsources the responsibility for ensuring the 'well-being' of the population. The primary recipient of this responsibility is derived from a strengthened notion of the subject as a rational individual. Indeed, these new subjectivities are expected to 'look after themselves'. This form of governmentality has an extremely diffuse form of rule whereby strategies and imperatives of control are distributed through a variety of media but are implicated in even the most mundane practice of everyday life. Indeed, we might connect these layers of power to that delegated power diffused through code objects and computational devices. As Schecter writes,

> Foucault regards the exercise of power and the formalisation of knowledge to be intimately bound up with the constitution of living individuals as

subjects of knowledge, that is, as citizens and populations about whom knowledge is systematically constructed. . . . Subjects are not born subjects so much as they become them. In the course of becoming subjects they are classified in innumerable ways which contribute to their social integration, even if they are simultaneously marginalised in many cases. (Schecter 2010: 171)

So, for example, the state promotes an ethic of self-care which is justified in terms of a wider social responsibility and which is celebrated through the examples given in specific moments represented as individual acts of consumption that contribute to a notion of good citizenship. So using recycling bins, caring for one's teeth, stopping smoking and so forth are all actively invested in by the state as both beneficial to the individual and as collective care, but most importantly they are the responsibilities of the citizen. They are also new sites for computational software apps that seek to promote a notion of the 'quantified self', such as that given in calorie-counting apps, and life-tracking hardware like the Nike Fuel or the Fitbit.

Neo-liberal governmentality also gestures towards the subordination of state power to the requirements of the marketplace, the implication being that 'political problems' are re-presented or cast in market terms. Within this framework, citizens are promised new levels of freedom, consumerism, customization, interactivity and control over their lives and possessions. In other words, they are promised an unfulfilled expectation as to the extent to which they are able to exert their individual agency. In order to facilitate this governmental practice, certain infrastructural systems need to be put in place, such as bureaucratic structures, computational agencies and so forth. For example, it has become increasingly clear that providing information to citizens is not sufficient for controlling and influencing behaviour. Indeed, people's ability to understand and manipulate raw data or information has been found to be profoundly limited in many contexts with a heavy reliance on habit understood as part of the human condition. Here, computational tools assist by providing mediation and advising and providing structure for a world full of data, real-time streams and complex calculations required from its citizens. This computational assistance or monitoring is backgrounded and often hidden from us.

Any study of computer code has to acknowledge that the performativity of software is in some way linked to its location in a capitalist economy. Code costs money and labour to produce and once it is written it requires continual inputs of energy, maintenance and labour to keep functioning. Thus code is socially constructed, historically specific and more or less socially embedded in broader networks of social relations and institutional ensembles. I have explored some of these issues in Berry (2008, 2011a.) It is crucial that the materiality and ownership of code is understood and the constraints that operate upon the production, distribution and consumption of code as software are noted. This has important implications when it is understood that much of the code that supports the internet, even though it is free software or open source, actually runs on private computer systems and networks (see Berry 2008).

We might say that a softwarized society is one in which society itself is computed. The term computation comes from the Latin *computare*, '*com* "together"' and *putare* – 'to reckon, to think or to section to compare the pieces'. To compute, then, is to 'to count, or to calculate' (see Berry 2011a). For computer scientists, computation (or information processing) is a field of research that investigates what can and what cannot be calculated. Understanding the theoretical, empirical and political economic aspects of 'computational cultures' in relation to the so-called knowledge economy, particularly through the lens of critical theory, requires us to engage with this computational dimension of the digital. Further, computation is the logic of the 'creative' economy and to understand the cultural outputs of computational structures (sometimes referred to as the 'softwarization of culture') we need a critical theory that can contribute to the understanding of the computational.

The internet itself is deeply saturated by both its historical compromises and its conditions of production. It is also increasingly penetrated by capitalist logics that are often imposed onto the technical layers and protocols of the internet. For example, the practice of surfing the web is a visual experience of seeing a collection of images, text, videos and animations that are presented in the browser. This is, however, only a portion of the web that is being shown. Concealed in the background are a group of hidden entities called 'web bugs', embedded in webpages across the internet, which allow advertisers, search engines, trackers and others to monitor our usage and page choices, in a system of monitoring I will call the 'dark Internet'. This enables a customized webpage to be delivered on the fly, which is personalized to the user, to a marketing group, or to a national population, etc. A good example of seeing the actions of these web bugs at work is to use the 'Cultural Differences' engine developed by Taryn Simon and Aaron Swartz (2012a). This javascript algorithm makes situated searches by requesting search queries from Google on different national versions of the search engine, such as Iran, America, Germany and France. Although only offering visual results as an image search, it places the top six results from each country next to each other and thus allows a comparative analysis of the image results to be made. It is striking how different the results can be depending on the national search engine used, and therefore how the search engine by localizing your search by IP address, for example, is delivering specific search engine results to the user. Usually, this would have been undertaken automatically, and supplemented by personalization data drawn from web bugs and the database of information collected about the user (Simon and Swartz 2012b).[1] This demonstrates that the internet is increasingly becoming subject to algorithmic pre-processing to create personalized versions of its content for capitalist exploitation.

The software we use is part of a wider constellation of software ecologies made possible by a plethora of computational devices that facilitate the colonization of code into the lifeworld. In other words, software enables access to certain forms of mediated engagement with the world. By being built on physical machinery that is distributed from global cloud data centres to highly mobile intimate technologies, huge logistical questions have to be addressed and solved. This mediation is achieved via the translucent surface interface, of the interactional layer, and enables a machinery to be engaged which computationally interoperates with the world. These engagements are enabled by processes we might call *compactants* (computational actants) which can be understood through a dual surface/machinery structure. That is, they are designed to function across the interactional and codal layers – as is much software in use today. Compactants are often constructed in such a way that they can be understood as having a dichotomous modality of data collection/visualization, each of which is a specific mode of operation. This may not necessarily be a visual component of the compactant, which may merely re-present data through computational analysis to a visual packager or visualization device/software system. This modal setting may be accessible to the user, or it may be a hidden function accessible only to certain people/coder/other compactants, etc. Compactants may also be layered across a technology stack forming complex networks of sensors, data processors and interface structures, rather like fishing nets or trellis, taking data from the bottom and processing it upwards in a process of curation or filtering.

Compactants are designed to *passive-aggressively* record data. I want to particularly draw attention to this passive-aggressive feature of computational agents, both in terms of their passive quality – under the surface, relatively benign and silent – and in terms of their aggressive quality in their hoarding of data – monitoring behavioural signals, social signals, streams of affectivity and so forth. The word *compact* also has useful overtones of having all the necessary components or functions fitted into a small package, and compact as in conciseness in expression. The etymology from the Latin *compact* for closely put together, or joined together, also neatly expresses the sense of what web bugs and related technologies are (discussed in greater detail in later chapters). The term compactants is also evocative in terms of the notion of 'companion actants' (see Harraway 2007). Here value-centred design and ethics of these systems offer an interesting moment of reflection in terms of the latitude usually granted to compactants by programmers. They will usually store more data, and this is considered a norm, hoarding user interactions and behaviour where possible, and to the fullest extent possible technically. Analytically, therefore, software can be said to have two faces:

Commodity: accessible via the interface/surface and providing or procuring a commodity/service/function. Provides a relative stability for the consumption of ends. The commodity is usually articulated at the level of the interactional layer, usually visually, although this may be through other sensory interfaces level.

Mechanism: accessible via textual source code, which contains the mechanisms and functions 'hidden' in the software (means). This can be thought of as the substructure for the overlay of commodities and consumption. The mechanisms are usually delegated within the codal layer, and thus hidden from the interactional.

Nonetheless, the complexity of the machinery of code is obscured by its interface, the commodity, which is often only loosely coupled to the underlying logics and therefore to the control of the system under use. It is here that the notion of *compactants* helps us to understand the way in which computationality has increasingly become constitutive of the understanding of important categories in late capitalism, like privacy and self-care. Here, we could say that we are interested in a transition from the juridicification, through the medicalization, to the 'computationalisation' of reason. This is the formation of discrete powers rather than power in general. That is, 'the processes through which subjects *become* subjects, the truth *becomes* truth, and then changing *conditions* under which this happens, which in the first instance is the discrepancy between the visible and the readable' (Schecter 2010: 173). Or as Foucault himself writes that what is at stake is,

> how the coupling of a series of practices with a truth regime form an operative knowledge-power system (*dispotif*) which effectively inscribes in the real something that does not exist, and which subjects the real to a series of criteria stipulating what is true and what is false, whereby these criteria are taken to be legitimate. It is that moment which does not exist as real and which is not generally considered relevant to the legitimacy of a regime of true and false. . . . It marks the birth of the asymmetrical bi-polarity of politics and economics, that is, of that politics and economics which are neither things that exist nor are errors, illusions or ideologies. It has to do

with something which does not exist and which is nonetheless inscribed within the real, and which has great relevance for a truth regime which makes distinctions between truth and falsity. (Foucault 2010: 19–20)

The way in which software and algorithms generate certain notion of truth and falsity is a topic requiring close investigation, both in terms of the surface interface generating a 'visible' truth, and in terms of the notion of a computational, or cloud, 'truth' that is delivered from the truth machines that lie somewhere on the networks of power and knowledge. Foucault suggests that if there is a 'system' or an ensemble of systems, the task is somehow to think systemic functioning outside of the perspective of the subject dominated by or in charge of the so-called system. Indeed, 'critical thinking can deconstruct the visible harmony between casual seeing and instrumental reason . . . in contrast with monolithic appearances, surfaces are characterised by strata and folds that can inflect power to *create* new truths, desires and forms of experience' (Schecter 2010: 175). The interactional layer is extremely plastic and enables the computational presentation of appearance as such, usually through a visual register, but which can hold particular types of visual rhetoric that can be deployed to support or produce preferred readings of the computational as such.

Here we can make the link between sight and power, and of course sight itself is deployed such that the 'visible' is not transparent nor hidden. Compactants certainly contribute to the deployment of the visible, through the generation of certain forms of geometric and photographic truths manifested in painted screens and surfaces, the availability of commodity surfaces, for example. One of the striking things about using this analytical model for thinking about software is that it draws attention to a source of stability in computational society. That is, the commodity layer, the interface, may stay relatively stable *vis a vis* the user (interactional, social, individuational layers), while, underneath at the level of the machinery, there can be rapid changes in terms of both hardware and software (codal, logical and physical layers). In a usual case, the user is unlikely to notice much difference in the usability of the device; however, the interface constantly allows for a de-freneticness or at least a looser coupling between rapid technical change and the user experience of technology. We should expect that when interfaces achieve a certain retinal quality, making them indistinguishable from other representational forms, such as high definition images or photography, then further developments will begin to be made in terms of the skeuomorphic/figurative/metonymic. Indeed, to some extent this is already starting to happen within UI design with the move to 'simple' or 'obvious' design principles (see Beecher 2010). The so-called 'flat design' is a visual design aesthetic and method that prioritizes a notion of *a priori* geons that structure the interface through a semi-platonic ideal drawn from geometric principles, this is then 'painted' onto layers of 'glass' which create a three-dimensional aesthetic which is highly kinetic and exploratory but moves away from 'fake' three-dimensional effects. The effect of this innovation is extremely visually pleasing and functions to enable the machinery level of the codal object to be hidden away more successfully. Later chapters will examine the extent to which new digital ontologies based on this process create profound challenges for the political.

The cyberstructure

Drawing on medium theory, I now want to explore the idea that to understand patterns in culture we are forced to look inside the structures of the machines – namely the notion that medial changes create epistemic shifts. Further, technology and, by extension, the medium of the computal itself create the conditions of possibility for particular cultural practices. These environments are prescribed – that is, they limit practices in certain ways that can be questioned through critical engagement with the technology. For example, entertainment technology is currently undergoing a radical shift due to the emphasis the industry places on restricting consumer use of content through digital rights management (DRM) technologies. This creates new practices and means of bodily engagement with the digital through the use of digital 'locks' and 'fences'. In effect it is the creation of an industrialized archive of culture placed behind corporate paywalls and gateways. Indeed, here Stiegler's notion of the 'Memory Industries' is suggestive of the extent to which code facilitates the rise of tertiary memory systems which are structured with industrial algorithm-mediated databases and content delivery networks (CDNs).

Attention to the materiality of software requires a form of reading/writing of these depths through attentiveness to the affordances of code. By attending to the ontological layers of software, that is the underlying structure and construction, we gather an insight into the substructure and machinery of software. But there is also a juridical and political economic moment here, where wealth and law are used to enforce certain control technologies, such as DRM, and the impossibility of opening them through legislation that criminalizes such access. Software is increasingly mediated not only by its surface or interface, but also by the underlying mechanisms which are not just difficult but also criminal to access. Software is therefore increasingly used/enjoyed without the encumbrance or engagement with its underlying structures due to this commodity/mechanism form – it becomes a consumption technology. For example, driven by rapid changes in technology, and particularly innovation in social media, we are now seeing a transition from static information to real-time data streams (Berry 2011). Real-time data streams are new ways to consume various media forms through data stream providers like Twitter. In fact, it can be argued that Twitter is now one of the *de facto* real-time message buses of the internet. This new way of accessing, distributing and communicating via the real-time stream is still being played out and raises interesting questions about how it affects politics, economics, social and daily life, but looking under the surface of these stream technologies is made more difficult than it already is as a complex technical artefact, by the control technologies, such as APIs, and the law.

The digital clearly has a functional dimension, in that it runs processes. But what is also radical about the digital is there is no real separation between data and execution. For the computer and the programmer, all are data flows. In contrast to a factory, where one might use leather and other tools that will allow the production of commodities such as shoes, leather is not used to reshape the tools themselves directly. In contrast, anything structured within code and software can be transformed. So the digital is not only changing the way things are classified and the way in which things and objects are recognized by the system, but also it changes what they are and how they can be used – that is, software acts upon software. This feedforward and feedback mechanism is an important part of software development implementation and creates rapid stages of innovation in computational systems.

We can think about shifts in mechanism, by exploring this process of digital transformation of the basic categories by which a system, process or object is understood, at the early and often public moments in the 'softwarization' process – before the technologies are completely formalized. This is when, for example, an industry reconfigures and reorganizes itself in order to meet the requirements of software systems' impetuous towards particular economic, structural forms and digital logics resulting in its re-articulation through the digital. I don't want to identify these technological changes as being the sole driver of economic change, of course, but rather highlight how these new forces of production are an important condition of mediation for and of social labour and the economy. For example, when media is incorporated into software, it is transformed into files – the content. When a song is taken from a physical medium, such as vinyl, CD or DVD, it is encoded into a digital file, for example MP3 or AAC. This is not a trivial process and is fraught with political and economic arguments, technical challenges and breakdowns, and institutional reconfigurations and innovations. It also requires an educative dimension in relation to the framing of the uses of these systems and formats – including the harvesting of user innovation back into the system, such as the Twitter use of @mention names and hashtags which were created by users themselves. We are very familiar with this concept when using PCs and laptops. However, as we rely less on discrete physical containers of digital (or analogue) media, we are now moving instead towards cloud-based information which is streamed to us. Gelernter argues,

> The traditional web site is static, but the Internet specializes in flowing, changing information. The "velocity of information" is important—not just the facts but their rate and direction of flow. Today's typical website is like a stained glass window, many small panels leaded together. There is no good way to change stained glass, and no one expects it to change. So it's not surprising that the Internet is now being overtaken by a different kind of cyberstructure. (Gelernter 2010)

This new 'cyberstructure' is the stream. This is also a move to transforming media content into 'apps' or media-rich software experiences and the reconstruction of a new gestural and contextualized interactional layer of computation. Taking the example of music again, rather than creating a series of MP3 files after encoding (ripping) the CD, some musicians are now experimenting with turning the album into a self-standing app for playing and interacting with the music itself (e.g. Bjork). This is important to note because these two ways of interacting with media are very different and draw on different repertoires within the computer interface and deeper at the level of the computal. Furthermore, it is introducing new practices for the user, who will have to be taught, and in many cases presented with, quite different ways of consuming and interacting with these new media forms. These new practices are also more amenable to the functioning of the computational, such as for collecting data about user preferences and activities. At the surface level, users play music structured around albums and singles; however, at the level of the underlying machinery, huge shifts are occurring computationally and organizationally. For example, the interface to the album may no longer be playing music files located on the user's device, but instead can be wirelessly connected to and seemingly stream music directly from the databanks and archives of the music companies, more so, these companies can control at a very fine granularity how and when they might be played. Such is the case with the power to 'skip' unwanted or unliked tracks, whereby the music labels literally dictate to companies like Spotify and Apple how many skips of music tracks a user can make in a specific period of time. It goes without saying that the user in such cases has little or no control over these variables.

These streaming systems also encourage a different means for recon- figuring the labour processes itself. Computational systems make possible a streaming form of labour, what we might call: *microlabour.* That is, tiny moments of people's labour computationally monitored and paid for in a process that can be seen as a massive intensification of the pin-making factory structure described by Adam Smith. Computation allows tasks to be broken down into small fragments that, using networked computational technology, can be distributed literally around the world and farmed out as piecework to workers for a few pence per job. This 'on-demand crowd work' allows a radical division of labour of informational and knowledge-based work. Crucially the workers in these microlabour projects are often unaware of the greater significance of the work they are undertaking (the totality), being given only incomprehensible fragments of a workflow or information process. Some examples of companies that undertake this mediation process include: micro-workers.com, which distributes online tasks like click-throughs; innocentive.com, which posts bounties for scientific and technical discoveries; liveops.com, which creates distributed call centres based in people's homes; and lastly, the most well-known, the Amazon Mechanical Turk, which purports to be 'artificial artificial intelligence', due to its reliance on millions of human 'computers' who undertake the labour that is distributed computationally to them. This process is 'the fragmentation of labor into hyper-temporary jobs . . . an intensification of decades-old US trends toward part-time, contingent work for employer flexibility and cost-cutting' (Irani and Silberman 2013).

These are all examples of intense microlabour practices that the new computational technologies make possible. Workers' labour power is literally incorporated and mediated through the software. For example, the word processor christened, Soylent, described as a 'Word Processor with a Crowd Inside', pays its 'workers' via the Amazon Mechanical Turk system to undertake word-processing functions (Bernstein et al. 2010: 1). So, the software contains a function that automatically summarizes a document, not by algorithmic compression, but by literally farming the sentences out to millions of human workers around the globe paid at piecework rates for editing. The programmers wanted to be 'slightly generous while matching going rates on Mechanical Turk, [so] we paid $0.08 per Find, $0.05 per Fix, and $0.04 per Verify' resulting in a piece work 'average paragraph cost [of] $1.41' (Bernstein et al. 2010: 6). But should this be considered too costly, Bernstein et al. (2010) helpfully explain:

> Were we instead to use a $0.01 pay rate for these tasks, the process would cost $0.30 per paragraph. Our experience is that paying less slows down the later parts of the process, but it does not impact quality [19]—it would be viable for shortening paragraphs under a loose deadline. (Bernstein et al. 2010: 7)

This notion of not only aggregating human beings through software, but also treating them as components or objects of a computational system is indicative of the kind of thinking that is prevalent in computational design. Production or consumption is mediated by the creation of code objects to represent activities in everyday life and translate them internally into a form the computer can understand. In many ways this is a discretization of human activity, but it is also the dehumanization of people through a computation layer used to mediate the use of social labour more generally. This also demonstrates how the user is configured through code objects as producer, consumer, worker or audience, a new kind of multiple subject position that is disciplined through computational interfaces and algorithmic control technologies. But it also serves to show how the interface reifies the social labour undertaken behind the surface, such that the machinery may be literally millions of humans 'computing' the needs to the software, all without the user being aware of it. In this case it is not that the machinery represents what Marx called 'dead labour', but in fact that it mediates living labour invisibly into the machinery of computation. Indeed, this is an example of where computation serves to hide social labour such that workers are hidden 'behind web forms and APIs [which] helps employers see themselves as builders of innovative technologies, rather than employers unconcerned with working conditions' (Irani and Silberman 2013).

So, for example, as old media forms, like TV, film and newsprint, are digitized, there is experimentation by designers and programmers on the best form to present media content to the user, and also the most profitable way that a subject position can be constructed such that its practices in relation to the interface are literally inscribed in algorithms. Traditional media are softwarized in this process and the way the content used is mediated through a software interface. When transformed into software, first, a new media object is subject to algorithmic manipulation. One thinks here of the so-called 'casual gaming' systems that are designed to not only present a non-linear entertainment system, but also use gamification techniques to create an addictive environment for users. Game mechanics, such as badges and levels, are used to manipulate the users and serve to maximize profit for the companies using these techniques. In short, media becomes programmable. Secondly, streaming media are any media built around a continuous data flow, and this will likely be the paradigmatic form of media for the future. This means that media will increasingly be subject to regular and repeating computation. Again Gelernter usefully explains,

> If we think of time as orthogonal to space, a stream-based, time-based Cybersphere is the traditional Internet flipped on its side in digital space-time. The traditional web-shaped Internet consists (in effect) of many flat

panels chaotically connected. Instead of flat sites, where information is arranged in space, we want deep sites that are slices of time. When we look at such a site onscreen, it's natural to imagine the past extending into (or beyond) the screen, and the future extending forward in front of the screen; the future flows towards the screen, into the screen and then deeper into the space beyond the screen. (Gelernter 2010)

To further explore this notion of real-time streams, I turn to Twitter, as the current instantiation of the real-time streaming message bus. As a form of computational media that is highly social, it presents an interesting case study in relation to our public/private experiences of communication through a computational platform. Here though, links need to be made between the aesthetic, the phenomenological and the digital. Indeed, the real-time stream is fundamentally a reconfiguration of temporality, a new construction of experience, which is structured around a desire for 'nowness'. But Twitter messages are never marked as 'now', instead they lie already in the past, whether one second ago, one hour or one day. Twitter is nonetheless oriented towards the future, the possibility of something else happening, others in the loop, pure potentiality or unfolding. This is partly constructed through an aesthetic experience of commitment to a radical now, an experience mediated in real time through Twitter's service requiring users to send tweets, twitpics and links that document the experiential aspects of their lives. So at the individuational layer we see profound changes in response to reconstructions of the levels of the interactional and social. So Twitter becomes, like all content-driven platforms, a vicarious experience; both in terms of the person who is live-tweeting his or her experience while, let's say, at an art exhibit, and in terms of the vicarious thrills of the followers – some of them located hundreds or thousands of miles away – who view the work through the eyes of the Twitterer.

So what does it mean when life is vicariously viewed? It's not dissimilar, at least formally, from watching an artwork being remediated through a visual medium, such as television. But the difference is that the television camera focuses attention towards the artwork, rarely able to capture the experiential quality of the presenter, who, using tried and trusted media structures, presents it as either a lecture, a documentary or a narrative. Within real-time streams, however, the artwork and the user merge, the pure singularity of the user – their wobbly half-focused photos, their exclamatory tweets, the geo-location updates – is fused with the artwork they are experiencing. A new kind of algorithmically mediated phenomenological code object. The two are therefore presented as one, less an object of attention rather transformed into a happening, an unfolding or a pure experiential social media event. In some senses then, this begins to highlight connections between the real time as constructed by digital technologies and Adorno's notion of identity thinking.

The other side of the coin, that of individuals using the real-time stream as a site or space for expression, is still nascent. It presents particular challenges to the user, particularly in relation to untethering the experience from the expression of tweeting it, more so if the expression is the collection of tweets themselves. The radical temporality, the short life span of the tweet, also presents interesting new challenges for an expression or intervention that might disappear in the blink of an eye. Additionally, the architecture of Twitter, its retweets, hashtags, URL shorteners, and @mentions, all subtract valuable real estate from the single tweet, which, being only 140 characters long, is already a terse real-time messaging format.

Some artists have already experimented with this medium – Cory Arcangel has appropriated its search function for *Great Twitter searches Volume #1* and *#2* (Archangel 2012); An Xiao has used it for art projects, like tweeting daily minutiae in Morse code for the Brooklyn Museum's '1stfans Twitter Art Feed' (NYFA 2012), and many artists from different disciplines use it as a soundboard for their work – these are interesting examples of art in the real-time stream, but perhaps future artistic practice is signposted in the ability of a tweet to remain on the surface of consciousness, to bob and dance across the real-time stream by raising the desire within the user to retweet and @mention it.[2] This points to aesthetic possibilities using the statistical clouds generated by the real-time streams of the industrial internet – as a form of 'social art' or 'social design' drawing from existing practices of social reading (see Hastac 2013 for a discussion of social reading).

One of the problems we have when thinking about the new real-time media streams, like Twitter and Facebook, is that our metaphors are usually based on old media forms (e.g. television or radio, or even, in some descriptions a cocktail party). For example, thinking about Twitter as television means that there is a tendency to think in terms of channels, programming, a passive audience and interactivity limited to selecting the channel to watch. It is no surprise that YouTube borrowed this 'comfortable' metaphor to explain to users how to use it. However, these metaphors can also stifle how we understand a new media platform, and perhaps even shape the way it is further used. Here, I want to argue that if we are to understand the medium of Twitter, then we should try to look at the properties and affordances that are particular to it as it currently stands: (1) it is a real-time medium; (2) information flows through it, if you miss it then the information passes by (although through data resellers you can purchase a Twitter archive and replay it); (3) it is based around an interest graph (things people find interesting rather than friends or colleagues) (Barnett 2010); (4) it is surprisingly flexible, if terse, and even with the 140 character restriction, the content of a tweet support urls, links to any other form of media (e.g. web/photos/video), etc.; (5) the entire tweet (as a JSON data entity) can carry location data, user data and other contextual data that makes it extremely powerful; (6) it has little active memory as a system, until 2012 you could only retrieve the most recent 3,200 tweets per person (Haines 2011). Twitter has recently allowed data reseller partners, like Datasift, to access Twitter's Tweet archives, however, Twitter also passes its entire archive of public Tweets over to the Library of Congress[3] for storage and research after 6 months for internal library use, for non-commercial research, public display by the library itself and preservation (Twitter 2010)[4]; (7) Twitter has a client/server structure rather than a peer-to-peer architecture, so should Twitter go down, then so would the ability to share on the network.[5]

These qualities seem to suggest a medium, or platform, that is more similar in some respects to a newswire system or news agency data feed, such as provided by Reuters or Bloomberg. These are extremely fast data transmission systems usually built around a proprietary data protocol generally for transmitting real-time news, data and financial market information, for example, Thomson Reuters uses RDF (Reuters Data Feed). These data feeds themselves are extremely low latency, in Reuters' case financial, text and numeric data took less than an average of half a millisecond to move through the system in 2005, and would be markedly faster today (Quinton 2005). We could therefore think of these streaming systems as, in effect, the mature mass-data versions of the system of original stock tickers introduced in the late nineteenth century, invented by Edward A. Calahan in 1867, an engineer associated with the American Telegraph Company.[6] This was,

> a printing telegraph with two independent type-wheels, placed under a glass bell jar (to keep off dust) and powered by a battery. The wheels were mounted face-to-face on two shafts and revolved under the action of an electromagnet. The first wheel had the letters of the alphabet on it; the second wheel had figures, fractions and some letters. The inked wheels printed on a paper tape divided into two strips: the security's name was printed on the upper strip and the price quote on the lower one, beneath the name. (Preda 2005: 755)

The stock ticker produced a constant flow of information that was sent by telegraph around the country about news and price movements on the stock exchange. The telegraph, of course, was also used to send personal messages as well as stock information. Indeed, Schott (2009) speculated that tweeting using the Telegraphic codes from 1891 might return within the terse format of a Tweet, he explains,

The 140-character limit of Twitter posts was guided by the 160-character limit established by the developers of SMS. However, there is nothing new about new technology imposing restrictions on articulation. During the late 19th-century telegraphy boom, some carriers charged extra for words longer than 15 characters and for messages longer than 10 words. Thus, the cheapest telegram was often limited to 150 characters. (Schott 2009)

With the growth of stock exchanges, the stock ticker companies developed a client/server structure with price changes being transmitted back to the centre as a hub, which were then resent, through spokes, to the provincial exchanges. For the users of the ticker service, unlike the telegraph, the stock ticker printed its message out as a continual unfolding stream of information on paper which could be read by anyone,

The flow of price variations visualized the results of ongoing conversational exchanges, and disassociated their results from the individual authority of the participants in those conversations. At the same time, the flow linked the results to each other, made the ties that bound them visible as the tape unfolded, and made the market in its turn visible as an abstract, faceless, yet very lively whole. All the felicity conditions that made the speech act valid (intonation, attitude, look, wording, pitch of voice, and so on) were blanked out. Authority and credibility was transferred from the broker's person to the machine. The flow of figures and letters on the ticker tape became an appresentation. . . . In other words, perception (of price rhythms) and representation (of floor transactions) fused together. (Preda 2005: 763)

This 'blanking out' of the speech act is, of course, very familiar to users of Twitter. This medium, due to its reliance on 140 character messages, ensures a terse text that tends towards a factual and news-like message. It is interesting to note that a great majority of tweets are found to be only around 40 characters in length (Ayman 2010, cf Hubspot 2009). It is, perhaps, little wonder that the news organizations have adapted to using it so easily.[7] Indeed, users have also taken to Twitter and Facebook in such a remarkable way, even more so with the growth of mobile app versions of the services. The similarity of ticker users becoming entranced by the information on the stock tickers to contemporary users of Twitter and Facebook, who also stop and stare at their screens and seemingly fall into a trance, is striking. In his reminiscences, Richard D. Wyckoff (1934a: 37), a stock operator and pioneer of financial chart analysis, wrote that 'in 1905 friends of his could sit and watch the tape for an hour and a half without any interruption' (Preda 2005: 766). Wyckoff had trained himself to sit still at the ticker so that he could watch the ticker tape for up to an hour. He also remembered how in 1907, James R. Keene, the financial speculator, fell into what he called a 'ticker trance',

> I used to stand facing him, my left elbow on his ticker while talking to him. He would hold the tape in his left hand and his eye-glasses in his right as he listened to me, then on went the glasses astride his nose as he bent close to the tape in a scrutiny of the length that had passed meanwhile. I might be talking at the moment his eye began to pick up the tape again, but until he finished he was a person in a trance. If, reading the tape, he observed something that stimulated his mental machinery, I might go on talking indefinitely; he wouldn't get a word of it. . . . He appeared to absorb a certain length of tape, and to devote to its analysis a specified interval, measured by paces. Sometimes he returned to the ribbon for another examination, followed by more pacing. (Preda 2005: 766)

The similarity of users absorbed in their mobile devices watching Twitter is striking and this 'Twitter trance', or attentiveness to the temporality of Twitter, disciplines the user to keeping ahead of the stream and by being 'in the stream'. The user has to develop a temporal awareness fitted and co-constructed by this technical device (or *agencement*), whether delivered via the browser or an app on a mobile phone. Again, the similarities to the stock ticker are remarkable.[8] In our increasingly financialized world this democratization of stream-based data flows as a disciplinary practice and its connection to financial flows is instructive, indeed,

> The stress on observation and attentiveness fitted in very well with the overall discourse of the "science of financial markets", so popular in late 19th century. It required of investors precisely those qualities preached by manuals: attention, vigilance and constant observation of financial transactions and of price variations. For the investor, it is only reasonable to follow the market movements and to try to be efficient. (Preda 2005: 773)

The temporality presented by Twitter, in particular, is a constant real-time social media flow, which is modulated by the activity of the users on the stream. Time is referred to in the past tense, with even the most recent tweet having happened a few seconds ago, and marked as such to the user. Each tweet is placed within its temporal box, neatly segmented in a structured textual format by the other tweets in the constant flow of time represented by technical time (see the raw Twitter public timeline here as JSON data).[9] As Preda (2005) described with the stock ticker,

> a ragged temporal structure was replaced by a smooth one, with the conse-
> quence that price variations became visualizations of market transactions

and objects of symbolic interpretation. The ticker made market exchanges visible as they happened, disentangled them from local conversations, and transformed them into something that is both abstract and visible in several forms to everybody at once. They are visible in the flow of names and prices on the paper strip, but also in the financial charts, which are nowadays also produced in real time. The quality of price data changed: instead of multiple, discontinuous, heterogeneous and unsystematically recorded prices, we now have single, continuous, homogeneous, nearly real-time price variations. (Preda 2005: 776)

Indeed, we could argue that the quality of media conversations is changing: instead of multiple, discontinuous, heterogeneous and unsystematic conversations, we now have single, continuous, homogeneous, nearly real-time updates of news, stories, lives, events and activities, all streamed through a common format that is distributed in real time around the world. But it is important to be attentive to the cadences of streams as clearly the pace of flow change dynamically over time in response to external events and activities. This, I think, helps us to think about the way in which a seemingly limited platform of data transmission has become a mass social media and in doing so is preparing/teaching users to cope with real-time streams of information, a key requirement for the kinds of services and technologies that are currently being developed in Silicon Valley. Thus, perhaps we should think of Twitter less as a radio, or as a television, but rather as a ticker, albeit one that contains information other than stock prices (although it does that too). Twitter as a ticker also reinforces its sense of temporality as a constant set of discrete 'ticks' that move dynamically around the world, and are connected to the activities and tweets of the users that use the service.[10] We might also note that the interactional layer of Twitter, as commodity surface, remains in the form of a flowing stream of information, which, while it may possibly move fast in and out of itself, hides the underlying mechanisms, which are constantly shifting at the levels of codal, logical and physical layers.

Financialization and software

Finally, I want to look at a particular case of the obscure objects of financial mediation, in particular the interesting notion of dark pools in finance. This is a useful case study due to the close relationship between a society which is softwarized and its financialization. With the financial crisis of 2008, the reliance of our societies upon software has become increasingly apparent, as the algorithms that formed the codal layers of financialization were found to be wanting in relation to the simplistic models of the world that they described. Nonetheless, it will come as little surprise that within a computational society, the answer to a crisis of computation is a turn to intensified computationality, that is greater use of softwarization in order to ensure that such technical failures are avoided. The irony of implementing more systems computationally, to the extent that the interactional, social and individuational layers are maximally softwarized, speaks of the powers of the computational imaginary. Here, I want to look at this counter-intuitive mode of object relationships that function by the very act of withdrawing and the way in which they represent a new higher level of financial expansion and profit in response to the opening of the black boxes of market exchanges.

One of the most innovative and softwarized industries globally is the financial services sector of the economy, including banking, financial trading, stocks, bond and government debt markets. These have become somewhat better known following high-profile crashes, such as with the 'Flash Crash' in May 2010, and other mini crashes that appear to have been triggered by algorithmic trading. Here, I want to look at the specific instance of counter-party credit risk as a site of softwarization, particularly due to its closeness to the everyday operation of the financial system, and by definition the 'real' economy. The intention is to move attention temporarily away from the concerns of everyday life and its relationship to subjectivity, software and new forms of computational being, to provide some structural analysis of the way in which software is a glue that holds together the economy through infrastructural systems.

Software/code can be used as an important resource for understanding and explaining many of the forces of capitalism operating today, particularly in relation to financial markets.[11] For example, software leaves traces through various forms of inscription and information cascades that can be analysed by scholars, from the software design documentation, to interviews with computer programmers, and even to the more dramatic examples of stock market volatility due to software errors and bugs. By careful close and distant readings of software/code, it is possible to see how particular forms of capitalism are embedded within the software/code layer to enable certain forms of market activity.

In order to fully understand these financialized practices and products, we need to develop methods to be more attentive to the software and computer code that acts as a condition of possibility for financial markets.[12] By learning how to read and decode the structures embedded within software, researchers could develop understandings of the dark arts of computer programmers and hackers and connect them more clearly to the way in which technology enables the diffusion of financialization practices.

Similarly, when understanding code there remain these difficult 'mysteries' and we must place them in their social formation if we are to understand how code and code work is undertaken. This is a very useful way of thinking about code, and draws attention to the way in which code and the practices associated with it are constantly evolving as new technologies are developed and introduced. We no longer program computers with a soldering iron, nor with punch cards. Due to improvements over the last 40 years or so, programmers can now take advantage of tools and modular systems that have been introduced into programming through the mass engineering techniques of Fordism. In the same way that studying the mechanical and industrial machinery of the last century can tell us a lot about the organization of factories, geographic movements, materials, industries and processes in industrial capitalism, through the study of code we can learn a lot about the structure and processes of our post-Fordist societies understanding the way in which certain social formations are actualized through crystallization in computer code. By reading the inscriptions in code that guide these behaviours, this opens exciting possibilities for the social scientist as the rules that govern certain kinds of institutional behaviour are laid out within the source code.

For example, it is surprising to know how similar the production of code is to practices of craftsmanship, such as carpentry. First the programmer starts with rough broad strokes to outline the general program ends, and then narrow it down through iterative processes of development to a more precise mechanism. Indeed, the programming environments are built to give the programmer the feedback on how the code is doing – something that is rather surprising to outsiders to programming who often view it in idealistic or unrealistic terms. Although programming is a lot more sophisticated too – in the visual programming environments it is becoming more like graphic design than the geeky 'programming' we often see in movies. As with carpentry, code is modular, programmers build it from bits (modules, snippets, fragments, classes, objects), each of which the programmer writes and tests separately, rather like the way a table is assembled from the different parts that make it up: top, legs, brackets, feet and so forth. Indeed, code is amply structured for the division of labour and the capitalist process of accumulation. Which is hardly surprising considering that it is an engineering process that has grown in lock step with the demands of what we might call cognitive capitalism.

Code/software is the 'doing of processing', which we can only understand by actually reading the code itself and watching how it operates, its *computationality* – this mostly we do at the level of the codal. It is interesting that after financialization came under attack following the credit crunch of 2008–10, digital technologies continue to be offered as a panacea – we could think of this as a computational economic imaginary. This certainly reveals the finance industry's commitment to a form of technological determinism or perhaps computational ideology. In other words, that technology can solve the problem of financial instability itself, but also a belief by traders and companies that the crash was caused, to some extent, by a *lack* of technology rather than a surfeit. Indeed, management, 'quants' and technical staff have continued to develop computational systems where statistical analysis and high-technology solutions can be leveraged to manage, if not mitigate counter-party risk, however misplaced that belief might be. For example, software which renders the display of a financial risk portfolio information in a very stylized, simplified form, often with colour codings and increasingly with rich graphics.[13] It is also increasingly clear that not only do few market participants fully understand risk as a statistical category, but also the familiar bell-shaped curve of Gaussian distributions displayed on mobile screens encourages a kind of 'domesticated' approach to risk that makes it appear familiarized and benign (see Langley 2008).

Here, following the credit crisis of 2008, which resulted in failures of relatively high-profile firms (Jorion and Zhang 2009), much more attention has been focused on counter-party risk and how it might be mitigated by a computational turn. With the collapse of Lehman Brothers between the 10th and 15th September 2008 following a reported $4 billion loss and unsuccessful negotiation to find a buyer, and with one of Wall Street's most prestigious firms filing for bankruptcy protection (Stampoulis 2010), concerns about counter-party risk were heightened still further.

> What is your real-time exposure at any point in time? That's the question that regulators will be asking," says Alan Grody, president of the New York-based risk advisory firm Financial InterGroup . . . The answers, especially urgent in light of the counterparty-risk deficiencies exposed by the 2008 collapse of Lehman Brothers, will require new and improved capabilities that bring about some form of real-time risk management. (Heires 2009: 35)

Counter-party credit risk has now emerged as a key issue for banks and other lenders, particularly following the losses associated with the high-profile failures of monoline insurers and investment banks. Many now argue that no counterparty can ever be considered immune to financial instability (including sovereign counterparties) (Gregory 2009a, b). The traditional approach of controlling counter-party credit risk has been to set limits against future risk exposures and to verify new trades against defined limits. For example, requiring a certain proportion of collateral to be 'posted' or else using an external measure of the credit-worthiness of the counterparty.

Increasingly, however, banks are moving towards dynamically pricing, in real time, the calculated counter-party credit risk directly into new trades. Credit Value Adjustment (CVA) uses computational processes to quickly determine an institution's credit risk at any moment (Algorithmics 2009; Beck n.d.). This 'real-time stream' of data is not just an empirical object; it also serves as a technological imaginary and enables new financial services, which produce and govern markets through a particular temporal order. For example, financial markets are undergoing an intensification of fast-moving data streams that measure time in microseconds, as such the moment under which a decision is taken whether to trade or not is getting shorter (Berry 2011a). For example, in the 'flash crash' on 6 May 2010, $500 billion dollars worth of value was momentarily erased from the market by high-frequency trading and the Dow plunged nearly 1,000 points in just a few minutes, a 9.2 per cent drop, half a trillion dollars worth of value was erased from the market and then miraculously returned again 20 minutes later (HTCWire 2010). This was largely due to 'quote stuffing' whereby huge streams of trades are pushed into the computer systems at an incredibly rapid rate, resulting in unexpected and chaotic algorithmic and human responses – in this case a partial sell-off.

Financial companies are rolling out new technologies all the time to give them an edge in the marketplace, such as 'dark pools' (also called 'dark liquidity'), which are off-market trade matching systems working on crossing networks which give the trader opaqueness in trading activities, such as when trying to sell large tranches of shares (Bogoslaw 2007). Dark pools are 'a private or alternative trading system that allows participants to transact without displaying quotes publicly. Orders are anonymously matched and not reported to any entity, even the regulators' (Shunmugam 2010). Dark pools are markets that by definition represent computal opaqueness in such a way as to facilitate a financial transaction whereby parties are matched within a non-transparent mode of off-exchange transaction (obfuscated markets). Dark pools are computationally created and algorithmically sustained opaque markets designed to be anonymous spaces for trading and financial flows.

These real-time data streams are created, managed, distributed and stabilized through the use of software/code, particularly software platforms that are custom built on low-latency hardware in order to enable rapid trading. In June 2010, Risk Professionals (from the Banking sector) reported that 50 per cent of their institutions calculated CVA monthly, 25 per cent daily and 25 per cent in real time (Stampoulis 2010). However, 'for many financial firms, achieving an institution-wide, real-time view of risk and profit-and-loss is the Holy Grail of risk management' (Heires 2009: 34).

This is the 'softwarization' of the problem of counter-party credit risk and forms the basis of the algorithms that finally generate visualized interface and reports. Indeed, it is very unlikely that either the traders or management have an active involvement in the software/code used and are unlikely to problematize the seeming 'objectivity' of the results it generates. This is where the computer as 'truth machine' becomes a highly trusted device for analyzing risk. Of course, widely shared algorithms of CVA equations also demonstrate a form of softwarized monoculture, whereby financial organizations are using very similar, if not almost identical algorithms for calculating their credit default exposure (see Zhu and Pykhtin 2007), although admittedly implemented in different programming languages. Even where the organization buys off-the-shelf credit counter-party risk analysis software, such as Murex, Kondor or Calypso, internally there are similar mathematized standardized algorithms and equations implemented from a small number of vendors. One wonders if the seeds of the next crisis in finance are already being laid in the code and software that lies hidden underneath these systems.

Here, we see the movement or translation between the temporal generation of the discrete elements of the stream and the computational storage through what Kittler calls *time axis manipulation*. This is the storing of time as *space*, and allows the linear flow to be recorded and then reordered, in this case financial data held as time-series data. The shifting of chronological time to the spatial means that things can be replayed and even reversed. This is the discretization of the continuous flow of time. For example, without it the complexity of financial markets would be impossible and the functions and methods applied to it, through for example the creation of new abstract classes of investment such as credit default swaps, collateralized debt obligations and asset backed securities, would be extremely difficult, if not impossible to create and trade. However, we must not lose sight of the materiality of computation which is nonetheless inscribed within a substrate on the physical, logical and codal layers.

Here, in risk calculation, computation is being applied to all counterparties of a financial trade by way of counter-party risk algorithms. This software/code attempts to quantify the likelihood of default, not only for corporations but also for sovereign nations, who were previously thought to be of only marginal risk as counterparties. Even more interesting is the development in using self-analysis, whereby in a curious process of *introspection*, the company performing counter-party risk analysis includes its own credit default likelihood in its own equations as a possible credit counter-party risk, so-called bilateral counter-party risk credit valuation adjustments.

In this more encompassing vision, a firm would obtain a real-time view of its risk exposures on a cross-asset, cross-trader and institution-wide basis, combined with profit and loss, coupled with the computerized ability to swiftly identify events that might introduce risk, instantly analyse those events against a variety of risk models and, if necessary, take appropriate risk-mitigating actions – all in the blink of an eye (Heires 2009: 34). The reliance on these systems to perform such mission-critical real-time decision analysis brings to the fore the problem of the great trust we are placing in these systems. It also shows how many of these systems that rely on 'finding alpha', that is 'the skill required to choose individual assets that will outperform the market', or 'beta', where it is the 'return achieved from exposure to the overall market, for example, via an index fund' or even the newer notion of 'smart beta' that uses quants and algorithms to beat traditional beta returns, are increasingly reliant on these software systems (Economist 2013).

There is no doubt at all that software is a hugely important global industry, and that software is critical to the functioning of financial companies, governments and non-governmental institutions (Berry 2008). In the case of financial markets, software has completely changed the nature of stock and commodity trading, creating 24/7 markets and enabling the creation of complex derivative products and services. Perhaps not surprisingly, sharp-eyed firms have also realized that credit counter-party risk is itself *hedgeable*, and consequently have begun to trade counter-party exposure itself as a category of financial instrument (Canabarro and Duffie 2004: 133). That is that risk itself as a computable function becomes subject to capitalist valorization.

More work is needed in this area to understand the ways software/code instantiates softwarized finance and particular computational imaginaries linked to finance capital. Equally important is the task of mapping and tracing the use of the computal in practice. Here, real-time credit counter-party risk and real-time data streams are a useful example of how algorithms tend to be delegated trust, and used to construct 'truth-machines' in finance and other areas of everyday life.[14] Indeed, more work is needed to critically explore the way in which software/code serves as the condition of possibility for stabilizing 'truth', risk, credit and financialized society more generally.

4

Computational ontologies

This chapter explores the question of ontology, particularly that presupposed by Cartesian ontology, which divides the world between *res cogitans* and *res extensa*, that is, spirit and matter. This was part of the Kantian legacy that, through Husserl, Heidegger attempted to critique. In this chapter I think it is fruitful to use Heideggerian concepts to refresh critical thinking through an encounter with the, often opposing, camps of critical theory and Heideggerian phenomenology to tentatively develop a critical phenomenology. Indeed, there are clear convergences with Heidegger's thought and Adorno, as each 'wishes to insist on the temporal-historical character of truth without taking this as a excuse for relativism; each resists reducing philosophy either to a method or a doctrine.' Lastly, and perhaps crucially, 'each is deeply concerned with a critique or questioning of modernity – and especially of the conversion of production into an absolute – without offering any simple return to tradition' (Jarvis 1998: 199). But, of course there are also clear political differences between the conservative Heidegger and Adorno, the critical theorist. In order to develop this notion of a critical phenomenology it is helpful to briefly review the corresponding positions of both Heidegger and Adorno. Thus the clarification of the relation to ontology of negative dialectics is needed in relation to the project outlined here, and to provide signposts for how this approach can be useful.

First, I want to briefly outline a brief position on Heidegger's relation to ontology and his project of deconstruction (*destruktion*). I will then examine Adorno's reaction to this and his position on ontology through negative dialectics. I am doing this for a number of reasons, but specifically because I use both Heidegger and Adorno as important touchstones for the development of a critical theory of the digital. Their work contributes to understanding how computationality has a specific and limited ontology which is nevertheless totalizing, and that needs to be historicized and read in relation to the kinds of contemporary philosophy that is practised under computational capitalism.

By this I am gesturing towards certain kinds of computationalism, but also the emergent philosophical work known as speculative realism, object-oriented philosophy or object-oriented ontology. Here, I shall group them under the term SR/OOO. While accepting that differences do exist between the various writers in this tradition, there are enough similarities in theorizing, not least due to their Heideggerian inheritance, that general contours of SR/OOO can be discerned. The aim is to explore how computationalism runs through the varieties of ontology that are deployed, and more specifically to connect them back to the critical theorists' treatment of philosophy as radically of its time.

Negative dialectics and fundamental ontology

Heidegger's philosophical project was an attempt to move beyond neo-Kantian transcendental idealism, without thereby accepting Hegelian 'speculative identification of subject and object or falling back into subjectivist or objectivist dogmatism' (Jarvis 1998: 201). In *Being and Time,* Heidegger argued that what he called 'the question of Being' has been forgotten about in contemporary life and philosophy. Heidegger was returning to a question that had been thought to no longer be an issue in 'modern' philosophy, as Being had been increasingly identified with a notion of the sum total of entities, or a classificatory concept regarding things that are. Heidegger, however, raised the problem that this understanding of Being was actually concerned with *beings*, rather than Being, and as such avoided the question of quite what entities are.

Heidegger argues that in modernity, the forgetting of Being took the form of an opposition between *res cogitans* and *res extensa*, which transformed the way in which modern humans acted and understood the world. In effect, humanity defined thus became a special kind of super being that had control over all other beings which were subject to technology to extract their resources and store them for later retrieval, which Heidegger terms *standing reserve*. Of course, this also led to the problem of humans slowly conceiving of themselves as just another kind of entity with particular properties and hence also amenable to conversion into a kind of standing resource, exemplified by the term 'human resources'. Heidegger argued that this problem could be addressed in a number of ways,

> Firstly, he suggested that a destruction or dismantling (*Destruktion*) of the previous history of ontology was a necessary precondition of any new "fundamental ontology". Such an ontology could not be built from scratch. It was inevitably implicated in the forgetting of being from which

it sought to wake up. Yet, secondly, Heidegger began to develop a new set of terms perculiar to his work (an idiolect) which were designed to avoid remaining for ever stuck in the presuppositions of previous ontology. (Jarvis 1998: 200–1)

Heidegger's attention to the question of the transcendence of Being concentrates on this issue, yet he argues that the meaning of Being can only be approached through an analysis of what he calls 'Dasein', the finite temporal character of human beings in their mortal and historical particularity. The ability of Dasein to think the truth of Being – that is, to ask the question of Being – requires the dismantling, both in our thought and in our relations with the world, of the previous ontology within which we are located. Here, the similarities with Adorno's work are clear, although Adorno continues to use the language of subject and object. This is because for Adorno, access to truth is always subjectively and historically mediated, and the subject does not create its object (Jarvis 1998: 202). Adorno argues we are not yet able to think the priority of the object, that is, not to confuse our concepts with the object itself, because to do so requires that we have already developed a critique of the fallacy of the 'constitutive subject' together with the demise of the 'absolutized production which this fallacy both reflects and sustains' (Jarvis 1998: 202). Again, Jarvis supplies a cogent overview of the differences between Heidegger and Adorno, he argues that,

> especially important is Adorno's contrast between Heidegger's interest in "historicity" and that of negative dialectics in history. For Adorno Heidegger's insistence on Dasein's historicity repeats the structure of the relation between the question of being and particular entities: *historicity* is prior to and qualitatively distinct from any merely ontic *history*. Historicity thus becomes the opposite of what it was supposed to be. It becomes a *de facto* invariant, because any historical particular is just as far away from "historicity" in general as it is from an invariant "nature". Heidegger's history thus becomes an "epochal history of Being"; for Heidegger, the succeeding ontologies testify to the structuring first principles (*archai*) of all life in the epochs which they govern. For Adorno, on the other hand, there can be no history of Being without a history of beings. (Jarvis 1998: 202, original emphasis)

Adorno claims that Heidegger's philosophy translates the problems of the current social reality into metaphysical questions; in other words, Heidegger ignores that metaphysics is historically and socially located. That is, that 'to speak about the meaning of Being as Heidegger's . . . attenuated metaphysical philosophy does is to miss the historical materialist conditions which, according to historical materialism, shape existence through and through' (O'Connor 2013: 95). Adorno further argues, 'the term "Being" means altogether different things to Marx and to Heidegger, and yet there is a common trait: in the ontological doctrine of Being's priority over thought, in the "transcendence" of Being, the materialist echo reverberates from a vast difference. The doctrine of Being turns ideological as it imperceptibly spiritualizes the materialist moment in thought by transposing it into pure functionality beyond any entity – as it removes by magic whatever critique of a false consciousness resides in the materialist concept of being' (Adorno 2004a: 200). In contrast to the dangers of what Adorno identifies as an unacknowledged theologically infused metaphysics in which Heidegger appears to be unable to accommodate the ability for humans to fundamentally alter the world in which they live, Adorno argues that 'the processes that unfold in the history of domination are not inevitable and they should not, for that reason, be construed to be irreversible' (O'Connor 2013: 100). Indeed, Adorno's work is an attempt to uncover the complex processes that operate under the 'appearances of a disconnected society' in order, through criticism, that they can be changed.

Adorno's materialism addresses the problem of givenness or immediacy. That is 'all attempts to get beyond idealism – claims of the type that thought constitutes, shapes, or is identical with, its objects appear to run the opposite risk of claiming access to immediacy, to a transcendence which is just a "given"' (Jarvis 1998: 149). We are therefore invited to 'have faith in some datum or framework for data which cannot be interrogated further. Our knowledge of the givens is mistakenly thought of as being purely passive. Inquiry must simply halt before them' (Jarvis 1998: 149). Thus,

> The lesson which Adorno draws is that whether thinking is really materialist is not decided by how often the word "materialism" is repeated, but by what actually happens in that thinking. Materialist thinking would need to ask how it would be possible to think about that which appears to escape conceptuality. (Jarvis 1998: 150)

We cannot ignore how problematic it is to attempt a metaphysical invocation of an immediate access to transcendence, nor by inventing a new philosophical language, rather the language of concept and intuition, subject and object will still need to be used but within a critical approach. Thus, the relation to history is crucially important in a materialist approach that recognizes its social-historical sources which mediate the possibility of meaning. Adorno explains,

> If it is the case that no metaphysical thought was ever created which has not been a constellation of elements of experience, then, in the present

instance, the seminal experiences of metaphysics are simply diminished by a habit of thought which sublimates them into metaphysical pain and splits them off from the real pain which gave rise to them. (Adorno, quote in O'Connor 2013: 105)

Metaphysics must nonetheless be defended as a space of thinking not reducible to sheer givenness. Indeed, metaphysics needs to be reformulated such that it still 'refer[s] to transcendence as an intramundane or immanent space. What [Adorno's concept of] nonidentity thinking aims at is the particularity of the object. That particularity lies beyond conceptuality – it is analogous to the absolute of traditional metaphysics . . . but is nonetheless within the space of historical-material reality' (O'Connor 2013: 108).

Glitch ontology

In this section, I want to look more closely at the computal and computational ontologies through what Adorno called 'cover concepts' and their distinction from 'emphatic concepts' (see Adorno 2004a: 148–51). That is,

A cover-concept is one which can be used to limit the members of a set. It is descriptive. But an emphatic concept is one which has inside it a promise. It is a promise which cannot be cut out of the concept without changing it. So that the concept of "art", it could be suggested, is not merely a cover-concept. It does not signify a certain set of properties, any object possessing which could count as an instance of the concept. To call something art is always not only to describe something but also to evaluate it. (Jarvis 2009: 88)

Adorno argues that emphatically conceived, a concept is 'one that is not simply the characteristic unit of the individual object from which it was abstracted' (Adorno 2004a: 150). That is, like the concept of freedom, these emphatic concepts are not merely descriptive, and therefore 'arbitrarily diminished', instead there is a 'more' of the concept, as it were, which offers the possibility of generating a contradiction between the concept of freedom and its realization, and therefore the possibility of critical thought itself. Concepts such as freedom, humanity, and justice are what Adorno calls 'emphatic' concepts in the sense that they are ineliminably both prescriptive and descriptive (Jarvis 1998: 66).

In the case of computational ontologies, and the use of computational concepts more widely within our ontological and everyday understanding of life, the question is: to what extent do these computational categories perform not merely as 'wretched' cover concepts? Indeed, do they have the possibility of generatively making possible contradictions that facilitate critical thought, within what we are calling here computationality, as emphatic conceptual resources?

Previously, in *The Philosophy of Software*, I outlined the emergence of computationality as an ontotheology drawing on the work of Heidegger (Berry 2011a, b). Computationality is understood as a specific historical epoch defined by a certain set of computational knowledges, practices, methods and categories. Computationality is therefore an *ontotheology*, which when read through Heideggerian categories can be understood as creating a new ontological 'epoch' or a new historical constellation of intelligibility. With the notion of ontotheology, Heidegger is following Kant's argument that intelligibility is a process of filtering and organizing a complex overwhelming world by the use of 'categories', Kant's 'discursivity thesis'. Heidegger historicizes Kant's cognitive categories arguing that there is 'succession of changing historical ontotheologies that make up the "core" of the metaphysical tradition. These ontotheologies establish "the truth concerning entities as such and as a whole," in other words, they tell us both what and how entities are – establishing both their essence and their existence' (Thomson 2009: 149–50). Metaphysics, grasped ontotheologically, 'temporarily secures the intelligible order' by understanding it 'ontologically', from the inside out, and 'theologically' from the outside in, which allows the formation of an epoch, a 'historical constellation of intelligibility which is unified around its ontotheological understanding of the being of entities' (Thomson 2009: 150).

Thus, as an ontotheology, computationality is a central, effective, increasingly dominant system of meanings and values that become operative and which are not merely abstract but which are organized and lived. Thus computationality cannot be understood at the level of mere opinion or manipulation. It is related to a whole body of computational practices and expectations, for example, the assignment of energy towards particular projects, the ordinary understanding of the 'nature' of humans, and of the world. This set of meanings and values is experienced as practices which appear as reciprocally confirming, repeated and predictable and also used to describe and understand the world – in some cases, software even becomes an explanatory form of explanation itself (see Chun 2011). This notion can be read through Heidegger, and shares some of the presuppositions and theoretical work undertaken by Horkheimer and Adorno, particularly in relation to the way in which the domination of nature is entangled with the 'mastery over human nature, the repression of impulse, but also the mastery over other humans' (Schecter 2007: 27).

Today there are rapid changes in social contexts that are made possible by the installation of code/software via computational devices, streams, clouds or networks, what Mitcham (1998: 43) calls a 'new ecology of artifice'. The proliferation of computal contrivances that are computationally based is truly breathtaking, and each year there is a large growth in the use of these computational devices and the data they collect. These devices, of course, are not static, nor are they mute, and their interconnections, communications, operation, effects and usage are increasingly prescriptive on the everyday life world. But as opaque devices they are difficult to understand and analyse due to their staggering rate of change, thanks to the underlying hardware technologies, which are becoming ever smaller, more compact, more powerful and less power-hungry, and also due to the increase in complexity, power, range and intelligence of the software that powers these devices. Within the algorithms that power these devices are embedded classificatory schemes and ontologies that pre-structure the world that is presented. Indeed, this formatting and mediating capacity directly encodes cover concepts into the device.

It should hardly come as a surprise that code/software lies as a mediator between ourselves and our corporeal experiences, disconnecting the physical world from a direct coupling with our physicality, while managing a looser softwarized transmission system. Called 'fly-by-wire' in aircraft design, in reality fly-by-wire is the condition of the computational environment we increasingly experience, hence the term computationality (Berry 2011a). This is a highly mediated existence and has been a growing feature of the (post) modern computational world. While many objects remain firmly material and within our grasp, it is easy to see how a more softwarized form of *simulacra* lies just beyond the horizon. Not that software isn't material, of course, certainly it is embedded in physical objects and the physical environment and requires a material carrier to function at all. Nonetheless, the materiality of software appears *uncanny* as a material and therefore more difficult to research as a *material* artefact. This is partly, it has to be said, due to software's increasing tendency to hide its depths behind glass rectangular squares which yield only to certain prescribed forms of touch-based interfaces. But also because algorithms are always mediated due to their existence as electric pulses and flows within digital circuits. We, therefore, only experience algorithms in their use through practices that rely on computers but also on screenic representation and so forth. Nonetheless, code/software is the paradigmatic case of computationality, and presents us with a research object which is fully located at all major junctures of modern society and is unique in enabling modern society and in also raising the possibility of reading and understanding the present situation of computationality.

These devices also enable the assemblage of new social ontologies and the corresponding social epistemologies that we increasingly take for granted in computational society, including Wikipedia, Facebook and Twitter. The extent to which computational devices, and the computational principles on which they are based and from which they draw their power, have permeated the way we use and develop knowledges in everyday life is simply breathtaking, had we not already discounted and backgrounded their importance. For example, computational methods like n-gramming are being utilized to decode everyday life by counting how word usage has changed over time, particularly over a large period of time (Zax 2011).[1] The ability to call up information instantly from a mobile device, combine it with others, subject it to debate and critique through real-time social networks, and then edit, post and distribute it worldwide would be incredible if it hadn't already started to become so mundane.

Drawing from and extending Heidegger's concepts we might reconstruct his notions of the mode of technicity and its 'challenging-forth' to one where computationality is central and has a classificatory structure we might call 'streaming-forth'. For Heidegger, 'challenging-forth' is understood as a relationship to the world whereby one treats the world, nature, culture, etc. as available for extraction, processing and storing as standing reserve. In doing so, the original entities are destroyed, transformed and reconstructed as a form of 'fuel'. A good example of this is a hill that produces coal, which in the process of being mined is destroyed, leaving behind only the coal as standing reserve (resources) and waste products. In computationality, however, it is data that is being 'mined', leaving the original entities in their original state, but with secondary information collected about them, a kind of second-order data or metadata, as a form of standing reserve. Thus, this data is 'extracted' without the destruction of the other. This data 'exhaustion' process, which here I call 'streaming-forth' is the creation of information from characteristics, properties and social epistemologies regarding the object under computational analysis.

Streaming forth generates second-order information and data to maintain a world which is itself *seen* and *computationally processed* as flow, but re-articulated within a screenic form which produces a universe which is increasingly understood as object-oriented and discrete. Collected information is processed together with feedback which creates part of the ecology of computationality. Adorno calls this an ontological moment, that is the emergence of a horizon or constellation of key concepts around a particular historical social formation linked to, in this case, computational capitalism. We can analyse the history of the changing forms of human alienation from nature by theorizing epistemological questions in relation to socio-economic, ethical and political issues. This is crucial in terms of a certain kind of historical *forgetting*, and reconstruction in computational categories, and even a forgetting of the computational as *the* horizon of thinking. Indeed, for Adorno, reification 'is as much about *forgetting* certain histories as it is about exploitation and projection' (Schecter 2007: 100). Adorno and Heidegger offer important concepts for thinking through these issues and with Heidegger's philosophy historicized, a newly historical Heideggerian phenomenology can begin to inform and explore notions of experience in relation to contemporary formations of computation. However, it is Adorno who, as the critical theorist, points the way to not only historicizing Heidegger's work, but also how the conditions under which we live today, being historical, can be changed and therefore are within the agency of individuals to critique and shift. Indeed, Schecter argues that Adorno,

> is a theorist of aesthetics and society interested in the (possibly utopian) conditions under which non-antagonistic knowledge and non-instrumental reason might be operative in practice rather than merely discernable in absence . . . a hermeneutics of *absent mediations*, and can be compared with Heidegger's affirmation of *Nichts* (nothingness) as a hermeneutic of *absolute origins*. (Schecter 2007: 112, fn 34, original emphasis)

This is a suggestive approach and helps thinking through the question of the absent mediations of the computational. Indeed, we might note again using historicized Heideggerian categories the way in which computation creates not only the conditions of possibility for this way of being in the world, but also points to computational experience within capitalism as constitutive of this ontology. Additionally, computational devices demonstrate a phenomenological experience of computation, that of the rapid oscillation between the categories Heidegger identified as *Vorhandenheit/Zuhandenheit* (present-at-hand/ready-to-hand) – and this I call a 'glitch' ontology. Thus the computational device constantly changes from being part of the everyday flow of reality, ready-to-hand and the objective 'paused' experience familiar from science, which he calls unready-to-hand, in quick alternation. As Weiser argued,

> Such a disappearance [in readiness-to-hand] is a fundamental consequence not of technology, but of human psychology. Whenever people learn something sufficiently well, they cease to be aware of it. When you look at a street sign, for example, you absorb its information without consciously performing the act of reading. Computer scientist, economist, and Nobelist Herb Simon calls this phenomenon "compiling"; philosopher Michael

Polanyi calls it the "tacit dimension"; psychologist TK Gibson calls it "visual invariants"; philosophers Georg Gadamer and Martin Heidegger call it "the horizon" and the "ready-to-hand", John Seely Brown at PARC calls it the "periphery". All say, in essence, that only when things disappear in this way are we freed to use them without thinking and so to focus beyond them on new goals. (Weiser 1991: 78)

Computers do not, nor have ever been able to, run themselves entirely without human assistance and therefore this computal disappearance is only ever partial. Computational devices are constantly suffering from breakdowns, bugs, errors and crashes. Well-engineered industrial machines do not tend to suffer these constant breakdowns. You could think of this then as an oscillation, perhaps due to the underlying fragility of the nature of code, that means it is always on the constant verge of breakdown (again car engines do not act like this, once they are working they are working, generally speaking). Software and code is thus always calling to us from a position of unreadiness-to-hand. Software programmers have a lovely term for what I am getting at when they say that code *throws an exception*, which causes the machine to pause and wait for further instruction or execute an alternative method, and if no such instruction is available or forthcoming, it is said that code is *unable to catch the exception* and it crashes in some way (sometimes gracefully and at other times catastrophically). When this happens we are left nursing a device that no longer contains the agency that animates the device – on Windows devices known as the 'Blue Screen of Death'. And by quick, this breakdown can be happening in microseconds, milliseconds or seconds, repeatedly, in quick succession. This aspect of breakdown has been acknowledged as an issue within human-computer design and is seen as one of the pressing concerns to be 'fixed' or made invisible to the computational device user (Winograd and Flores 1987).

However, it is not necessarily the case that computation is different from 'other' equipment by being a 'third mode' or middle between presence and absence. For example, there is much to learn by exploring how computational devices engender an experience generated by this rather novel feature/bug of oscillating rapidly between *Vorhandenheit* and *Zuhandenheit;* indeed it highlights the phenomenological specificity of the computal. Thus, how absence and presence are experienced in this very specific and curious way, enabled by computational devices (and by extension code and software), can give a great deal of insight into the experience of the user of computational devices. This *quantitative* micro/millisecond oscillations between *Vorhandenheit* and *Zuhandenheit* might therefore be said to translate into an odd mediated 'pseudo-mode' which is, perhaps, *qualitatively* experienced as 'uncanny' and which might analytically be referred to as 'radically unready-to-hand' or as *fractured objects*. This is generated by the so-called 'closed world' of computation. Certainly, this is part of the specificity of the phenomenological experience that I am gesturing towards with the concept of glitch ontology.

The oscillation creates the 'glitch' that is a specific feature of computation as opposed to other technical forms (Berry 2011a). This is the glitch that creates the conspicuousness that breaks the everyday experience of things, and more importantly breaks the flow of things being readily at hand. This is a form that Heidegger usefully outlined using the term unreadyness-to-hand (*Unzuhandenheit*). Heidegger defines three forms of unreadyness-to-hand: Obtrusiveness (*Aufdringlichkeit*), Obstinacy (*Aufsässigkeit*) and Conspicuousness (*Auffälligkeit*), where the first two are non-functioning equipment and the latter is equipment that is not functioning at its best (see Heidegger 1978, particularly fn 1). In other words, if equipment breaks, you have to think about it and consider it as a 'present-at-hand' object. Nonetheless, it is crucial to historicize this notion, in relation to a specific historically located understanding of the subject-object relationship and particular conceptions of how an object appears or changes within a historical epoch. Within the computational constellation of historical intelligibility outlined here, objects are both constituted through a computational register, and, crucially, are increasingly mediated through computer software, code and algorithms.

In this ontology, it is important to note that conspicuousness is not partially or temporarily broken-down equipment. As Heidegger puts it, it requires 'a more precise kind of circumspection, such as "inspecting", checking up on what has been attained, [etc.]' (Dreyfus 2001: 70). Conspicuousness, then, 'presents the available equipment as in a certain unavailableness' (Heidegger 1978: 102–3), so that, as Dreyfus (2001: 71) explains, we are momentarily startled, and then shift to a new way of coping. However, if help is given quickly or the situation is resolved, then 'transparent circumspective behaviour can be so quickly and easily restored that no new stance on the part of Dasein is required' (Dreyfus 2001: 72).

In other words, computation due to its glitch ontology continually forces a contextual slowing down at the level of the experience of the user. This is suggestive of the possibility for a micro-phenomenology that could fully explore the breaks in perception that the computer generates. The continuity of flow or practice is interrupted by minute pauses and breaks (these may be beyond conscious perception, as such). This is not to say that analogue technologies do not break down. The difference in the conspicuousness of digital technologies is at a resolution of breakdown beyond conscious perception whereas our everyday experience of the obstinacy or obtrusiveness of analogue technologies is that they tend to work or not at a 'macro' scale.

The discrete granularity of the conspicuousness of digital technologies raises interesting questions in relation to basic questions about our experiences of computational systems and the way in which micro-phenomenological interrupts can structure consciousness in a number of ways. It also suggests a research programme related to the new high-speed adaptive algorithmic interfaces (algorithmic GUIs) that can offer contextual information, and even reshape the entire interface itself, through the monitoring of our reactions to computational interfaces and feedback and sensor information from the computational device itself. This method of producing computational devices has been christened 'context aware programming' which 'just as the switch from the command line to the GUI required new UI skills and sensibilities, mobile and sensor-based programming creates new opportunities to innovate, to surprise and delight the user, or, in failing to use the new capabilities, the opportunity to create frustration and anger' (O'Reilly 2013).

The use of Heideggerian concepts is also helpful in contesting the methodological distinction of concept from intuition in Kant's thought where Neo-Kantian readings of Kant's first critique, *Critique of Pure Reason* have read it as an epistemology (Jarvis 1998: 203). Heidegger argues,

> What is philosophically primary is neither a theory of the concept-formation of historiology nor the theory of historiological knowledge, nor yet the theory of history as the Object of historiology; what is primary is rather the Interpretation of authentically historical entities as regards their historicality. Similarly the positive outcome of Kant's *Critique of Pure Reason* lies in what is has contributed towards the working out of what belongs to any Nature whatsoever, not in a "theory" of knowledge. (Heidegger 1978: 31)

For both Heidegger and Adorno, Kant's schematism chapter (Kant 1998: 271–7) is an important contribution to philosophy and to thinking. For Heidegger 'the idea that the transcendental imagination itself makes possible both understanding and sensibility – and that it does so through "transcendental determinations of time"' – is a radically new insight which . . . opens up the possibility of a fundamental ontology whose "horizon" is time' (Jarvis 1998: 203). Heidegger and Adorno both,

> Suggest that critical thinking may itself already contain the resources for an ontology (or ontological moment, in Adorno's case) in which Being need not be transfigured into an invariant. Secondly, they take it to indicate an awareness of the metaphysical presuppositions of epistemology. It is to these presuppositions that Heidegger refers when he remarks that "possibility of experience is therefore synonymous with transcendence". (Jarvis 1998: 204)

For Heidegger, the reciprocal relationship between concepts and intuition is expressed in terms of the 'priority of (categorical) intuition over concepts' (Jarvis 1998: 204). This is problematic for Adorno, as it suggests that 'mediation through concepts which is necessary for our knowledge of objects to be *knowledge* of objects is in some way a dependent or inferior element, "in the service" of what is given in intuition' (Jarvis 1998: 204). Indeed, for Adorno, 'the mediated non-identity of subject and object is not even potentially knowable without thinking the priority of the object against the background of anticipated reconciliation in epistemology and politics' (Schecter 2007: 119). Thus,

> Heidegger distinguishes between epistemological *subjects* knowing objects without thinking the being of their beingness, and *Dasein* thinking that difference ontologically. Adorno insists that there is a difference between *thinking* and more or less successful modes of *adaptation* to social norms and structures. That difference is also a historical and libertarian difference for Adorno that is not thinkable in isolation from the repressive socio-economic, political and juridical institutions which make the difference between thought and mere adaptation apparent. (Schecter 2007: 120, original emphasis)

In contrast to Heidegger's fundamental ontology, Adorno offers negative dialectics. Adorno argues that critical theory must be grounded in philosophy, and as such the distinction between appearance and reality is crucial to understand that 'society determines social phenomena (the appearances of society)' (O'Connor 2013: 51). By doing so Adorno stands against positivistic and empirical approaches that argue that research into appearance is sufficient to describe society (O'Connor 2013: 51). Indeed Adorno,

> Conceives society as a totality. Society is not a collection of disconnected facts. Rather facts (what things supposedly are) are interconnected – mediated – by the social totality, the character of which impresses itself on each fact . . . society has become a totality: it is now a coercive system. (O'Connor 2013: 52)

Thus, Adorno seeks to criticize society and part of this criticism is to explore how the 'conditions of society that can be shown to distort or deform the possibilities for human flourishing' can be examined through the notion of immanent critique. Here, immanent critique is understood as a critique which "remains within" what it criticizes in contrast to a transcendental critique, a critique from outside, which first establishes its own principles, and then uses them as a yardstick by which to criticize other theories (Jarvis 1998: 6). Immanent critique seeks not just to provide a criticism of individual arguments, 'but also the way those arguments fit together . . . so as to understand the significance of the particular kinds of contradiction present . . . to understand what these contradictions tell us about the social experience' (Jarvis 1998: 6). Thus, Adorno is interested in analysing the changing forms of human alienation in contrast to Marx's political economy of reification based on alienated labour (Schecter 2007: 99) and in contrast to Heidegger's fundamental ontology. So, for example, Horkheimer and Adorno examine the 'simultaneous homogenization and isolation of individuals in the industrial–democratic era', such that 'enlightenment, which presents itself as the secular modern movement par excellence, becomes secular mythology in the course of its unfolding' (Schecter 2007: 94).

While Marx orients his project towards the re-appropriation of alienated labour, Adorno and Horkheimer, in contrast, develop a genealogy of reification based on alienated nature. Indeed, this move towards the industrial subjective objectification is, within late capitalism, the measure of reality itself. While,

> Marx clearly regards the re-appropriation of alienated labour as the condition of a humanized world oriented towards emancipation, Horkheimer and Adorno regard such re-appropriation as the condition of a subjectivized world oriented towards manipulation and distortion. On this reading the commodified version of objectification prevalent in capitalism simply takes over from the successive forms of religious objectification which dominated consciousness and society prior to the advent of industrial production. (Schecter 2007: 94)

Thus, the question they pose is: how does the project of enlightened autonomy and freedom become instead a reality of radical heteronomy and domination? This takes place, they argue, when increasingly advanced forms of rationalization as *ratio* become institutionalized, and the project of autonomy is sacrificed in relation to homogenization, standardized thinking and social control. This means that human beings become fungible and useful only in as much as they are trained towards the requirements of a corporate, industrial world of commodity production. For the Enlightenment thinkers, human power triumphs over nature, enabling freedom from physical necessity and hardship. For Kant, 'humanity creates the conditions of its autonomy in consciousness by ordering the chaos of nature in concepts and categories, for Marx it creates the political conditions of its autonomy by ordering the chaos of nature through labour and collective social action' (Schecter 2007: 96). In contrast, Horkheimer and Adorno argue that these processes are instead taken over by money and capital, creating the possibilities for oppressive social structures.

I now want to examine in detail what I see as one possible manifestation of the reification associated with computationality and which is sedimented in a philosophy that has come to be known as speculative realism/object-oriented ontology (SR/OOO). This we might call a contemporary configuration. While accepting that there are differences in the way in which different participants within SR/OOO present their work and articulate their ontology, here I present a general overview of SR/OOO. The aim is not to engage substantively with SR/OOO's chosen fields of debate and investigation, indeed, the wide range of publications are outside the scope of this book. Rather, I want to tentatively explore the links between my own notion of computationality as ontotheology and how SR/OOO unconsciously reproduces some of these structural features that I think are apparent in its ontological and theological moments. In order to do this, I want to begin outlining some of the ways one might expect the 'ontological moment', as it were, to be dominated by computational categories and ideas which seem to hold explanatory power. SR/OOO is marked by its focus on the priority of the 'object' for thought and the insistence on a heterogeneous multiplicity of entities as objects. The priority of objects as a fundamental notion in their work together with the inability within the philosophical systems grouped together as SR/OOO to critically distinguish between the products of alienated labour congealed into objects and subjects gives SR/OOO a problematic form. Indeed, SR/OOO has a limited notion of reification as the insistence of objects stymie attempts to think about the objectification practices of capitalism, if as SR/OOO proponents claim, the object is pre-defined as an ontological category.

It is interesting to note that these philosophers do not tend to take into account the possibility that the computational medium itself may have transformed the way in which they understand the ontological dimension of their projects – even as they invoke McLuhan in their work. Indeed, the taken-for-granted materiality of digital media is clearly being referred to in relation to a form of communication theory – as if the internet were merely a transparent transmission channel – rather than understanding the affordances of the medium encouraging, shaping or creating certain ways of thinking about things, as such. It is revealing that discussions about computation by members of SR/OOO have been limited to the importance of a computational medium for facilitating SR/OOO's dissemination (see Bryant 2012; Harman 2012). Nonetheless, SR/OOO might be termed the first computational medium-based philosophy, even if it is not fully reflexive of its own historical context in its self-understanding of the computation milieu in which it resides.

For SR/OOO, the speed and publishing affordances of digital media allow them to get their philosophical reflections out more quickly, correct them and create faster feedback and feedforward loops. However, I would argue that the computational layers (software, applications, blogs, tweets, etc.) also discipline the user/writer/philosopher to think within and through particular computational categories. I think it is not a coincidence that what is perhaps the first internet or born-digital philosophy has certain overdetermined characteristics that reflect the medium within which they have emerged. Indeed as Galloway (2012) asks,

> why, within the current renaissance of research in continental philosophy, is there a coincidence between the structure of ontological systems and the structure of the most highly-evolved technologies of postfordist capitalism? I am speaking, on the one hand, of computer networks in general, and object-oriented computer languages (such as Java or C++) in particular, and on the other hand, of certain realist philosophers such as Bruno Latour, but also more pointedly Quentin Meillassoux, Graham Harman, and their associated school known as "speculative realism." Why do these philosophers, when holding up a mirror to nature, see the mode of production reflected back at them? Why, in short, a coincidence between today's ontologies and the software of big business? (Galloway 2013: 347, original emphasis)

Indeed, I would argue that it is no surprise that reification is central to both SR/OOO and object-oriented programming. Indeed, both have deep similarities and, I argue, draw from a computational imaginary that conceptualizes what things *are*, or *how* they should be categorized. In other words, it is an ideology of reification informed through a computational ontotheology. For example, Harman argues that 'the movement of philosophy is less an unveiling . . . than a kind of *reverse engineering*. Teams of industrial pirates often lock themselves in motel rooms, working backward from a competitor's finished product in an effort to unlock and replicate the code that generates it. In the case of the philosopher, the finished product that must be reverse-engineered is the world as we know it . . . one should reverse engineer, so as to unlock the infrastructure of objects' (Harman 2002: 196, original emphasis). It is striking to note the extent to which human productive activities are re-presented as reified and object-like, that is, as something strange and alien within the contours of SR/OOO. Ian Bogost's (2012) *Alien Phenomenology* is perhaps the most recent case where the links between his computational approach, reification and SR/OOO philosophical system are deeply entwined as objects, units, collections, lists, software philosophy, carpentry (as programming), etc. Indeed, the subtitle, *what its like to be a thing*, gestures towards their strangeness and the autonomy of things that are given agency, even as humans are in contrast sharply restricted in their autonomy. As Galloway argues,

> Philosophy and computer science are not unconnected. In fact they share an intimate connection, and have for some time. For example, set theory, topology, graph theory, cybernetics and general system theory are part of the intellectual lineage of both object-oriented computer languages, which inherit the principles of these scientific fields with great fidelity, and for recent continental philosophy including figures like Deleuze, Badiou, Luhmann, or Latour. Where does Deleuze's "control society" come from if not from Norbert Wiener's definition of cybernetics? Where do Latour's "actants" come from if not from systems theory? Where does Levi Bryant's "difference that makes a difference" come from if not from Gregory Bateson's theory of information? (Galloway 2013)

The recent work within SR/OOO reflects the society and historical conditions under which they were written, particularly in their fetishization of the object as both ontological and epistemological sources of truth and reality. Galloway further argues,

> (1) If recent realist philosophy mimics the infrastructure of contemporary capitalism, should we not show it the door based on this fact alone, the assumption being that any mere repackaging of contemporary ideology is, by definition, anti-scientific and therefore suspect on epistemological grounds? And (2) even if one overlooks the epistemological shortcomings, should we not critique it on purely political grounds, the argument being that any philosophical project that seeks to ventriloquize the current industrial arrangement is, for this very reason, politically retrograde? (Galloway 2013)

Computational metaphors share a lot of similarity in object-oriented software to the principles expressed by SR/OOO speculations about objects as objects. Indeed the appeal of SR/OOO becomes tautological when it discusses computation itself, as the philosophical principles sometimes too neatly intersect with the reality of software systems. This is where Bogost's work on alien phenomenology becomes interesting to focus on, in relation to its attempt to apply SR/OOO to understanding computational systems even as it claims to cast a new light on wider questions about other kinds of objects. After all, every entity is an 'object', in the ontology of object-oriented ontology. Galloway explains,

Granted, merely identifying a formal congruity is not damning in itself. There are any number of structures that "look like" other structures. . . . Nevertheless are we not obligated to interrogate such a congruity? Is such a mimetic relationship cause for concern?. . . . What should we do so that our understanding of the world does not purely and simply coincide with the spirit of capitalism? (Galloway 2013)

In response SR/OOO argues that we must no longer make the 'correlationist' error of privileging the being of humans within ontology, instead we should be moving towards a 'democracy of objects' (see Bryant 2011). By correlationist they mean any subjectivist position, or attempt to place humanity or human cognition or understanding central in relation to a philosophy of reality. This is to follow from the work of Quentin Meillassoux (2009) who argued in *After Finitude*:

Such considerations reveal the extent to which the central notion of modern philosophy since Kant seems to be that of the *correlation*. By "correlation" we mean the idea according to which we only ever have access to the correlation between thinking and being, and never to either term considered apart from the other. We will henceforth call *correlationism* any current of thought which maintains the unsurpassable character of correlation so defined. Consequently, it becomes possible to say that every philosophy which disavows naive realism has become a variant of correlationism. (Meillassoux 2009: 5, original emphasis)

Meillassoux, in particular, is interested in the production of claims about reality that are extra-human, either *ancestral*, that is, any reality anterior to the emergence of the human species, or shown as *arche-fossil,* particularly through materials indicating the existence of an ancestral reality, the material support such as an isotope whose rate of radioactive decay enables the dating of things (Meillassoux 2009: 10). How then can we make claims about things that are not only non-human, but that also temporally predate the very existence of humans at all. While Meillassoux was careful to delimit his philosophical investigations to those that pre-date humans, and thus the problematic of a correlationist claim in relation to it, here there isn't space to explore the problematic nature of the formulation of a realist science which underpins his claims, it does open the door for philosophically speculative work on the nature of the universe *per se*. Indeed, this is where object-oriented ontology comes into play, particularly with the work of Bryant et al. (2011) – although here we should note that Meillassoux rejects the labels of both object-oriented ontology and speculative realism. Bryant et al. claim,

[In] "The Speculative Turn", one can detect the hints of something new. By contrast with the repetitive continental focus on texts, discourses, social practices, and human finitude, the new breed of thinkers is turning once more towards reality itself. While it is difficult to find explicit positions common to all the thinkers . . . all have certainly rejected the traditional focus on textual critique . . . all of them, in one way or another, have begun speculating once more about the nature of reality independently of thought and of humans more generally. (Bryant et al. 2011: 3)

Indeed, Meillassoux argues,

For it could be that contemporary philosophers have lost the *great outdoors*, the *absolute* outside of pre-critical thinkers: that outside which was not relative to us, and which was given as indifferent to its own givenness to be what it is, existing in itself regardless of whether we are thinking it or not; that outside which thought could explore with the legitimate feeling of being on foreign territory – of being entirely elsewhere. (Meillassoux 2009: 7, original emphasis)

While there are significant differences between the various 'speculative realism' positions, this attempt to develop a strong anti-correlationist approach seems both significant and interesting philosophically, and something, I should add, that I am broadly sympathetic to. To my mind, however, there remains a significant problem of theorizing non-human relations while simultaneously being constrained within the categories and limitations of human thought, what we might call the *anti-correlationist paradox*, even when mediated through mathematics, physics or technical apparatus that gives the appearance of objectivity or non-human thought.

In this, they develop a notion of a form of 'flat ontology' or a variant described by Bogost (2012: 11) as, 'all objects equally exist, but not all objects exist equally'. This ontology insists on equal *ontological status* but difference in *ontic status*, and bears a striking resemblance to a reductionist universe described by science, albeit perhaps differing in not seeking reductionist explanations in terms of causation, etc. Bogost and others have argued that because they recognize difference at the level of the ontic this demonstrates that they do not have a flat ontology as such – however, it seems to me that the category of *object* as the *de facto* ontological entity is demonstrative of a flattened ontology.

My critique echos the critical theorists position on Kant, and particularly Lukác's critique of Kant' introduction of a dialectical moment into epistemology which superseded the inadequacies of 'the rationalist dualism between humanity and nature and the empiricist identity between humanity and nature' (Schecter 2007: 52). Indeed, Kant's epistemology posits the limit to human knowledge which reflects the political reality that 'freedom can only be rational if it is formal and juridical'. Thus, Kant's epistemology and political thought more generally are trapped in a series of dualisms such as theory/practice, phenomenon/thing-in-itself, subject/object, ethics/politics, etc., which 'reveal themselves to be dependent on the mode of production and the forms of consciousness that correspond to it' (Schecter 2007: 53). Indeed it is striking that the ontology of objects that SR/OOO describe is sharply reminiscent of the flatness represented by objects within object-oriented programming, and the post-Fordist capitalism that is proper to it.

Additionally, there is a dismissal of the notion of World, in the Heideggerian sense, for SR/OOO, which, observing the relative position of philosophy *vis a vis* science within *human* culture, endeavours to replicate or supplement scientific inquiry *without* human culture, by providing a speculative and philosophical description of the universe through the notion of withdrawn or partially visible objects – Morton calls this *ekphrasis* or 'ultra-vivid description' (Morton 2011: 170). That is, to refute the presumed correlationism of scientific practice. In most varieties of SR/OOO, therefore, I think that they are actually undertaking object-oriented *onticology*. That is, a position more interested in beings, rather than Being, something I discuss further below. For example, Bogost (2012a) outlines a system of thought in which no object has precedence or hierarchy over another, and yet all share a commonality which, following Heidegger, Bogost calls *being* and we might understand as 'objectness' or 'being an object'. This suggests a revealing paradox raised by trying to place a general case (being) as equivalent to the particular (beings) within this flat ontology, and which is justified by virtue of the singularity of what he calls a 'tiny ontology' (Bogost 2012a: 22).

So, what is at stake in the project of SR/OOO – a philosophy whose readers consist of humans who are actively solicited? Indeed, as part of this project, object-oriented ontology seeks to convince the reader of her own experiential *equality* in relation to the quantitative variety of experiences of different beings within the universe, human and non-human (see Charlesworth 2012). This, of course, has political implications. Here, I want to explore how and why this group of self-defined 'anti-correlationists' work so hard at a rhetorical attempt to convince its readers as to the importance of the SR/OOO project. We might also note that the term object-oriented philosophy has knowingly borrowed its label from object-oriented programming, a method of structured computer software design and programming. I argue that there appears to be an ontotheology of computationality underlying object-oriented ontology (see Bogost 2009b for a related discussion of this; also Berry 2011; Galloway 2013).

But even while expressing a disavowal of the human (as correlationist) there is a practice undertaken of philosophy, an extremely human activity, in relation to humans and objects but directed to the human readers. It is useful again to again turn to Bogost (2012) where he indicates a readership that is unmistakably human. He writes,

> We ought to think in public. We ought to be expanding our spheres of influence and inspiration with every page we write. We ought to be trying to influence the world, not just the blinkered group that goes to our favorite conference. And that principle ought to hold no matter your topic of interest, be it Proust or videogames or human factors engineering or the medieval *chanson de geste*. No matter your field, it can be done, and people do it all the time. They're called "good books". . . . And I've tried very hard as an author to learn how to write better and better books, books that speak to a broader audience without compromising my scholarly connections, books that really ought to exist as books. (Bogost 2011; see also Bogost 2012: 88–91)

Bogost here acknowledges that the practices of reading and writing, and by extension, that of a reading public – the 'we', is an activity that lies within the purview of humanity. By implication then, humans are a special kind of entity that is able to understand, and by understand I am gesturing towards the notion of *Verstehen*, or interpretative understanding (Outhwaite 1975). So, rather than asking what it is like to be a thing, I want to explore what is the *use* of knowing what it is to be a thing. In other words, we might ask *what are the uses of SR/OOO?* What are the practices of SR/OOO, and how do they reflect upon their own, mostly discursive practices, and their relationships with 'objects'? Although I cannot hope to provide a complete answer to this question here, it is helpful to examine the contours of SR/OOO in relation to these key questions.

Indeed, I would argue that SR/OOO can be understood as a descriptive project for philosophy, which Bogost, following Harman, christens ontography (Bogost 2012a: 36), a 'name for a general inscriptive strategy, one that uncovers the repleteness of units [Bogost's term for objects] and their interoperability' (Bogost 2012a: 38). For Bogost, this project involves the creation of *lists*, a 'group of items loosely joined not by logic or power or use but by the gentle knot of the comma', he explains, 'ontography is an aesthetic set theory, in which a particular configuration is celebrated merely on the basis of its existence' (Bogost 2012a: 38). Here, we see why Bogost is keen to draw out the similarities to the creation of aesthetic collections, such as with the new aesthetic discussed below (see Berry 2012; Bogost 2012b). Drawing on Harman, Bogost describes why the 'rhetoric of lists' is useful to a philosophical project:

> Some readers may tire (or pretend to tire) of these frequent lists, dismissing them as an "incantation" or "poetics" of objects. But most readers will not soon grow tired, since the rhetorical power of these rosters of beings stems from their direct opposition to the flaws of current mainstream philosophy. We cannot imagine Kant or Hegel invoking such a roll-call. . . . The best stylistic antidote to this grim deadlock is a repeated sorcerer's chant of the multitude of things that resist any unified empire. (Harman 2009a: 102)

Thus, Bogost argues that making lists 'hones a virtue: the abandonment of anthropocentric narrative coherence in favor of worldly detail' (Bogost 2012a: 42). An attempt, we might say, to get closer to the buzzing variety of the 'real'. Harman further argues that 'human-centred philosophy is a Hiroshima of metaphysics, one that annihilates . . . objects'. Instead, Bogost explains, 'lists of objects without explication can do the philosophical work of drawing our attention towards them with greater attentiveness' (Bogost 2012a: 45). This Bogost calls an ontograph, which is, he says, a 'crowd' (Bogost 2012a: 59). They are also, we might note in passing, extremely partial lists, reflecting the rhetorical intentions of the litany reciter and only a 'description' in the weakest sense. For example, in the following three litanies taken from Bogost (2012a), objects are invoked with no particularity, rather they remain abstract – the signified rather than the referent,[2]

> "molded plastic keys and controllers, motor-driven disc drives, silicon wafers, plastic ribbons, and bits of data", "Subroutines and middleware libraries compiled into byte code or etched onto silicon, cathode ray tubes or LCD displays mated to be insulated, conductive cabling, and microprocessors executing machine instructions that enter and exit address buses", "African elephant or the Acropora coral", "computer or a microprocessor, or a ribbon cable". (Bogost 2012a: 10)

> The unicorn and the combine harvester, the color red and methyl alcohol, quarks and corrugated iron, Amelia Earhart and dyspepsia. (Bogost 2012a: 11)

> quarks, Harry Potter, keynote speeches, single-malt scotch, Land Rovers, lychee fruit, love affairs, dereferenced pointers, Mike "The Situation" Sorrentino, bozons, horticulturalists, Mozambique, Super Mario Bros. (Bogost 2012a: 12)

One striking aspect to the project outlined within *Alien Phenomenology* is the aim towards what Bogost calls a phenomenological *practice*. Bogost writes, 'as philosophers, our job is to amplify . . . the noise of objects. . . . Our job is to write the speculative fictions of their processes, of their . . . operations. . . . Our job is to get our hands dirty . .' (Bogost 2012a: 34). In contrast to Marx's dictum that philosophers have hitherto tried to *understand* the world, and that philosophers should therefore aim to *change* it, Bogost proposes that we should *describe* it or create other actors to describe it for us, by *making* philosophical software (see Bogost 2012a: 110). A form of second-order epistemology, quite in keeping with the computational approaches of distantiation and second-order data collection and the importance of control via a computational system, even if only used as a 'method' to 'access' the objects themselves. As Bogost himself notes,

> Why do *we* give the Civil War soldier, the guilty Manhattan project physicist, the oval-headed alien anthropomorph, and the intelligent celestial race so much more credence than the scoria cone, the obsidian fragment, the gypsum crystal, the capsicum pepper, and the propane flame? When *we* welcome these things into scholarship, poetry, science, and business, it is only to ask how they relate to human productivity, culture, and politics. *We've* been living in a tiny prison of *our* own devising, one in which all the stuff that concerns *us* are the fleshy beings that are *our* kindred and the stuffs with which we stuff *ourselves.* (Bogost 2012a: 3, emphasis added)

Putting to one side the somewhat doubtful claim that the former litany is given more credence by anyone except, perhaps, humanities scholars, here we see a claim to a collective 'we' that Bogost wishes to speak for and to. Further, he adds, 'let me be clear: we need not discount human beings to adopt an object-oriented position – after all, we ourselves are of the world as much as musket buckshot and gypsum and space shuttles. But we can no longer claim that our existence is special *as existence*' (Bogost 2012a: 8). Thus the flatness denied in relation to the ontological 'specialness' or uniqueness of humans is reinforced. Entities and humans have equal place in the metaphysics presented by Bogost, in other words humans have no specific existence, contra Heidegger, that would enable them to have any claim over or in distinction to other kinds of objects.

However, there is a performative contradiction presented here in as much as 'musket buckshot and gypsum and space shuttles' cannot be the addressees of this text as patently they do not read. It seems that SR/OOO is trying to do two things here: on the one hand SR/OOO denies the specialness of humans' *existence* in relation to other objects, while simultaneously having to write a special kind of writing – philosophy – to make arguments supporting their claims – thereby acknowledging the very special existence that humans possess, namely qualities of understanding, taking a stand on their own being, etc. This is a classic performative contradiction. While it would be perfectly legitimate to outline a formalist theory or methodological position that, for the sake of the approach, limits the requirement to treat human actors as particular or special in relation to others (this is the methodological innovation within actor-network theory), it is quite another to then extend this claim into a philosophical ontology, which is part of a special order of discourse particular to human beings, that is, *philosophy*. The implications of a so-called philosophical non-human turn are interesting for its nihilistic and conservative implications but for his part, Bogost (2012a) rejects that nihilism is present in his work, remarking,

> [object-oriented ontology] "allows for the possibility of a new sort of humanism," in which, as Harman adds, "humans will be liberated from the crushing correlational system." For his part, Nick Srnicek offers opprobrium in place of optimism. . . . "Do we need another analysis of how a cultural representation does symbolic violence to a marginal group? This is not to say that this work has been useless, just that it's become repetitive". (Bogost 2012a: 132)

In this 'liberation' therefore, we are saved from the 'crushing' problem of repetitive accounts of marginal inequality and suffering. This is achieved by a new 'humanism' that seems to reject the human as having any special case, such that the marginal problems of women, LGBT, immigrants, asylum seekers and the poor are seemingly replaced with the problem of a litany of objects such as 'quarks, Elizabeth Bennet, single-malt scotch, Ford Mustang fastbacks, lychee fruit, love affairs, dereferenced pointers, Care Bears, sirocco winds, the Tri-City Mall, tort law, the Airbus A330, the five-hundred drachma note' (Bogost 2012a: 133).

Bogost notes, 'if we take seriously the idea that all objects recede interminably into themselves, then human perception becomes just one among many ways that objects might relate. To put things at the centre of a new metaphysics also requires us to admit that they do not exist just for us' (Bogost 2012a: 9). Leaving aside the question as to why we would want to apply that hypothesis, the question arises as to how one is to judge between the different forms of perception in order to (re)present the litanies, let alone recognize them. In other words, if human perception is 'correlationist' is itself suspect and to be rejected, then why should we accept litanies and sets, which themselves are creations of the human mind? Indeed, it seems that litanies as a method for forming a collection of objects are extremely partial and are a result of a particular and limited capacity of the human mind. The question of how SR/OOO theorists are able to make a claim to the litany as a device free of the contagion of correlationism is never firmly established. Nor indeed is Bogost's attempt to sidestep this problem by the composition of litanies using algorithms, which merely moves the human intervention to that of a second-order function by writing the very algorithm that generates the lists. This issue of litanies as a rhetorical structure and claim to a certain kind of 'objectivity', as if a list of things were more concrete, is a problem within the domain of SR/OOO and is hardly dealt with by Harman's notion of 'metaphor' or 'alluding' to things (Harman 2009b).

However, Bogost wants to move away from the tricky epistemological problem of access, and instead also argues for 'metaphor' as a means of understanding the way in which objects, within this system, interact. This, oddly, avoids the very real problem of mediation in SR/OOO and moves the focus onto a form of *information transfer* between objects, rather than the practice of *mediating* those objects and SR/OOO's claims about them. In effect, 'metaphor' describes an operation whereby the properties of an object are 'represented' within another object in order to facilitate some form of interaction (which might be vicarious). Bogost writes,

> Ontology is the philosophical study of existence. Object-oriented ontology ("OOO" for short) puts *things* at the center of this study. Its proponents contend that nothing has special status, but that everything exists equally—plumbers, cotton, bonobos, DVD players, and sandstone, for example. In contemporary thought, things are usually taken either as the aggregation of ever smaller bits (scientific naturalism) or as constructions of human behavior and society (social relativism). OOO steers a path between the two, drawing attention to things at all scales (from atoms to alpacas, bits to blinis), and pondering their nature and relations with one another as much with ourselves. (Bogost 2009; see also Bogost 2012: 6)

This definition is helpful in a number of ways, first it demonstrates that in the move towards a flat ontology the attention has shifted from ontology (being) to things/objects (beings). Indeed, the definition of everything as a single thing, in this case an object/unit – is precisely the danger that Heidegger identified for philosophy – the 'Being' that explains everything, the 'Good' for Plato, 'Substance' for Spinoza and 'Object' for SR/OOO. As Bryant remarks, 'there is only one type of being: objects. As a consequence, humans are not excluded, but are rather objects *among* the various types of objects that exist or populate the world, each with their own specific powers and capacities' (Bryant 2011: 20, original emphasis). This raises a further problem of 'correctness', in other words in correctly identifying objects as beings, as Heidegger argues the focus on entities is a mistake for philosophy and that,

> what is essential is not what we presumably establish with exactness by means of instruments and gadgets; what is essential is the view in advance which opens up the field for anything to be established. (Heidegger 1995: 60)

Bogost's work is exemplary and highly suggestive for the work of studying software and code, however, I feel that this work is an example of what we might call object-oriented *onticology*, rather than ontology as such. This is important work, we do need to map certain kinds of objects and their inter-relations, however, we also need to be aware of the consequences of certain ways of seeing and categorizing the world else we fall prey to identity think-ing. The problem seems to be that object-oriented ontology has no notion of an exemplar, no special case, no shining examples. Indeed, the cover concept, 'object' has been generalized to a remarkable degree in this work. As such, it quickly descends into endless lists and litanies. As Heidegger observes,

> So it happens that we, lost as we usually are in the activities of observing and establishing, believe we "see" many things and yet do not see what really is. (Heidegger 1995: 60)

Bogost attempts to circumvent this problem by the application of a method he calls *carpentry*, after Harman and Lingis who use the term to refer to the way in which 'things fashion one another and the world at large' (Bogost 2012a: 93). Bogost introduces *philosophical software carpentry* to implement the creation of what he calls 'ontographic tools to characterize the diversity of being' (Bogost 2012a: 94). A move he characterizes as pragmatic speculative realism. One of these tools he calls the *Latour Litanizer*, which generates 'random' litanies based on randomized selections of Wikipedia pages (although it doesn't appear to have been used within *Alien Phenomenology* itself, which has a constant refrain in the choice of items in the litanies, see above). While an interesting example of software litany creation, it is hardly divorced from its programmer (see Berry 2011a). This is further demonstrated in the example of the 'image toy' programmed by Bogost that selected random photographs of 'objects' from the Flickr website, and occasionally therefore showed images of women, one of which happened to be wearing a playboy bunny suit. In response to criticism, Bogost was required to hand-code a specific query that *prevented* the operation of certain aspects of philosophical software carpentry, namely *no women in bunny suits*, defined in the code as:

```
Options.Tags = '(object OR thing OR stuff) AND NOT (sexy
OR woman OR girl)'. (Bogost 2012: 99)
```

So there is certainly agency at work here, but it is a delegated agency, and one that is circumscribed both by the programmer, in this case Bogost, and by norms and values of society. For example, human notions of what an acceptable image is. But also there is an interesting question of how images of woman become 'objects' when mediated through code, in this case 'sexy or woman or girl' are not the kinds of 'objects' that the 'image toy' is allowed to find and display. And just to reiterate, these requirements are delegated to the code in the image toy by Bogost, they require the very correlationism that SR/OOO tries so hard to avoid. Indeed the agency of these objects, and how this agency plays out in relation to the selectivity that goes into making the litanies of SR/OOO are mediated by human programmers. Indeed, when software code objects are unmonitored and given the opportunity to exercise their (limited) agency very strange results can occur, such as with the financial Flash Crash of 2010 discussed earlier, or for example, the case of offensive computer-generated t-shirts, where

> The American clothing company Solid Gold Bomb blamed an automated computer dictionary for its series of the items emblazoned with offensive phrases such as "Keep Calm and Rape a Lot" and "Keep Calm and Hit Her", based on the much reproduced "Keep Calm and Carry On" second world war poster . . . [they claimed it was] the result of "a scripted computer process", which used an algorithm to generate hundreds of slogans. (Guardian 2013)

The founder of Solid Gold Bomb explained,

> I then generated word lists that were called using simple scripting methods to generate image based art of the modified slogans. These were subsequently scripted to position themselves on t-shirts and the associated product data was derived simply from the product name and the 16 word combinations like "On" and "Off" and "Him" or "Her" and so forth . . . it was the result of a scripted programming process that was compiled by only one member of our staff. (Fowler 2013)

It is interesting to consider within the flat ontology of objects, and to which SR/OOO generally subscribes, how SR/OOO is able to square the ontological claims of its philosophical position with unintended ethical and political outcomes. For example, Bogost argued 'the change [to excluding problematic images of women etc.] risks excluding a whole category of units from the realm of being! Are women or girls or sexiness to have no ontological place alongside chipmunks, lighthouses, and galoshes?' (Bogost 2012: 99). But the act of referring to women and girls as 'units' or 'objects' even if, as he is keen to emphasize, they are objects among a plenitude of other objects remains problematic. Indeed, it raises the question of whether it is possible within SR/OOO to condemn an *object* or its outcomes, and from what normative position would one critique it? In the case where the computer code is clearly at fault, for example, by producing offensive output, where is the standpoint whereby one object (humans) can critique another object (computer code)? Is there such a thing as a *bad* object in SR/OOO, or are all objects equal to the extent that no such distinctions can be made? Certainly the critique of correlationism seems to imply that humans are not in such a position to make such judgements, and certainly not able to exercise a moral or ethical superiority in relation to the objects that surround them, code objects included. Bogost states 'being is unconcerned with issues of gender, performance, and its associated politics' (Bogost 2012: 99). Harman explains,

> Often when this question is asked, people want to know what the *political* ramifications of object-oriented philosophy would be, and I think this is the wrong place to start. Intellectuals have become far too aggressively *political*, in almost puritanical fashion, as if there were something immoral about looking for beauty or fascination in the world as long as there is still exploitation somewhere. Philosophers have tried to save the world; the point, however, is to explore it. (Kimbell 2013: 7)

It seems then that SR/OOO reflects a worrying spirit of conservatism. They discount the work of human activity and place it alongside a litany of naturalized objects – a method that points less at the interconnected nature of things, and gestures more towards the infinity of sameness, the gigantic of objects, the relentless distanceless of a total confusion of beings. In short, experience is conceived of as disoriented and overwhelming, what Heidegger described as the 'terror' of pure unmitigated flatness. And with that, philosophy becomes 'cold' philosophy, instead of understanding, we have lists and litanies of objects. Not so much philosophy as *philosography*, where rather than *understanding* the world, there is an attempt to *describe* it. A description that is taken to be objective, in as much SR/OOO claims a special kind of access to the ontology that it uncovers, a position that is strangely unreflexive about its own historical grounding. SR/OOO is, then, a descriptive philosophy that attempts to conceptualize a universe of objects while simultaneously disavowing conceptualization as correlationist. It attempts to provide a speculative, but nonetheless realist and ahistorical ontology which claims to be philosophically untimely, but in fact is extremely timely, mirroring, as it does, the objectification of both computation and capitalism.

This lack of historical awareness is common in the SR/OOO approach, and one that is rejected by claiming to be writing 'metaphysics' disconnected from the social and political. I want to challenge this claim on three grounds: first, a performative contradiction in relation to the selection of intended readers capable of being influenced by the persuasive discourse of object-oriented ontology. Secondly, on the basis of what I perceive to be an unexamined formalism which is implicit in the construction of the SR/OOO philosophical system, this is, indeed an example of identity thinking. Lastly, it seems to me that as Golumbia (2012) convincingly argues, there are 'profound philosophical contradictions posed by the refusal to distinguish between epistemology and metaphysics and simultaneous use of arguments from both philosophical discourses' (Golumbia 2012). These objections I believe are highly damaging to the claims of SR/OOO, but the second criticism points towards a potential political conservatism at work within the project of speculative realism more generally. These are not the only weaknesses in the object-oriented ontology position, but I think they are significant enough to warrant discussion. Indeed, Blake (2012) argues these strands have a common root of the 'necessary but repressed "anthropologism" required to make sense of our singularity as bearers of and contributors to the practice of science. . . . Thus [SR/OOO] philosophy addresses itself to the anthropological Subject of science . . . a structural subject instantiated, as far as we know, only by human beings' (Blake 2012). Even if, as Harman claims,

> Speculative Realism is not post-human in the sense of *privileging entities other than humans*. Humans are still in the picture as entities, even very interesting entities, they simply aren't a full half ontology anymore. (Harman 2013)

The litanies by which SR/OOO practitioners proclaim their commitment to heterogeneity of entities – cascades and tumbling threads of polythetic classification – are linked merely by sequence, in which each item has no need to bear any resemblance to the ones before or after. They posit few relationships, and offer few narrative connections, and are therefore 'essentially uncontrollable: at the limit so indeterminable that anything can be connected with anything' (Anderson 2012). But of course there is a connection, a link, a thread, performed by the *philosographer* as the human who chooses, consciously or unconsciously, the elements that make up the chain, and which are inscribed in countless books and articles. And more so, undertakes the work of constructing the litany or the collection as a means of discussing the very notion of the 'object'. The *use* of object-oriented ontology, then, is bound up in an apparent conservatism that rallies at the temerity of human beings to believe in themselves, their politics and their specialness. Instead of World, SR/OOO posits universe, and collapses object and concept into ontology.

To see what 'shows up' to the *philosographer,* a critical examination of the lists shows that they are often contaminated by the products of neo-liberal capitalism, objects which could not just appear of themselves, but required the actual concrete social labour of human beings to mediate their existence. This is the lack of historical and social context in both the types of objects found and the choices that SR/OOO makes in its selection of exemplar objects, not that it accepts that these are 'exemplars', they just 'happen' to be the objects chosen in this particular litany. There is also the tendency to attempt to shock the reader by the juxtaposition of objects that would normally be thought to be categorically different – see Bogost (2009) for a discussion of whether including Harry Potter, blinis and humans in a list was a striking enough example. These rhetorical strategies are interesting in themselves, but I do not see them as replacements for critical philosophy. This demonstrates that SR/OOO has not escaped the so-called 'correlationist circle' (Harman 2009b), nor provided a model for thinking about the anti-correlationist paradox which remains present in their own work. Indeed, it reinforces the extent to which SR/OOO practices identity thinking.

We should therefore ask SR/OOO to move beyond merely 'exploring' the objects they see around them and catch sight of *what* is being listed in their descriptive litanies. That is, examining the lists they produce, we can see what kind of objects they see as near, and which they see as far, and therefore question their claims to see objects *all the way down* (see Bogost 2012: 83–4). Yet, as we examine these lists there appears to be a profound forgetting of *Being*, as it were, as they write both for and as *subjects* of computational capitalism – a fact which remains hidden from them – and a seemingly major aporia in their work – that is, the wider capitalist order, post-Fordist or informational capitalism. For some reason, SR/OOO is attracted to the ephemerality of certain objects, as if by listing them they doubly affirm their commitment to realism, or that the longer the list, the more 'real' it is. And this ephemerality is often represented by objects that are the creation of computational capitalism, such as,

> molded plastic keys and controllers, motor-driven disc drives, silicon wafers, plastic ribbons, and bits of data. . . . Subroutines and middleware libraries

compiled into byte code or etched onto silicon, cathode ray tubes or LCD displays mated to be insulated, conductive cabling, and microprocessors executing machine instructions that enter and exit address buses. (Bogost 2012: 10)

Indeed, this highlights the important distinction between materialism and realism, that materialism must be historical and critical, whereas realism tends towards an ahistoricism. By historicizing SR/OOO, we are able to discern the links between the underlying computational capitalism and its theoretical and philosophical manifestations. Indeed, in the spirit of the critique made by the Frankfurt School of Kant's work, it is apparent that SR/OOO is a timely philosophy that uncritically re-presents claims that mirror capitalism, for example, that SR/OOO is in some sense outside the realm of humans, eternal, unchanging, apolitical or naturalized, even as concepts and litanies are hypostatized in metaphysical claims.

More work needs to be done to trace the trajectories that are hinted at, particularly the computationality I see implicit in SR/OOO more generally. But I also want to tentatively gesture towards SR/OOO as one discourse contributing to a new bifurcation (as Whitehead referred to the nature/culture split), in this case, not between nature and culture, which today have begun to reconnect as dual hybridized sites of political contestation – for example, climate change – but rather as computation versus nature-culture. Here, nature-culture becomes a site of difference, disagreement, political relativism and a kind of 'secondary' quality, in other words 'values' and 'felicity conditions'. Computationality, or some related ontological form, becomes the site of primary qualities or 'facts', the site of objectivity, and is foundational, ahistorical, unchanging and a replacement for nature in modernity as the site of agreement upon which a polity is made possible – a computational society.

The abstract nature of objects within computer programming, formal code objects which interrelate to each other and interact (or not), and yet remain deeply computational, mathematical and discrete, is more than suggestive of the ontology that SR/OOO outlines. The purification process of object-oriented design/programming is also similar to the gradual emptying of the universe of 'non-objects' by SR/OOO, in other words subjects become objects too, but this serves to create the possibility of shared consensus by SR/OOO practitioners about this new bifurcated world. This creates a united foundation, understood as ontological, a site of 'objectivity', 'facts', and with a strict border control to prevent this pure realm being affected by the newly excised nature-culture. Within this new bifurcation, we see pure objects placed in the bifurcated object-space and subjects are located in the nature-culture space. Such as demonstrated by the litanies that SR/OOO practitioners share and which describe abstract names of objects, not concrete entities. This is clearly ironic in a philosophical movement that claims to be realist.

This ontological claim also points thought towards a cartography of what are claimed to be 'purer' objects, often provocatively listed in the litanies, such as 'angels', 'Popeye' and 'unicorns'. These textual attempts to capture and describe the real – without ever venturing into the 'great outdoors' that SR/OOO claims to respect. Galloway rightly shows us how to break this spell, reflected also in the SR/OOO refusal to historicize, through a concrete analysis of the historical and material conditions of production. He writes,

> One might therefore label this the postfordist response to philosophical realism in general and Meillassoux in particular: after software has entered history, math cannot and should not be understood ahistorically . . . math itself, as algorithm, has become a historical actor. (Galloway 2013)

A critical approach to SR/OOO raises the suspicion that the claims are a metaphysical reflection of computational capitalism. Indeed, it raises important questions of how the SR/OOO position on ontological questions, and here I am thinking in terms of the ontological notion of the political, creates certain conditions of possibility for an SR/OOO politics at the level of the ontic. In other words, ontological claims imply choices which serve to delimit certain kinds of action in the specific realm of politics. Which is not to say, of course, that the construction or categories used to define the ontological, as such, are not political in themselves. This points the way to understanding the way in which SR/OOO manifests identity thinking in its claims to 'explore' the 'real' object, and simultaneously disavow the human subject as correlationist error. Indeed, this tendency towards reification within SR/OOO mirrors in many ways the reification of computational processes, which excels in creating discrete objects within its systems. A discussion we now turn to in relation to the reification of everyday life in the next chapter.

5

The reification of everyday life

From its early days as a mechanism used to perform data processing, the digital is becoming the *de facto* medium for transmitting information, communicating and for sharing social life. Through these important functions the digital becomes a privileged site for social and political engagement and therefore it is increasingly important that we understand the digital and offer the possibility of a critical theory of the digital. This allows us to think about the digital, and contest the many forms of control and regulation that are currently being implemented around the world using digital technology. Most importantly, it allows social movements that are increasingly turning to the digital to help with social critique and mobilization to critically understanding the medium within which they are working. Indeed, questions of resistance, or possibilities for 'lines of flight', need also to be explored in and through the contestation of the digital as a site of politics through an immanent critique of the digital.

In this chapter I want to look specifically at how computational agencies act to transform social relations and labour into computational or code objects. Indeed, 'such is its pervasiveness that . . . it is impossible to now live outside of its orbit (even if one does not directly interact with software, much code is engaged, at a distance, in the provision of contemporary living)' (Kitchin and Dodge 2011: 260). We are therefore surrounded by code objects and a world that is transformed into code objects for processing or re-presentation to us. This is a process of reification, both ideologically and materially. Reification is understood as drawn from Marx's analysis of the structure of commodities, Simmel's notion of the commodification of culture and Weber's account of rationalization. For the critical theorists, reification permeated all levels of society and spheres of life. Lukács argued that,

> Reification involves a process whereby social phenomena take on the appearance of things, it is not . . . simply a subjective phenomenon; rather it arises from the productive process which reduces social relations themselves to thing-like relations – reduces, that is, the worker and his or her products to commodities. Reification is a socially necessary illusion – both reflecting the reality of the capitalist exchange process and hindering its cognitive penetration (Held 1997: 22)

New computational technologies increasingly make up an important part of our urban environment, and indeed also stretch from very remote areas of the world to outside the world into space. Code and software thus have become the conditions of possibility for human living, creating computational ecologies, which we inhabit with non-human actors (see Fuller 2005). This ecology of code objects, code infrastructure and coded spaces, 'divulges and affords new kinds of automated agency, opening up new possibilities in the world' (Kitchin and Dodge 2011: 248). This computational world and how we live today in a highly mediated code-based world make up an everyday life that is deeply inscribed by the results of computational processes and also by the frameworks that are associated with such computal structures. These structures and processes enable a reification of the world and the re-presentation of the world as discrete objects subject to control and management. Indeed, Lash and Lury are correct in their assertion that 'culture, once in the base, takes on a certain materiality itself. Media become things. Images and other cultural forms from the superstructure collapse into the materiality of the infrastructure. The image, previously separated in the superstructure, is thingified, it becomes *matter-image*' (Lash and Lury 2007). However, the reification is not just literally into matter, but also into code, as a second-order form of materiality, that is, while the digital is material in form, encoded onto magnetic hard disks, computer flash memory or distributed in the network of cables that are weaved around the world, it is also true that what we used to call media is suspended within a digital medium, software, and enveloped by algorithms and code.

The critical theorists sought to critically analyse and describe processes of reification, as it was understood as 'the central structural problem in capitalist society in all its aspects' (Lukács 1971: 83). This process leads to alienation, a key theme in Horkheimer and Adorno's *Dialectic of Enlightenment*, where,

> Something does not fit; human beings are doing violence to nature, and ultimately themselves. Workers spend their lives trapped in occupations they

hate, creating products nobody needs and which destroy the environment they live in, engaged in futile and enervating conflicts with their families, their neighbours, other social groups, and nations. (Robert 2004: 60)

They argued that unchecked alienation eventually leads towards a catastrophe and 'terminal explosion of the entire system' (Roberts 2004: 60). This is the end result of a system of rationalization that creates a societal struggle to keep ahead of a system that enforces the need to earn a wage and which, due to the pressures of capitalism, generates a more inhospitable environment in which to work. In contrast to alienation, Horkheimer and Adorno offer the 'sanctity of the *hic et nunc*' (Horkheimer and Adorno 2002: 6). The 'here and now' is what alienation disconnects us from, alienation causes the state whereby human beings have an 'inability to see or feel what is here, now, in front of us [and] that characterizes our ability to think about our future and to incorporate the present and the past into schemes of life' (Robert 2004: 60). Thus, under capitalism, consciousness is shaped and moulded within the frame of identity thinking, that is, 'the subsumption of all particular objects under general definitions and/or unitary systems of concepts' (Held 1997: 202). As a result, the particular is usually dissolved into the universal. Today the unitary system of concepts is supplied by computation, and more specifically by the computational categories and total system of computationality, which is increasingly manifested in a mediated 'now' supplied by real-time streams.

Computer code and software are not merely mechanisms, they represent an extremely rich form of media (e.g. see Servin 2010). They differ from previous instantiations of media forms in that they are highly processual. They can also have agency delegated to them, which they can then prescribe back onto other actors, but which also remain within the purview of humans to seek to understand. As Kitchin argues:

The phenomenal growth in software creation and use is due to its emergent and executable properties: how it codifies the world into rules, routines, algorithms, and databases, and then uses these to do work in the world to render aspects of everyday life programmable. Whilst it is not fully sentient and conscious, software can exhibit some of the characteristics of "being alive". . . . This property is significant because code enables technologies to do work in the world in an autonomous fashion – that is, it can process data, evaluate situations, and make decisions without human oversight or authorization. (Kitchin 2011: 945)

This autonomy of code and software makes it highly plastic for use in everyday life, and as such it has inevitably penetrated more and more into the lifeworld.

This has created, and continues to create, specific tensions in relation to old media forms, as well as problems for managing and spectacularizing the relations of the public to the entertainment industry and politics. This is something that carries over the interests of previous century's critical theorists, particularly concern with the liquidation of individuality and the homogenization of culture. Nonetheless, there is also considered to be a radical, if not revolutionary kernel within the softwarization project (see Berry 2008; Antonelli 2011). This is due to the relative affordance code/software appears to give for individual autonomy within networks of association to share information and communicate. Indeed, as Deuze et al. have argued:

> Considering the current opportunity a media life gives people to create multiple versions of themselves and others, and to endlessly redact themselves (as someone does with his/her profile on an online dating site in order to produce better matches), we now have a entered a time where . . . we can in fact see ourselves live, become cognizant about how our lifeworld is "a world of artifice, of bending, adapting, of fiction, vanity, a world that has meaning and value only for the man who is its deviser". . . . But this is not an atomized, fragmented, and depressing world, or it does not have to be such a world. (Deuze et al. 2012)

This new data ecology is an environmental *habitus* of both human and non-human actors. It is a world deeply informed by the machinery of computing which is under constant ferment and innovation but which is not always apparent to a user used to interacting with computational devices at the level of the screen interface. Another way of putting this, as N. Katherine Hayles (2004) has argued, is that print is flat and code is deep. This depth enables a machinery that is able to function rapidly and invisibly to collect and analyse data about its user. Of course, we should also be attentive to the over-sharing or excessive collection of data too within these device ecologies that are outside of the control of the user to 'redact themselves'. But this is not just historical data and information, such as is found in Big Data, for example, as Borthwick (2013) argued:

> As autonomous human beings, we hate the idea that our lives and choices are predictable, but it turns out they mostly are. A few years ago the Chief Marketing Officer at American Express asked me how long I had had my Amex card . . . he wagered he could tell me where I was going to have dinner that night. His ability to predict was based on analyzing a time-series of transaction information, and is therefore limited to actions and activities that I've done before. That kind of predictive analysis is interesting, but it's yesterday's news.

Indeed, computation of data is entering a new phase, and in many ways due to the growth in computing power that we have witnessed over the past decade, new computationally intensive calculations can be done on the fly. In some instances on the mobile device, which change the conditions and contexts under which computation takes place, Borthwick explains,

> The new world we're entering is different. I'm talking about a layer of data that exists over reality, one that is real-time and whose signals are highly diverse and redundant. One that has history, one that learns, one that can ascertain intent. Combining the data layer with simple prompt-based navigation, it becomes possible to tell a person exactly what (or even whom) she is going to want to know in a particular place at a particular time, before she even forms the thought. (Borthwick 2013)

It is important that in order to undertake a critique of everyday life in terms of computationality there will need to be attention paid to how conversions and integrations are achieved 'without resorting to conspiracy theories or notions of structural determination and other flawed accounts of history and society' (Schecter 2007: 152). Indeed, the aim is to further develop a notion of computational systems and the computational categories that lie behind them in order to develop an understanding of power, knowledge and how reason and thinking are understood in a computational context. It is striking to note the extent to which technocratic thinking continues to be prevalent today and therefore there is often a deficit of democracy, particularly in a computational context. In other words, computationality has important implications for thinking about instrumental reason and how the instrumental is legitimized.

To understand computation better, it is important to appreciate the importance of *patterns* that provide a particular capacity for computation systems to provide recognition in some form of another, whether in data, visual material, texts or some other form of computable material. Patterns are crucial because they enable us to map the relationship between what Adorno called identity thinking and the computational. Identity thinking attempts to know an object by classification, through the application of a set of classifications that correctly identify it.

> For this kind of thinking we would know an object once all possible correct classifications of it have been completed. But for Adorno, there is an element of untruth in the very form of classificatory judgement itself. When truth is conceived according to the model of such judgements the concepts become purely classificatory, merely the common denominator of what is gathered under them. The objects become merely illustrative, of interest only as examples of the concept. (Jarvis 1998: 166)

Thus, by aggregating or combining these classifications one may only state 'what [an entity] comes under, of what it is a representative or an example, and what therefore it is not itself' (Jarvis 1998: 166). Indeed, here Adorno is pointing towards the insufficiency of correspondence models of truth, and raising the importance of mediation as a process and the production of truth through a method that does violence to the object. Indeed, 'in the exchange of commodities Adorno finds the epitome of an identificatory judgement. That which is not merely quantitatively unequal but qualitatively incommensurable is misidentified as though it were equal and commensurable' (Jarvis 1998: 167). In a similar vein, we can see that computation in its need to classify identifies all things as code objects, raw data, which it is able to conceptualize as distinct objects, with properties that are all amenable to processing through their flattening via a computational ontology. Hence, dialectical thinking crucially enables the recognition of the insufficiency of any given classification or identification.

One of the striking features of computation is the extent to which forms of pattern matching are required in computer processing. Pattern recognition can be described as a means of identifying repeated shapes or structures which are features of a system under investigation. While we tend to think of patterns as visual, of course they can also be conceptual, iterative, representational, logical, mathematical, etc. in form provided the underlying computational system can be programmed to recognize the distinctive shape of the pattern from the data. They can also consist of meta-patterns, as described by Gregory Bateson as patterns that can be detected across different spheres, such as culture, humanities, science and the social or 'the pattern that connects' (see Bateson 1979; Dixon 2012). The recognition of patterns and uncovering their relationships in sets of data was called 'abductive reasoning' by Charles Peirce, who contrasted it with inductive and deductive reasoning. Indeed, Peirce described abduction as a kind of logical inference akin to *guessing*. This he called the leap of abduction, whereby one could *abduce* A from B if A is sufficient (or nearly sufficient) but not necessary for B. The possible uses of this within a computational context should be fairly obvious, especially when software is handling partial, fuzzy or incomplete data and needs to generate future probabilistic decision points, or recognize important features or contours in a data set.

Computers classify according to the patterns which have already been programmed within them. Thus patterns serve to create a language, a *pattern language*, which is a set of classificatory means for the identification of the type of thing an object presented to the computer is. Not the particular object, but the abstract class of the object and therefore the abstract properties and understandings that are pre-coded into the computer and provide its basis of comprehension.

Computational thinking formats things into objects as an automated process and prescribes it back onto reality, both in terms of the cognitive pre-formatting that is presented to the user of the computer, and in terms of the fetish of computational capitalism to remake the world in its computational image. This classificatory flattening eases market exchange, in addition to computer processing, and hence it is of no surprise that computation is widely seen as a saviour of capitalism and the capitalist. Indeed, computationalism calls for everyday objects and life to be radically reshaped under the terms of a computational classificatory process (Golumbia 2009), whether materially, that all things become objects in physical form, or informatically, such that they are encoded, inscribed or implanted with identification tags, RFID (Radio Frequency Identification), bluetooth beacons, or some other form of encoding device that enables them to be read.

Peirce argued that pattern matching, which he called *abduction* or *retroduction* (he also used the terms *presumption* or *hypothesis*), was a type of hypothesis formation. The crucial function of 'a pattern of abduction . . . consists in its function as a search strategy which leads us, for a given kind of scenario, in a reasonable time to a most promising explanatory conjecture which is then subject to further test' (Schurz 2008: 205). Peirce argued,

> Abduction is the process of forming an explanatory hypothesis. It is the only logical operation which introduces any new idea; for induction does nothing but determine a value, and deduction merely evolves the necessary consequences of a pure hypothesis. Deduction proves that something must be; Induction shows that something actually is operative; Abduction merely suggests that something may be. (Peirce 1958: 5.171)

Or perhaps better:

> The abductive suggestion comes to us like a flash. It is an act of *insight*, although extremely fallible insight. It is true that the different elements of the hypothesis were in our minds before; but it is the idea of putting together what we had never before dreamed of putting together which flashes the new suggestion before our contemplation. (Peirce 1988: 227)

In effect, abduction is the process of arriving at an explanatory hypothesis or a process of generating a hypothesis. As Eldridge explains,

> For Peirce, abduction works from these surprising facts to determine a possible, plausible explanation. Furthermore, Peirce stresses the fact that

the logic of abduction is fallible – abductive inferences, like induction, can, and do, lead us to the wrong result. However, as a part of the triad, abduction is able to correct itself, once it is investigated by deduction and tested by induction. Because of this, we should never take the conclusion of an abductive inference to be a fact in and of itself until it is tested. (Eldridge n.d.)

Patterns were made popular as a heuristic for thinking about the new problematics introduced by software systems through the work of the architect Christopher Alexander (1936–), particularly *Notes on the Synthesis of Form* (Alexander 1964), *The Timeless Way of Building* (Alexander 1979) and *A Pattern Language* (Alexander et al. 1977) which influenced computer scientists, who found useful parallels between building design and the practice of software design (Rybczynski 2009). Alexander's central premise in his books, 'is that there is something fundamentally wrong with twentieth century architectural design methods and practices' (Lea 1997). Indeed, *A Pattern Language* was originally written to enable any citizen to design and construct their own home, although he has arguably had more influence on computer scientists than architects. As Appleton explains, patterns 'are a literary form of software engineering problem-solving [approach] that has its roots in a design movement of the same name in contemporary architecture . . . [they enable a] common vocabulary for expressing its concepts, and a language for relating them together. The goal of patterns within the software community is to create a body of literature to help software developers resolve recurring problems encountered throughout all of software development' (Appleton 2000). As Lea explains, Alexander's *The Timeless Way of Building* and *A Pattern Language* were written together,

with the former presenting rationale and method, and the latter concrete details. They present a fresh alternative to the use of standardized models and components, and accentuate the philosophical, technical and social-impact differences between analytic methods and the adaptive, open, and reflective (all in several senses) approach to design. The term pattern is a preformal construct (Alexander does not ever provide a formal definition) describing sets of forces in the world and relations among them. In *Timeless*, Alexander describes common, sometimes even universal patterns of space, of events, of human existence, ranging across all levels of granularity. *A Pattern Language* contains 253 pattern entries. . . . Each entry links a set of forces, a configuration or family of artifacts, and a process for constructing a particular realization. (Lea 1997)

Patterns are therefore reusable, structured or formalized ways of doing things or processing information and data. Alexander himself defined each pattern as:

> a three-part rule, which expresses a relation between a certain context, a problem, and a solution. As an element in the world, each pattern is a relationship between a certain context, a certain system of forces which occurs repeatedly in that context, and a certain spatial configuration which allows these forces to resolve themselves. As an element of language, a pattern is an instruction, which shows how this spatial configuration can be used, over and over again, to resolve the given system of forces, wherever the context makes it relevant. The pattern is, in short, at the same time a thing, which happens in the world, and the rule which tells us how to create that thing, and when we must create it. It is both a process and a thing; both a description of a thing which is alive, and a description of the process which will generate that thing. (Alexander 1979: 247)

The antithesis to a pattern is called an anti-pattern, that is, patterns that describe (i) a bad solution to a problem which resulted in a bad situation, or (ii) how to get out of a bad situation and how to proceed from there to a good solution (Appleton 2000; Brown et al. 1998). Patterns and pattern languages provide a broader framework to think about questions of paradigmatic means of designing and implementing computational systems. In many cases, patterns are used in this way to indicate a set of means for the development of software at a macro-level. It should also be noted that patterns can be combined with other patterns to produce new patterns at a higher level of complexity, indeed, this is the idea behind Alexander's (1977) notion of a 'pattern language'. Within software design, it is quite common to see three levels noted, namely from most abstract to more concrete: Architectural Patterns, Design Patterns and Implementation Patterns, the last being detailed, programming-language-specific patterns as *idioms* (Microsoft 2012).

Within computer science, and particularly related to the more micro-level problem of recognizing patterns themselves within data sets automatically using computation, this is an important and challenging area of research. The main forms of pattern recognition (we can think of these as patterns to find patterns) used in computation are usually enumerated as template matching, prototype matching, feature analysis, recognition by components, Fourier analysis, and lastly bottom-up and top-down processing. The six main approaches are: *Template Matching*: This is where a computational device uses a set of images (or templates) against which it can compare a data set, which itself might be an image, for instance (for examples of an image set, see Cole et al. 2004). *Prototype Matching*: This form of pattern matching uses a set of prototypes, which are understood as an average characteristic of a particular object or form. The key is that there does not need to be a perfect match, merely a high probability of likelihood that the object and prototype are similar (for an example, see Antonina et al. 2003). *Feature Analysis*: In this approach a variety of approaches are combined including detection, pattern dissection, feature comparison and recognition. Essentially, the source data is broken into key features or patterns to be compared with a library of partial objects to be matched with (e.g. see Morgan n.d.). *Recognition by Components*: In this approach objects are understood to be made up of what are called 'geons' or geometric primitives. A sample of data or images is then processed through feature detectors which are programmed to look for curves, edges, etc., or through a geodetector which looks for simple 2D or 3D forms such as cylinders, bricks, wedges, cones, circles and rectangles (see Biederman 1987). *Fourier Analysis*: This form of pattern matching uses algorithms to decompose something into smaller pieces which can then be selectively analysed. This decomposition process is called the *Fourier transform*. For example, an image might be broken down into a set of twenty squares across the image field, each of which being smaller is made faster to process. As Moler (2004) argues, 'we all use Fourier analysis every day without even knowing it. Cell phones, disc drives, DVDs, and JPEGs all involve fast finite Fourier transforms.' Fourier transformation is also used to generate a compact representation of a signal. For example, JPEG compression uses a variant of the Fourier transformation (discrete cosine transform) of small square pieces of the digital image. The Fourier components of each square are then rounded to lower arithmetic precision, and weak components are discarded, so that the remaining components can be stored in much less computer memory or storage space. To reconstruct the image, each image square is reassembled from the preserved approximate Fourier-transformed components, which are then inverse-transformed to produce an approximation of the original image, this is why the image can produce 'blocky' or the distinctive digital artefacts in the rendered image, see JPEG (2012). And lastly, *Bottom-up and Top-down Processing*: in the Bottom-up and Top-down methods an interpretation emerges *from the data.* This is called data-driven or bottom-up processing. Here, the interpretation of a data set is determined mostly by information collected, not by prior models or structures being fitted to the data, hence this approach looks for repeated patterns emerging from the data. The idea is that starting with no prior knowledge, the software is able to learn to draw generalizations from particular examples. Alternatively, in an approach where prior knowledge or structures are applied, data is fitted into these models to see if there is a 'fit'. This approach is sometimes called schema-driven or top-down processing. A schema is a pattern formed earlier in a data set or drawn from previous information (Dewey 2011).

What should be apparent from this brief discussion of the principles of *abduction* and pattern matching in computer science is their creative possibilities for generating results from data sets. The ability to generate hypotheses on the basis of data, which is fallible and probabilistic, allows for computational devices to generate forecasts and predictions based on current and past behaviours, data collection, models and images. It is this principle of abductive reason which makes computational reasoning different from instrumental reason, and particularly from the iron cage of logical implication or programmatic outcome that instrumental reason suggests. Nonetheless, it shares the classificatory impulse to sort things into specific types, classes or sets, within which their identity is ascertained.

Within computation, patterns are a useful concept because they discretize the process of creating software and therefore are connected in some ways to a Taylorist notion of modularity and the division of labour. Patterns serve as computational classificatory templates that are crucial for understanding computation itself. This computational system of classification results in an abstract machine for classifying and organizing and as such reifies everyday life. The site of computation can thus become a site of conflict between forces that attempt to capture and process such patterns, and others who seek to escape from these classificatory processes.

For Adorno, the struggle for emancipation relied upon particular historical and material conditions to be in place. Thus the use of concepts as mechanisms for classification should be rigorously critiqued, particularly its tendency not to say what something is, but rather what can it be classified under. This is undertaken through a notion of a constellation of concepts, Adorno explains,[1]

> The unifying moment survives without a negation of negation, but also without delivering itself to abstraction as a supreme principle. It survives because there is no step-by-step progression from the concepts to a more general cover concept. Instead, the concepts enter into a constellation. The constellation illuminates the specific side of the object, the side which to a classifiying procedure is either a matter of indifference or a burden. (Adorno 2004a: 162)

Thus at this historical juncture we should not be surprised to see the emergence of spaces where these conflicts are currently playing out in a number of interesting and sometimes surprising ways. One of these is the increasing collection of data about everyday life through the use of overt and covert monitoring technologies. As they collect, these systems classify and store information in various aggregated and raw forms which are themselves subject to pattern-matching and filtering activities. This practice of monitoring, aggregating and sorting data is called *dataveillance*, due to the way it relies on cross-referencing of users identified through tags, codes and cookies (Raley 2013). It is a practice that is growing in intensity as the cost of computation and storage is correspondingly shrinking creating the conditions for a new collection of reification technologies that record our lives through time and place them into code objects.

Reification technologies: Web bugs, beacons and trackers

The notion of using time for the collection of data and representing it back to the user was originally an idea from David Gelernter and Eric Freeman in the 1990s (Freeman 1997; Gelernter 2010) which they called a lifestream,

> a time-ordered stream of documents that functions as a diary of your electronic life; every document you create and every document other people send you is stored in your lifestream. The tail of your stream contains documents from the past (starting with your electronic birth certificate). Moving away from the tail and toward the present, your stream contains more recent documents – papers in progress or new electronic mail; other documents (pictures, correspondence, bills, movies, voice mail, software) are stored in between. Moving beyond the present and into the future, the stream contains documents you *will* need: reminders, calendar items, to-do lists. You manage your lifestream through a small number of powerful operators that allow you to transparently store information, organize information on demand, filter and monitor incoming information, create reminders and calendar items in an integrated fashion, and "compress" large numbers of documents into overviews or executive summaries. (Freeman 2000)

Gelernter originally described these 'chronicle streams' (Gelernter 1994), highlighting both their narrative and temporal dimensions related to the storage of documentation and texts. Today we are more likely to think of them as 'real-time streams' (Berry 2011) and the timeline functions offered by systems like Twitter, Facebook and Google+ (see Bucher 2012, for a discussion of the EdgeRank algorithm, for example). This is increasingly the model of interface design that is driving the innovation in computation, especially in mobile and locative technologies. However, in contrast to the document-centric model that Gelernter and Freeman were describing, there are also the micro-streams of short updates, epitomized by Twitter, which has short text message sized 140 character updates. Nonetheless, this is still enough text space to incorporate a surprising amount of data, particularly when geo, image, weblinks and so forth are factored in. Stephen Wolfram was certainly one of the first people to collect their data systematically as he explains he started in 1989:

> So email is one kind of data I've systematically archived. And there's a huge amount that can be learned from that. Another kind of data that I've been collecting is keystrokes. For many years, I've captured every keystroke I've typed—now more than 100 million of them. (Wolfram 2012)

This kind of self-collection of data is certainly becoming more prevalent, and in the context of reflexivity and self-knowledge, it raises interesting questions. The scale of data that is collected can also be relatively large and unstructured.[2] Nonetheless, better data management and techniques for searching and surfacing information from unstructured or semi-structured data will no doubt be revealing about our everyday patterns in the future.[3]

It is clear too, for example, that the growing phenomena of what are called 'web bugs' (also known as 'web beacons') that are covertly collecting data and information about us is becoming more contentious while it also becomes ubiquitous. These 'web bugs' are computer algorithms that are embedded in seemingly benign computal surfaces but which collect data relentlessly.[4] As Madrigal (2012) explains:

> This morning, if you opened your browser and went to NYTimes.com, an amazing thing happened in the milliseconds between your click and when the news about North Korea and James Murdoch appeared on your screen. Data from this single visit was sent to 10 different companies, including Microsoft and Google subsidiaries, a gaggle of traffic-logging sites, and other, smaller ad firms. Nearly instantaneously, these companies can log your visit, place ads tailored for your eyes specifically, and add to the ever-growing online file about you . . . the list of companies that tracked my movements on the Internet in one recent 36-hour period of standard web surfing: Acerno. AdaraMedia. Adblade. Adbrite. ADC Onion. Adchemy. ADiFY. AdMeld. Adtech. Aggregate Knowledge. AlmondNet. Aperture. AppNexus. Atlas. Audience Science. . . . And that's just the As. My complete list includes 105 companies, and there are dozens more than that in existence. (Madrigal 2012)

Web bugs are automated data collection agents that are secretly included in the web pages that we browse. Often held within a tiny one-pixel frame or image, which is therefore far too small for the naked eye to see, they execute code to secrete cookies onto your computer so that they can track user behaviour, and send various information about the user back to their servers. Web bugs can be thought of as reification technologies, that is, they convert social relations, experience and activities into relations between objects. Here, the objects are code objects, but nonetheless they function in similar ways to everyday objects, in as much as they are understood to have properties and remain relatively stable and therefore in some sense persistent. They are also a product of capitalism both in terms of their function as providing means for the creation and maintenance of exchange, and in terms of generating consumer feedback and generating desire as part of a system of advertising and marketing.

Originally designed as 'HTTP state management mechanisms' in the early 1990s, these data storage processes were designed to enable webpages and sites to store the current collection of data about a user, or what is called 'State' in computer science, known as 'web bugs for web 1.0' (Dobias 2010: 245). They were aimed at allowing website designers to implement some memory of a user, such as a current shopping basket, preferences or username. It was a small step for companies to see the potential of monitoring user behaviour by leaving tracking information about browsing, purchasing and clicking behaviour through the use of these early 'cookies'.[5] The ability of algorithms to track behaviour, collect data and information about users raises important privacy implications but also facilitates the rise of so-called behaviour marketing and nudges (see Eyal 2012 for a behaviourist approach). However, it is important to note that the extent of the 'nudge' that the system can provide can range from the libertarian paternalism of defaults and formatting advocated by Thaler and Sunstein (2009) to post-human distributed aids to cognition, or even collective notions of cognition, as described by Hutchins (1996). These technologies have become much more sophisticated in the light of Web 2.0 technologies and developments in hardware and software, in effect web bugs for web 2.0 (Dobias 2010: 245).

Fortunately, we are seeing the creation of a number of useful software projects to allow us to track the trackers, such as, Collusion, Foxtracks and Ghostery.[6] For example, if we look at the Betaware ChartBeat web bug, a key company in the collection of this form of data, the Ghostery log for the Betaware ChartBeat company describes it as providing real-time analytics via an interface that tracks visitors, load times and referring sites on a minute-by-minute basis. This therefore allows real-time tracking and monitoring of users (Ghostery 2012b).[7]

These trackers are used to collect and aggregate user data, in effect they attempt to identify either the user or the type of user. For website owners, especially those interested in using behavioural nudges and other persuasive techniques, customizing the website pages that are served up to the user according to their profile vastly improves the 'stickiness' of the website, but also its profitability. Web bugs perform these analytics by running code run in the browser without the knowledge of the user, and which if it should be observed, looks extremely opaque.[8]

It is noticeable, however, that newer web bugs are complicated and difficult to understand, even for experienced computer programmers. They are larger, more complex in their processing capabilities and far more intrusive in the data they attempt to collect. Indeed, one suspects an element of obfuscation, a programming technique to reduce the readability of the code and which is used to essentially shield the company from observation. So far in checking a number of web bugs on a variety of websites, I have been unable to find one that supplies any commentary on exactly what the code is doing, beyond a short privacy policy statement. Again Ghostery (2012b) usefully supplies us with some general information on the web bug, such as the fact that it may been found on 'over 100,000 websites' across the internet and that the data collected is 'anonymous (browser type), pseudonymous (IP address)', or that the data is not shared with third parties but no information is given on their data retention policies. In March 2012, Ghostery reported that it was tracking 829 different web bugs across the internet and by July 2013 it reported over 1,400 web bugs. Likewise, Kennish (2011) found 6,926 third-party web-bug code fragments on 201,358 Web pages (see Efrati 2011; Milian 2011). This is a relatively unregulated market in user behaviour, tracking and data collection, which currently has a number of voluntary self-regulatory bodies, such as the Network Advertising Initative (NAI). As Madrigal reports:

> In essence, [the NAI] argued that users do not have the right to not be tracked. "We've long recognized that consumers should be provided a choice about whether data about their likely interests can be used to make their ads more relevant," [they] wrote. "But the NAI code also recognizes that companies sometimes need to continue to collect data for operational reasons that are separate from ad targeting based on a user's online behavior." . . . Companies "need to continue to collect data," but that contrasts directly with users desire "not to be tracked." (Madrigal 2012)

These web bugs, beacons, pixels and tags, as they are variously called, form part of the dark-net surveillance network that users rarely see even though it is profoundly changing their experience of the internet in real time by attempting to second guess, tempt, direct and nudge behaviour in particular directions.[9] Google is clearly the biggest player in the area of the collection of user data and statistics but other companies are aggressively moving into this area. This data is important because, as JP Morgan's Imran

Khan explained, a unique visitor to each website at Amazon (e-commerce) is generating $189 per user, at Google (search) it is generating $24 per user and although Facebook (social networking) is only generating $4 per user, this is a rapidly growing number (Yarrow 2011). Keeping and holding these visitors, through real-time analytics, customer history, behavioural targeting, etc. is increasingly extremely profitable. Indeed, Amazon has calculated that knowing and responding to customer needs is very important for profitability and 'that a page load slowdown of just one second could cost it $1.6 billion in sales each year' (Eaton 2012a). Correspondingly, 'Google has calculated that by slowing its search results by just four tenths of a second they could lose 8 million searches per day – meaning they'd serve up many millions fewer online adverts,' and hence make less money (Eaton 2012a).

Where companies are more explicitly collecting data and information they often have in place data collection and privacy policies, for example, see Facebook (2012) or Google (2012a). An analysis by Cranor and McDonald (2008) found that it would take on average 201 hours per year to read the privacy policies that users find in connection with their everyday use of the internet and which are extremely complicated legal documents. Unsurprisingly, few read them. Users are therefore often agreeing to certain data usage, collection, reselling and aggregation without explicitly being aware of it. For example, while you are logged in, Facebook collects,

> a timestamped list of the URLs you visit and pair it with your name, list of friends, Facebook preferences, email address, IP address, screen resolution, operating system and browser. When you're logged out, it captures everything except your name, list of friends, and Facebook preferences. Instead, it uses a unique alphanumeric identifier to track you (Love 2012).

Of course, all of these web bugs are active in some level of user surveillance, and indeed it is no surprise that web bugs perform part of the tracking technologies used by companies to monitor staff. For example, in 2006, Hewlett Packard used web bugs from readnotify.com to trace insider leaks to the journalist Dawn Kawamoto and later confirmed in testimony to a U.S. House of Representatives subcommittee that it's 'still company practice to use e-mail bugs in certain cases' (Evers 2006; Fried 2006).

This is an extremely textured environment that currently offers little in terms of diagnosis or even warnings to the user. The industry itself, which prefers the term 'clear GIF' to web bug, certainly is keen to avoid regulation and keeps itself very much to itself in order to avoid raising too much unwarranted attention. Some of the current discussions over the direction of regulation on this issue have focused on the 'do not track' flag, which would signal a user's opt-out preference within an HTTP header. Unfortunately, very few companies respect the 'do not track header' and there is currently no legal requirement that they do so in the United States, or elsewhere (W3C 2012). There have been some moves towards *self-regulation* in the technology industry with a recent report from the US Federal Trade Commission (Tsukayama 2012). Although, see the current debate over the EU ePrivacy Directive, where the Article 29 Working Party (A29 WP) has stated that 'voluntary plans drawn up by Europe's digital advertising industry representatives, the European Advertising Standards Alliance and IAB Europe, do not meet the consent and information requirements of the recently revised ePrivacy Directive' (Baker 2012). Legislation may therefore be introduced into the European Union before elsewhere – indeed in the United Kingdom the *Privacy and Electronic Communications (EC Directive) (Amendment) Regulations (PECR) 2011* has already come into force and covers all website owners with a UK presence, who are now required to obtain informed consent from website users and subscribers in order to store information on their devices, although this is often merely a warning that the web site uses 'cookies', which is meaningless to most members of the public (see ICO 2012).

With the greater use of computational networked devices in everyday life, from mobile phones to GPS systems, these forms of tracking systems will only become more invasive and more aggressive in collecting data from our everyday life and encounters. There is growing concern by users and the media itself about what they should do to protect themselves against this growing web-bug surveillance industry. Indeed, it is unsurprising to find that Americans, for example, are not comfortable with the growth in use of these tracker technologies, Pew (2012) found,

> that 73 percent of Americans said they would "not be okay" with being tracked (because it would be an invasion of privacy). . . . Only 23 percent said they'd be "okay" with tracking (because it would lead to better and more personalized search results). . . . Despite all those high-percentage objections to the idea of being tracked, less than half of the people surveyed – 38 percent – said they knew of ways to control the data collected about them (Garber 2012; Pew 2012).

The ability of these computational systems to supply a service commodity to the user, while needing to raise income through the harvesting of data, which is sold to advertisers and marketing companies, shows that this is a potentially conflictual situation. It also serves to demonstrate the extent to which users are just not aware of the subterranean depths of their computational devices and the ability for these general computing platforms to disconnect the user interface from the actual intentions or functioning of the device, while giving the impression to the user that they remain fully in control of the computer. As Garber observes, 'underground network, surface illusion. . . . How much do we actually want to know about this stuff? Do we truly want to understand the intricacies of data-collection and personalization and all the behind-the-screen work that creates the easy, breezy experience of search . . . or would we, on some level, prefer that it remain as magic?' (Garber 2012). Indeed, as Aron (2012) reports, 'up to 75 per cent of the energy used by free versions of Android apps is spent serving up ads or tracking and uploading user data.' That is, on free versions of popular apps most of the processing work in the app is spent in monitoring user activities and reporting that data back home to servers (see also Pathak et al. 2012). This ability for code/software to monitor the user covertly and even obscure its processing activities will undoubtedly become a growing political and economic as well as technical issue (see some examples from Goodale 2012).[10]

In terms of covert code objects acting or obscuring their activities, Stuxnet, a computer worm, is a fascinating example.[11] Experts now believe that Stuxnet was aimed at the Iranian uranium-enrichment facility at Natanz, Iran.[12] The Stuxnet worm, a subclass of computer virus, copied itself repeatedly across computer systems until it found the host that met its 'strike conditions', that is, the location it was designed to attack, and activated its 'digital warhead', which could monitor, damage or even destroy its target. The name, 'Stuxnet', is 'derived from some of the filename/strings in the malware – mrxcls.sys, mrxnet.sys', the first part, 'stu', comes from the (.stub) file, mrxcls.sys; and the second part, 'xnet', comes from mrxnet.sys (Kruszelnicki 2011; mmpc2 2010). Due to the sophistication of the programming involved, this worm is considered to have reached a new level in cyberwarfare. Stuxnet has been called the first 'weaponized' computer virus, and it would have required huge resources, like a test facility to model a nuclear plant, to create and launch it (Cherry 2010). As Liam O'Murchu, an operations manager for Symantec, explained,

> Unlike the millions of worms and viruses that turn up on the Internet every year, this one was not trying to steal passwords, identities or money. Stuxnet appeared to be crawling around the world, computer by computer, looking for some sort of industrial operation that was using a specific piece of equipment, a Siemens S7-300 programmable logic controller. (60minutes 2012b)

The Stuxnet worm works by undertaking a very complex stealth infection and covers its tracks by recording data from the nuclear processing system which it then plays back to the operators to disguise that it is actually gently causing the centrifuges to fail. This is known as a 'man-in-the-middle attack', because it fakes industrial process control sensor signals so an infected system does not exhibit abnormal behaviour and therefore raise alarm. Cleverly, the faults created in the plant are likely to occur weeks after the sabotaged effort, and in a targeted way, through the fatiguing of the motors – making it look like a standard failure rather than an attack. Indeed, Iran later confirmed that a number of its centrifuges had been affected by an attack (CBSNews 2010). Later, a 'senior Iranian intelligence official said an estimated 16,000 computers were infected by the Stuxnet virus' (AP 2012). The Stuxnet worm is also interesting because it also has built-in *sunset code* that causes the worm to erase itself (in this case after 24 June 2012), and hence hide its tracks. As Zett (2011) explains:

> once the code infects a system, it searches for the presence of two kinds of frequency converters made by the Iranian firm Fararo Paya and the Finnish company Vacon, making it clear that the code has a precise target in its sights. . . . Stuxnet begins with a nominal frequency of 1,064 Hz . . . then reduces the frequency for a short while before returning it back to 1,064 Hz. . . . Stuxnet [then] instructs the speed to increase to 1,410 Hz, which is "very close to the maximum speed the spinning aluminum IR-1 rotor can withstand mechanically," . . . [but] before the rotor reaches the tangential speed at which it would break apart . . . within 15 minutes after instructing the frequency to increase, Stuxnet returns the frequency to its nominal 1,064 Hz level. Nothing else happens for 27 days, at which point a second attack sequence kicks in that reduces the frequency to 2 Hz, which lasts for 50 minutes before the frequency is restored to 1,064 Hz. Another 27 days pass, and the first attack sequence launches again, increasing the frequency to 1,410 Hz, followed 27 days later by a reduction to 2 Hz. (Zetter 2011)

Stuxnet disguises all of this activity by overriding the data control systems and sending commands to disable warning and safety controls that would normally alert plant operators to these dangerous frequency changes. Stuxnet is interesting because it is not a general purpose attack, but designed to unload its digital warheads under specific conditions against a specific threat target. It is also remarkable in the way in which it disengages the interface, the screen for the user, from the underlying logic and performance of the machine.

Due to the complexities involved in being able to test such a worm before releasing it into the wild, there has been a great deal of speculation about whether a state would have been required to develop it (Markoff and Sanger 2010). Richard Clarke, the former chief of counter-terrorism under Presidents

Clinton and Bush, argues that the built-in fail-safes are an important clue to Stuxnet's source and that they point to the kinds of procedures found in a Western government. Clarke stated, 'if a [Western] government were going to do something like this . . . then it would have to go through a bureaucracy, a clearance process, [and] somewhere along the line, lawyers would say, "We have to prevent collateral damage," and the programmers would go back and add features that normally you don't see in the hacks. And there are several of them in Stuxnet' (Gross 2011). Indeed, the complexities and structure of the worm mean that estimates are that at least 30 people would have been working on it simultaneously to build such a worm (Zetter 2010). Especially one that launched a so-called 'zero-day attack', that is, using a set of techniques that are not public nor known by the developer of the attacked system, in this case Microsoft and Siemens – in actuality it was remarkable for exploiting four different zero-day vulnerabilities (Gross 2011). There is now a large and growing secondary market for these kinds of exploits with prices ranged between $50,000 and $100,000 (Naraine 2012a). Indeed,

> [these] customers . . . don't aim to fix Google's security bugs or those of any other commercial software vendor. They're government agencies who purchase such "zero-day" exploits, or hacking techniques that use undisclosed flaws in software, with the explicit intention of invading or disrupting the computers and phones of crime suspects and intelligence targets. In that shady but legal market for security vulnerabilities, a zero-day exploit that might earn a hacker $2,000 or $3,000 from a software firm could earn 10 or even 100 times that sum from the spies and cops who aim to use it in secret. (Greenberg 2012)

Companies that specialize in the trade in cybersecurity information and technology vulnerabilities have been described as 'modern-day merchant[s] of death,' selling 'the bullets for cyberwar' (Greenberg 2012). Combined together into cleverly written code digital warheads these vulnerabilities can be exploited to create serious attacks on infrastructure and technical equipment, although the skills to do this would require a sophisticated project team. Indeed, with Stuxnet the layered approach to its attack and application of multiple vulnerabilities, combined with the detailed knowledge required of Microsoft Windows, supervisory control and data acquisition (SCADA) and programmable logic controllers (PLCs) systems, this would have been a very large project to develop and launch. Indeed, Eric Byres, chief technology officer for Byres Security, has stated: 'we're talking man-months, if not years, of coding to make it work the way it did' (Zetter 2010). The 'weaponization' of code vulnerabilities is a growing problem as Brad Arkin argues, 'I'm not saying we should outlaw offensive research. However, it's clear that these [intellectual] offensive advances very much change the game. Once something gets published, it's only a matter of time before real-world bad guys put them into their operations' (Naraine 2012b).[13] In order to counter the anarchy of a free market in zero-day vulnerabilities, some Western governments are pushing for 'designed exploits' to be built into their systems, as Morozov (2012a) explains,

> [The] surveillance business keeps booming. The FBI [has made] attempts to convince Internet companies to build secret back doors into their services. . . . At the same time . . . developing countries—and especially Russia, China, and Iran—have begun making efforts to limit their dependence on American technology, in part because they feel it may contain secret back doors or be strategically exploited to foment unrest. (Morozov 2012)

Indeed, these security concerns are shown to have some truth in relation to Stuxnet, whose two chief capabilities are: (1) to identify its target precisely using a number of software-based markers that give the physical identity of the geographic location away. Indeed, 'attackers [had] full, and I mean this literally, full tactical knowledge of every damn detail of [the Natanz] plant' (60minutes 2012b) and (2) the capability to disengage control systems from physical systems and to provide a stealth infection into the computers that would fool the operators of the plant (a 'man-in-the-middle attack'). This was achieved through the use of two 'digital warheads', called 417 and 315. The smaller, (315), was designed to slowly reduce the speed of rotors leading to cracks and failures, and the second larger warhead, (417), manipulated valves in the centrifuge and faking industrial process control sensor signals by modelling the centrifuges which were grouped into 164 cascades (Langner 2011). Indeed, Langner (2011) described this evocatively as 'two shooters from different angles'. The Stuxnet worm was launched some time in 2009/2010 and shortly afterwards,[14]

> the all-important centrifuges at Iran's nuclear fuel enrichment facility at Natanz began failing at a suspicious rate. Iran eventually admitted that computer code created problems for their centrifuges, but downplayed any lasting damage. Computer security experts now agree that code was a sophisticated computer worm dubbed Stuxnet, and that it destroyed more than 1,000 centrifuges. (60minutes 2012a)

The origin of the name Stuxnet is hypothesized from an analysis of the approximately 15,000 lines of programming code in the worm. Langner undertook a close reading and reconstruction of the programming logic by taking the machine code, disassembling it and then attempting to convert it into the C programming language. The code could then be analysed for system function calls, timers and data structures, in order to try to understand what the code was doing (Langner 2011). As part of this process, a reference to 'Myrtus' was discovered, and the link made to 'Myrtus as an allusion to the Hebrew word for Esther. The Book of Esther tells the story of a Persian plot against the Jews, who attacked their enemies pre-emptively' (Markoff and Sanger 2010).[15] While no actor has claimed responsibility for Stuxnet, there is a strong suspicion that either the United States or Israel had to be involved in the creation of such a sophisticated attack virus. Its attack appears to have been concentrated on a number of selected areas, with Iran at the centre.

Clearly, this kind of attack could be mobilized at targets other than nuclear enrichment facilities, and indeed the stealth and care with which it attempts to fool the operators of the plants shows that computational devices will undoubtedly be targets for monitoring, surveillance, control and so forth in the future. Of course, once the code for undertaking this kind of sophisticated cyberattack is out in the wild, it is relatively trivial to decode the computer code and learn techniques that would have taken many years of development in a very short time. As Sean McGurk explains, 'you can download the actual source code of Stuxnet now and you can repurpose it and repackage it and then, you know, point it back towards wherever it came from' (60minutes 2012b). Indeed, a different worm, called Duqu, has already been discovered, albeit with purposes linked to the collection of the data on industrial control systems and structures, a so-called 'Trojan' (Hopkins 2011).[16] As Alexander Gostev, reports,

> There were a number of projects involving programs based on the "Tilded" [i.e. Stuxnet] platform throughout the period 2007–2011. Stuxnet and Duqu are two of them – there could have been others, which for now remain unknown. The platform continues to develop, which can only mean one thing – we're likely to see more modifications in the future (Gostev 2012).[17]

The increased ability of software and code to covertly monitor, control and mediate, both positively and negatively, is not just a case of interventions for deceiving the human and non-human actors that make up part of these assemblages. However, below, I want to look at the willing compliance with data collection, indeed, the enthusiastic contribution of real-time data to computal systems as part of the notion of lifestreams, and more particularly the quantified self-movement – what Searls (2013) has called 'life management platforms'.

The growth in the use of self-monitoring technologies often called lifestreaming, or the notion of the quantified self, is rapidly expanding as the public has become more comfortable with the computational monitoring possible with intimate computational devices.[18] These technologies have expanded in recent years as the 'real-time streams' like Twitter and Facebook platforms have expanded, enabling users to upload and share their data and statistics. Indeed, some argue that 'we're finally in a position where people volunteer information about their specific activities, often their location, who they're with, what they're doing, how they feel about what they're doing, what they're talking about. . . . We've never had data like that before, at least not at that level of granularity' (Rieland 2012). Indeed the Economist argues that the,

> idea of measuring things to chart progress towards a goal is commonplace in large organisations. Governments tot up trade figures, hospital waiting times and exam results; companies measure their turnover, profits and inventory. But the use of metrics by individuals is rather less widespread, with the notable exceptions of people who are trying to lose weight or improve their fitness. . . . But some people are doing just these things. They are an eclectic mix of early adopters, fitness freaks, technology evangelists, personal-development junkies, hackers and patients suffering from a wide variety of health problems. What they share is a belief that gathering and analysing data about their everyday activities can help them improve their lives—an approach known as "self-tracking", "body hacking" or "self-quantifying". (Economist 2012)

This phenomenon of using computational devices to monitor health signals and to feed them back into calculative interfaces, data visualizations, real-time streams, etc. is the next step in social media. This closes the loop of personal information online, which, although it remains notionally private, is stored and accessed by corporations who wish to use this biodata for data mining and innovation surfacing. For example, The Zeo (headband) has already generated the largest-ever database on sleep stages, which apparently reveals gender differences in REM-sleep quantity; Asthmapolis which hopes to pool aggregated data from thousands of inhalers fitted with its Spiroscout (asthma inhaler) sensor in an effort to improve the management of asthma; and data from the Boozerlyzer (alcohol counting) app which investigates the variation in people's response to alcohol, while collecting data about these drinking habits (Economist 2012).

This way of collecting and sending data has been accelerated by the use of mobile 'apps', which are small, relatively contained applications that usually perform a single specific function. For example, the Twitter app on the iPhone allows the user to send updates to their timeline, but also search other timelines, check out profiles, streams and so on. When created as apps, however, they are also able to use the power of the local device, especially if it contains the kinds of sophisticated sensory circuitry that is common in smartphones, to log GPS geographic location, direction, etc. This is when lifestreaming becomes increasingly similar to the activity of web bugs in monitoring and collecting data on the users that are active on the network (Hill 2011).[19] Indeed, activity streams have become a standard which is increasingly being incorporated into software across a number of media and software practices (see ActivityStreams n.d.). An activity stream essentially encodes a user event or activity into a form that can be computationally transmitted and later aggregated, searched and processed,

> In its simplest form, an activity consists of an *actor*, a *verb*, an *object*, and a *target*. It tells the story of a person performing an action on or with an object – "Geraldine posted a photo to her album" or "John shared a video". In most cases these components will be explicit, but they may also be implied. (ActivityStreamsWG 2011, original emphasis)

This data and activity collection is only part of the picture, however. In order to become reflexive data it must be computationally processed from its raw state, which may be structured, unstructured or a combination of the two. At this point it is common for the data to be visualized, usually through a graph or timeline, but there are also techniques such as heat maps, graph theory and so forth that enable the data to be processed and reprocessed to tease out patterns in the underlying data set. In both the individual and aggregative use cases, in other words for the individual user (or lifestreamer) or organization (such as Facebook), the key is to pattern match and compare details of the data, such as against a norm, a historical data set, or against a population, group, or class or others.[20]

The patterned usage is therefore a dynamic real-time feedback mechanism in terms of providing steers for behaviour, norms and so forth, but it is also offering a documentary narcissism that appears to give the user an existential confirmation and status.[21] Even in its so-called gamification forms, the awarding of competitive points, badges, honours and positional goods more generally is the construction of a hierarchical social structure within the group of users, for example, Foursquare. It also encourages the users to think of themselves as a set of partial objects, fragmented dividuals or loosely connected properties, collected as a time series of data points and subject to intervention and control. This can be thought of as a computational care of the self, facilitated by an army of oligopticans (Latour 2005) in the wider computational environment that observe and store behavioural and affective data. However, this self is reconciled through the code and software that visualizes the data so that it makes sense. The code and software are therefore responsible for creating and maintaining the meaning and narratives through a stabilization of the web of meaning for the actor.[22]

One of the most interesting aspects of these systems is that users are actively downloading apps that advertise the fact that they collect this data and seem to genuinely find existential relief or recognition in their movements being recorded and available for later playback or analysis. Indeed, web bugs are in many ways themselves facilitating life streams, albeit life streams that have not been authorized by the user whom they are monitoring. This collection of what we might call *compactants* is designed to *passive-aggressively* record data.[23] It is this passive-aggressive feature of computational agents – that is, collecting information, both in terms of their passive quality of being under the surface, relatively benign and silent, and in terms of the aggressiveness in their hoarding of data by monitoring behavioural signals, activity streams, affectivity streams, social signal data and so forth.[24]

Interestingly, compactants are structured in such a way that they can be understood as having a dichotomous structure of data collection/visualization, each of which is a specific mode of operation. Naturally, due to the huge quantities of data that is often generated, the computational processing and aggregation is often offloaded to the 'cloud', or server computers designed specifically for the task, and accessed via networks. Indeed, many viruses, for example, often seek to 'call home' to report their status, upload data or offer the chance of being updated, perhaps to a more aggressive version of themselves or to correct bugs.

There is also a telos within these wider computational systems made up of arrays or networks of compactants, which in many cases is a future user, or an ideal version of the present user. It also raises the problem of what we might call, the *cognitive capture* of the user (or institution) whereby algorithmic systems, with their speed and breadth of information analysis, present us with suggestions that we accept because we are not in a position to cognitively check that the proposal proffered is the best one. Within the quantified self-movement there is an explicit recognition that the 'future self' will be required to undo bad habits and behaviours of the present self (see Hill 2011). There is an explicit normative context to a *future* self, who you, as the *present* self may be treating unfairly, immorally or without due regard to, what has been described as 'future self continuity' and who can speak to the present through algorithms (Tugend 2012). This inbuilt tendency towards the *futural* is a fascinating reflection of the internal temporal representation of time within computational systems, that is, time-series structured streams of real-time data, often organized as lists.

Therefore, the past (as stored data), present (as current data collection, or processed archival data) and future (as both the ethical addressee of the system and potential provider of data and usage) are often deeply embedded in the code that runs these systems. In some cases the future also has an objective existence as a probabilistic projection, literally a *code object*, which is updated in real time and which contains the major features of the future state represented as a model; computational weather prediction systems and climate change models are both examples of this. This code object (or perhaps better, code-subject) may be better placed to work out what is best for its user than the users themselves, as proposed with software-based personal assistants, such that 'it understands you so well, that it can make really good suggestions to make your life much better' (Mac 2012). Although these compactant systems also raise concerns, such as 'the inability for consumers to anticipate how their information is being used, [there is] a potential chilling effect on personal behavior that comes with monitoring and the possibility of the government using [this] data' (Mac 2012).[25]

Indeed, recent revelations about the comprehensive collection of data by the US NSA and the UK GCHQ demonstrate the extent to which everyday life is now reified into computational systems creating a kind of quantified public. Indeed, '[Edward] Snowden, the former NSA contractor, among other things revealed a secret order from the surveillance court directing Verizon Business Services Inc. to turn over "comprehensive communications routing information" to the NSA' (Valentino-Devries and Gorman 2013). This forms part of a collection strategy that essentially hoovers up all information that passes over the internet, for example, 'Britain's Government Communications Headquarters (GCHQ) [uses a system called] Tempora [which] is the signal intelligence community's first "full-take Internet buffer," meaning that it saves all of the data passing through the country' (Spiegel 2013). Indeed, the fact that so much of our data is sent via the internet in the 'clear', that is as easily readable textual information, has led Assange (2013) and others to claim 'strong cryptography is a vital tool in fighting state oppression', indeed, he argues,

> cryptography can protect not just the civil liberties and rights of individuals, but the sovereignty and independence of whole countries, solidarity between groups with common cause, and the project of global emancipation. (Assange 2013)

Even so, within institutional contexts, code/software is still being fully incorporated into the specific logics of these systems, and in many ways may undermine these structural and institutional forms.[26] We must remain attentive to the fact that software engineering is a relatively recent discipline and its efforts at systematization and rationalization are piecemeal and incomplete, as the many hugely expensive software system failures attest. Code/software design and implementation is not easy, many techniques needed are still in their relative infancy, and while it is clear that these large surveillance systems are being built, their efficacy still remains to be shown although there is a clear and present danger to democratic life. But this should give hope and direction to the critical theorists, both of the present looking to provide critique and counterfactuals, but also *of* the future, as code/software is a particularly rich site for intervention, contestation and the *unbuilding* of code/software systems.[27] Indeed, I tentatively suggest that a future critical theory of code and software is committed to *un*building, *dis*assembling and *de*formation of existing code/software systems, together with leaking, glitching and overloading these systems. But additionally, it requires a necessary intervention in terms of a positive moment, such as the Turkopticon project which allows workers to 'create and use reviews of employers when choosing employers on Amazon Mechanical Turk . . . as an example of systems design incorporating feminist analysis and reflexivity . . . a system to make worker-employer relations visible and to provoke ethical and political debate' (Irani and Silberman 2013). But also needed are the formation and composition of future and alternative systems, using civil society movements, public encryption, the democratization of cryptography, megaleaks and the education of citizens about these systems and the dangers of massive data archives, whether in the hands of companies or governments.

6

Computational aesthetics

For the critical theorists, as capital becomes increasingly concentrated and the state and economy become ever more interdependent, traditional political economy becomes insufficient as an explanatory framework for understanding the new forms of emerging capitalism. Hence, the critical theorists turned their attention to the 'assessment of the mode in which ideas and beliefs are transmitted by "popular culture" – the way in which the personal, private realm is undermined by the external (extra-familial) socialization of the ego and the management and control of leisure time' (Held 1997: 77). Indeed, in a similar fashion to the way in which corporations now seek to intervene in consciousness through computational persuasive technologies, the critical theorists identified the way organizations began encroaching upon individuals' consciousness and unconsciousness. As Held explains,

> For Horkheimer, Adorno, and Marcuse, in particular, sociology and critique are inseparable: to analyse a work of art, or a particular cultural artifact, is to analyse and assess the way it is interpreted. This entails an inquiry into its formation and reception. Such an inquiry seeks to understand given works in terms of their social origins, form, content and function – in terms of the social totality. The conditions of labour, production and distribution must be examined, for society expresses itself through it cultural life and cultural phenomena contain within themselves reference to the socio-economic whole. (Held 1997: 77)

This is to explore the way in which society itself and its organization are 'crystallized' in cultural phenomenon. However, in contrast to most Marxist accounts of culture, the critical theorists did not think of culture as merely the superstructure, which was in some sense determined by a base. Indeed, the critical theorists rejected such a model altogether. They also rejected 'traditional cultural criticism' that disconnected it from society, as if it could be understood in and of itself, divorced from its social production and practices. Indeed, they argued that 'culture emerges from the organizational basis of society as the bundle of ideas, mores, norms and artistic expressions – the heritage and practices of intelligence and art' (Held 1997: 80). Marcuse, when discussing culture, makes the following useful distinction,

> The spheres of *material* culture and *intellectual* (artistic, "higher") culture. Material culture comprises "the actual patterns of behaviour in 'earning a living'", the system of operational "values", and includes the social, psychological and moral dimensions of family life, leisure time, education and work. Intellectual culture refers to the "higher" values, science and the "humanities", art, religion. (Held 1997: 80)

For Adorno, the concept of the 'new' within art is understood with reference to the determinate negation of the old. In other words, only by reference to that which has gone before can a distinction be developed which enables a 'new' to be articulated as such. This is crucial in understanding that the 'new' will always involuntarily repeat the old, even if there is a disavowal of previous work and claims to a decisive break. Nonetheless, Adorno does not take the view that artworks can be an instrument in the cause of social justice. Adorno argues instead,

> That works of art, rather than being instrumental "interventions", offer a criticism of instrumental reason and action as such. In so far as art is autonomous, it does not criticize some particular good or bad action, as though actions could be weighed outside their increasingly total context, but the whole framework within which practice takes place. . . . As sheer instruments they could no longer offer a critique of instrumental reason. . . . The danger for politically committed art is that it will end up as bad art without becoming good politics either. (Jarvis 1998: 121)

Artistic culture represents the 'perennial protest' of the 'particular against the universal', that is, 'culture, in the true sense, did not simply accommodate itself to human beings; but it always simultaneously raised a protest against petrified relations under which they lived' (Adorno 2005b: 100). That is, the artistic transformation of objects such that they reveal the conditions under which they exist. Through the power of negation, objects are thereby released from their surroundings and images are created which become difficult to reconcile with everyday existence (Held 1997: 86). Indeed in relation to our contemporary experience of digital technologies and computationality, Bishop cogently argues, the most prevalent trends in contemporary art since the '90s seem united in their apparent eschewal of the digital and the virtual. Performance art, social practice, assemblage-based sculpture, painting on canvas, the "archival impulse," analog film, and the fascination with modernist design and architecture: At first glance, none of these formats appear to have anything to do with digital media. . . . But when we examine these dominant forms of contemporary art more closely, their operational logic and systems of spectatorship prove intimately connected to the technological revolution we are undergoing. . . . I am suggesting that the digital is, on a deep level, the shaping condition—even the structuring paradox—that determines artistic decisions to work with certain formats and media. Its subterranean presence is comparable to the rise of television as the backdrop to art of the 1960s. One word that might be used to describe this dynamic—a preoccupation that is present but denied, perpetually active but apparently buried—is disavowal. (Bishop 2012)

In this chapter I want to explore the digital in relation to the aesthetic – and its disavowal – particularly in relation to the way in which digital works are acknowledged or rejected as forms of art. Here, I do not necessarily mean purely formal art production, nor in terms of institutionalization of art through gallery curation necessarily. Rather, I want to look at claims to an aesthetic moment itself revealed in and through aesthetic practice and popular culture surrounding the digital. Indeed, it is interesting in terms of the refusal of new aesthetic practitioners to abide by the careful boundary monitoring between the art world and the 'creative industry' more generally, really bringing to the fore the questions raised by Liu (2004) regarding how design and art might be conceptually linked through a notion of what he calls 'cool'. Indeed, here the computational propensity towards dissolving of traditional boundaries and disciplinary borders is manifested on an aesthetic register and includes practices such as Live Coding, Hacklabs, Hackmeets and Free/Libre Open Source Software (FLOSS) models of 'practitioner-led collaborative practice' (see Yuill 2008).

In a similar fashion to Adorno, I do not necessarily want to examine these moments as 'interventions' as such; instead I want to look at how digital aesthetic works are presented for no obvious purpose, in contrast to a world in which things are normally presented as being for the sake of other things, and by this I mean instrumentally (see Jarvis 1998: 121). The key point for Adorno is not to oppose a contemplative ideal of the work of art against that of an instrumentalized one, but rather to criticize an entire framework within which artist practice takes place, such that 'the critique exercised a priori by art is that of action as a cryptogram of domination. . . . The effect of artworks is not that they present a latent praxis that corresponds to a manifest one, for their autonomy has moved far beyond such immediacy; rather, their effect is that of recollection, which they evoke by their existence' (Adorno 2004b: 241). I take two main cases of aesthetics and the computational, the 'new aesthetic', a constellation of objects and practices that bear the traces of the computational within them, for example, through digital artefacts, breakdown or structure, and the argument that code and algorithms are themselves in some sense aesthetic.

The New Aesthetic

The 'New Aesthetic' was initially introduced at South By South West (SXSW) on 12 March 2012, at a panel organized by James Bridle.[1] The panel was called 'The New Aesthetic: Seeing Like Digital Devices' and was primarily concerned with 'giv[ing] examples of these effects, products and artworks, and discuss[ing] the ways in which ways of [computer/robot] seeing are increasingly transforming ways of making and doing' (SXSW 2012). A number of post-panel write-ups were made by the participants, including Bridle (2012b), Cope (2012), Davies (2012), McNeil (2012) and Terrett (2012), who described what they saw as a digital aesthetic linked to the ubiquity of modern computation. Bruce Sterling who also attended the original panel consequently discussed how struck he was by the new aesthetic and how it went beyond a mere concern with computer/robot vision (Sterling 2012).

The new aesthetic can be described as an aesthetic that revels in seeing the grain of computation or, perhaps better, seeing the limitations or digital artefacts of a kind of digital glitch, sometimes called the 'aesthetic of failure' (see Jones 2011). Indeed,

> the debate on the aesthetic of digital code has been predominantly focused, on the non-representational and non-functional performativity of coding and its infinite possible infractions (errors, glitches and noise), emphasising that it is precisely these infractions that give code its real aesthetic value . . . [or] the sensorial alterations or affects produced by technology on the human body-subject. (Parisi and Portanova 2012)

Enabling robot/computer algorithms to 'see' by imposing computational 'pixels' on reality is also part of this new aesthetic (see Catt 2012). However, there is also an element of representation of a kind of digital past, or perhaps digital *passing*, in that the kinds of digital glitches, modes and forms that are chosen, are very much located historically where we are moving into a high-definition world of retina displays and high-pixel density experience (e.g. see Huff 2012). Sterling explains that the new aesthetics,

> concerns itself with "an eruption of the digital into the physical." That eruption was inevitable. It's been going on for a generation. It should be much better acculturated than it is. There are ways to make that stark, lava-covered ground artistically fertile and productive. (Sterling 2012)

Using a flâneur-like approach, James Bridle collected objects, artworks, buildings, places and images in a growing blog-based accumulation of things that he presents as exemplars of this new aesthetic (a collection or litany being an interesting computational form) (Bridle 2011a, b). Indeed there is an unmonumentality, a lo-res assemblage quality about these works, as forms of 'precarious' objects and artworks formed by digital 'unskill' (see Smith 2007). Bridle explains,

> I started noticing things like this in the world. This is a cushion on sale in a furniture store that's pixelated. This is a strange thing. This is a look, a style, a pattern that didn't previously exist in the real world. It's something that's come out of digital. It's come out of a digital way of seeing, that represents things in this form. The real world doesn't, or at least didn't, have a grain that looks like this. But you start to see it everywhere when you start looking for it. It's very pervasive. It seems like a style, a thing, and we have to look at where that style came from, and what it means, possibly. Previously things that would have been gingham or lacy patterns and this kind of thing is suddenly pixelated. Where does that come from? What's that all about? (Bridle 2011a)

His website, titled 'The New Aesthetic', displays an archival impulse and links to or archives found objects from across the internet (and which he captures in everyday life), piled together into a quantitative heap of computational aesthetic objects (Bridle 2012). Sterling (2012) explained,

> the "New Aesthetic" is a native product of modern network culture. It's from London, but it was born digital, on the Internet. The New Aesthetic is a "theory object" and a "shareable concept". . . . The New Aesthetic is "collectively intelligent." It's diffuse, crowdsourcey, and made of many small pieces loosely joined. It is rhizomatic, as the people at Rhizome would likely tell you. It's open-sourced, and triumph-of-amateurs. It's like its logo, a bright cluster of balloons tied to some huge, dark and lethal weight. (Sterling 2012)

Sterling rightly sees this as a symptomology with constituent parts including, 'information visualization. Satellite views. Parametric architecture. Surveillance cameras. Digital image processing. Data-mashed video frames. Glitches and corruption artifacts. Voxelated 3D pixels in real-world geometries. Dazzle camou. Augments. Render ghosts. And, last and least, nostalgic retro 8-bit graphics from the 1980s' (Sterling 2012). But the question that arises in relation to the writings of both Bridle and for Sterling is: what is going on here? What does this seemingly new computational aesthetic signify and what is its critical location? Sterling correctly, in my mind, rejects the notion of an aesthetic of the machines, or of computer vision, etc., what has been called *sensor-venacular* elsewhere, equally rejecting a kind of *hauntology* of the 1980s (Jones 2011), or *sensor-aesthetic* (Sloan 2011; see also Ellis 2011; Gyford 2011). Nor does an explicit link between this new aesthetic and SR/OOO necessarily help us understand this *pattern aesthetic* – although, perhaps, this is also revealing in SR/OOO's relation to computationality (Borenstein 2012; Kaganskiy 2012).

Ironically, this is happening at a time when most people's command of digital technology is weak and their understanding of the politics of technology is minimal. The new aesthetic might then, in its popular manifestations, and as evidenced by Bridle and Sterling, actually represent a weak form of understanding of the computational and its representation – perhaps even an attempt at a *domestication*. This seems especially true when we look at the examples often given, which at their most basic represent not the presently existing computationalism but a cartoon version, for example, 8-bit graphics or blocky lo-res visuals.

Inevitably there have been attacks on the notion of the new aesthetic which have tended to focus on its seeming 'internet meme', 'buzz', 'promotional strategy' and this I see as indicative of a wider set of concerns in relation to computation as a hegemonic order. Many of these discussions have a particular existential flavour, questioning the existence and longevity of the new aesthetic, for example, or beginning to draw the boundaries of what is 'in' or 'out' of the domain of new aesthetic things (See Twitter 2012). Grusin (2012), for example, claims: '[t]he "new aesthetic" is just the latest name for remediation, all dressed up with nowhere to go'. At such an early stage there is understandably some scepticism and, being mediated via Twitter, some sarcasm and dismissal, rather than substantive engagements with the questions raised by a moment presaged by the eruption of the digital into the everyday lifeworld, but there is also some partial support (e.g. see, Berry 2012b; Exinfoam 2012; Fernandez 2012; Owens 2012).

Nonetheless, it is certainly the case that one of the themes particular to the new aesthetic is a form of cultural practice related to a postmodern and fundamentally paranoid vision of being watched, observed, coded, processed or formatted. If Lash (2007) is correct that 'a society of ubiquitous media means a society in which power is increasingly in the algorithm', then the new aesthetic could be the aesthetic of the algorithm, and by extension a representation of these new forms of power. Indeed, this aspect of algorithmic surveillance and being subject to data collection is clearly a very timely experience, as we understand more and more the extent to which we are being tracked. The representational practices of the new aesthetic are often (but not always) retro showing computational processes as blocky and pixelated visually. So surveillance footage is usually low resolution, with the kinds of digital artefacts we expect to see in a computer-generated surveillance image – even if this is mere ornamentation in actuality. But the fact that computer vision, as a kind of scopic experience by the computer, is nonetheless an aesthetic that remains firmly human mediated, contrary to the claims of 'seeing like machines' means that the new aesthetic is an aestheticization of computational technology and computational techniques more generally.

Nonetheless, the new aesthetic is also important in a critical vein because it appears to have an inbuilt potentiality towards critical reflexivity, not only towards itself (does it exist?) but also towards its own artistic practice (is this art?), curation (should this be in galleries?) and technology (what is technology?). While these critical moments are often alienated into a supposed question posed by computational devices themselves, this moment offers the new aesthetic a critical sensitivity that is often absent in aesthetic practice. Indeed, we might say that there is an interesting utopian kernel to the new aesthetic, in terms of its visions and creations – what we might call the paradigmatic forms – which mark the crossing over of certain important boundaries, such as culture/nature, technology/human, economic/aesthetic and so on. Here I am thinking particularly of the notion of augmented humanity, or humanity 2.0 – a latent post-humanism that is intrinsic to the discourses of the new aesthetic (Fuller 2011). This criticality is manifested in the new aesthetic continually seeking to 'open up' black boxes of technology, to look inside at developments in science, technology and technique and to try to place them within histories and traditions – in the emergence of social contradictions, for example. But even an autonomous new aesthetic, as it were, highlights the anonymous and universal political and cultural domination represented by computational techniques which are now deeply embedded in systems that we experience in all aspects of our lives.

The new aesthetic, of course, is as much symptomatic of a computational world as itself subject to the forces that drive that world. This means that it has every potential to be sold, standardized and served up to the willing mass of consumers as any other neatly packaged product, perhaps even more so, with its ease of distribution and reconfiguration within computational systems, such as Twitter and Tumblr. But even in an impoverished consumerized aesthetic form, the new aesthetic still serves notice of computational thinking and processes. This is certainly one of the interesting dimensions to the new aesthetic both in terms of the materiality of computationality and in terms of the need to understand the logics of postmodern capitalism, even ones as abstract as obscure computational systems of control. The new aesthetic can be said to mediate the computational and its relationship to a particular way-of-being in the world and its instantiation in technical media (here specifically concerned with computational technology). This aspect of the new aesthetic lends itself to contributing to creating what Lash called 'crystalline intellectuals, who work less as an organ in the body of a social class and more as coders, writing algorithms, as designers and the like' by continuing to open up and question the internal structures of computationality and creating a ubiquitous politics (Lash 2007: 75).

The new aesthetic is particularly a visual form showing digital *surfaces* in a number of different places and contexts. It is also not purely a digital production or output, it can also be the concepts and frameworks of digital that are represented (e.g. voxels or three-dimensional pixels in everyday life). We could perhaps say that the new aesthetic is a form of 'breakdown' art linked to the *conspicuousness* of digital technologies; not just the use of digital tools, of course, but also a language of new media (as Manovich would say), the frameworks, structures, concepts and processes represented by computation, that is, both the presentation of computation and its representational modes. It not only represents computation, but also draws attention to this glitch ontology to a striking extent, for example, through the representation of the *conspicuousness* of glitches and other digital artefacts (also see Menkman 2010, for a notion of critical media aesthetics and the idea of glitch studies). Beaulieu et al. (2012) have called these approaches 'Network Realism' and sought to draw attention to some of these visual practices, particularly the way of producing these networked visualizations. However, the new aesthetic is interesting in remaining focused on the aesthetic in the first instance (rather than the sociological, etc.). This is useful in order to examine the emerging visual culture, but also to try to discern aesthetic forms instantiated within it.

The new aesthetic then might be the herald of a new kind of comprehensive digital archive, what we might call an *archive in motion* – what Bernard Stiegler called the *Anamnesis* (the embodied act of memory as recollection or remembrance) combined with *Hypomnesis* (the making-technical of memory through writing, photography, machines, etc.) (Stiegler n.d.). Thus, particularly in relation to the affordances given by the networked and social media within which it circulates, combined with a set of nascent practices of collection, archive and display, the new aesthetic is distinctive in a number of ways.

First, it gives a description and a way of representing and mediating the world in and through the digital, that is understandable as an infinite archive (or collection). Secondly, it alternately highlights that something digital is *happening* in culture – and which we have perhaps only barely been conscious of – and the way in which culture is happening to the digital. Lastly, the new aesthetic points the direction of travel for the possibility of a *Work of Art* in the digital age – something Heidegger thought impossible under the conditions of technicity, but which conceivably remains more open under computationality.

In this, the new aesthetic shows us that computation is a *pharmakon*, in that it is both potentially poison and cure for an age of pattern matching and pattern recognition. If the archive was the set of rules governing the range of expression following Foucault, and the database the grounding cultural logic of software cultures into the 'permanent extendibility' of software (Manovich 2013: 337), we might conclude that the New Aesthetic is the cultural eruption of the grammatization of software logics into everyday life. The new aesthetic can be seen as surfacing computational patterns, and in doing so articulates and represents the unseen and little-understood logic of computation, which lies under, over and in the interstices between the modular elements of an increasingly computational society.

The *pattern aesthetic* of the new aesthetic is deeply influenced by and reliant on patterns and abductive reasoning more generally. This is a common thread that links the lists and litanies of objects that seem to have nothing more in common than a difficult-to-reconcile and tenuous *digitality*, or perhaps a seeming retro towards older forms of digital rendering and reproduction. In actuality, it is no surprise that we see a return of 8-bit retro as it could perhaps be described as the abductive aesthetic par excellence, in as much as it enables an instant recognition of, and indeed serves as an important representation for the digital, even as the digital becomes high definition and less 'digital' by the day.

Patterns are also deeply concerned with computer pattern recognition, repeated elements, codes and structural elements that enable *something* to be recognized as a *type* of *thing* (see Harvey 2011 for a visualization of facial pattern recognition). This is not just visual, of course, and patterns may be recognized in data sets, textual archives, data points, distributions, non-visual sensors, physical movement or gestures, haptic forces, etc. Indeed, this points to the importance of information visualization as part of the abduction aesthetic in order to 'visualise' the patterns that are hidden in sets of data. This is also the link between the new aesthetic and the digital humanities (see Berry 2012b; Gold 2012).

The fact that *abduction aesthetics* are networked, sharable, modular, 'digital' and located in both the digital and analogue worlds is appropriate as they follow the colonization of the lifeworld by the technics of computationality. We could look at David Hockney's Fresh Flowers (Grant 2010) and the fact that he links the artwork he produces to the medial affordances of the computational device, in this case an iPad, stating 'when using his iPhone or iPad to draw, the features of the devices tend to shape his choice of subject. . . . The fact that it's illuminated makes you choose luminous subjects' (Freeman 2012). Parisi and Portanova further argue for an algorithmic aesthetic with their notion of 'soft thought',

> the aesthetic of soft thought precisely implies that digital algorithms are autonomous, conceptual modes of thinking, a thinking that is always already a mode of feeling ordered in binary codes, and is not to be confused with sensing or perceiving. Numerical processing is always a feeling, a simultaneously physical and conceptual mode of feeling data, physical in the actual operations of the hardware-software machine, conceptual in the grasp of numbers as virtualities or potentials. (Parisi and Portanova 2012)

The point I want to make is that Bridle's (2012a) collection is symptomatic of an emerging real-time aesthetic of the algorithm, and that the digital requires representation. It is also significant that the means of collecting these litanies of digital and pseudo-digital objects is through a computational frame and further that the collection is made possible through new forms of computational curation tools, such as Tumblr and Pinterest (2012). The real-time as an aesthetic concern was discussed by Jack Burnham as far back as 1969, who explained that '[r]eal-time systems gather and process data from environments, in time to effect future events within those environments' (Shanken 2012). Here, value is produced on the basis of an 'immediate, interactive, and necessarily contingent exchange of information'. Burnham juxtaposed this model with the 'traditional aesthetic notion of "ideal time", in which the contemplation of beauty occurs in theoretical isolation from the societal and temporal contingencies' (Shanken 2012). Although Burnham has a particularly cybernetic notion of the real-time, even for computation, and by definition its carriers, code and software, which withdraws into the background of our experience, it is probable that we will increasingly see the foregrounding of a representation of, and for, the real-time digital/computational in the way that Burnham suggests. Indeed Burnham,

> observed that, paralleling the introduction of computerised real-time systems into the operations of government, finance, and the military, some experimental artists . . . were increasingly approaching art with an

emphasis on real-time issues. "What a few artists are beginning to give the public is real time information, information with no hardware value, but with software significance for effecting awareness of events in the present." (Shanken 2012)

In some ways, 8-bit images and domesticated real-time streams are perhaps reassuring and still comprehensible as different from and standing in opposition to the everyday world people inhabit – the source of the 'digital divide' identified by Bishop (2012). In actuality, however, the glitches and retro 8-bit-esque look that we see in new aesthetic pixelated works are far away from the capabilities of contemporary machines, and their blocky ontologies provide only limited guidance on the way in which software now organizes and formats our shared, and sharable, world (Berry 2011a). Indeed, in some senses we might be experiencing a transition from an object-oriented to a software-oriented culture due to the processual nature of these real-time streams and their post-object construction of algorithmic relations. So ironically, just as digital technologies and software mediate our experience and engagement with the world, often invisibly, so the 'digital' and 'software' is itself mediated and made visible through the representational forms of pixelation and glitch.

While today we tend to think of the 8-bit pixelation, satellite photos, CCTV images and the like, it is probable that alternative, computational forms may prevail, such as increasing use of geons and other geometric representation forms. The importance of patterns in computation capitalism will likely produce a kind of cognitive dissonance with individuals expecting *pattern aesthetics* everywhere, understood as a form of apophenia, that is, the experience of seeing meaningful patterns or connections in random or meaningless data (called a Type-1 error in statistics). Indeed, they may seek digital or abductive *explanations* for certain kinds of aesthetic, visual or even non-visual experiences which may not be digital or produced through computational means at all, a *digital pareidolia*. Pareidolia involves seeing importance in vague and random phenomenon, for example, a face in a random collection of dots on paper. By 'digital pareidolia' I am gesturing towards seeing digital causes for things that happen in everyday life. Indeed, under a regime of computationality in the future it might be considered stranger to believe that things might have non-digital causes. Thus apophenia would be the norm in a highly digital computational society, perhaps even a significant benefit to one's life chances and well-being if finding patterns becomes increasingly lucrative.[2]

This representation of the digital is, of course, an interesting feature of the new aesthetic as much as (1) there may be the mediation of the computal in the creation of aesthetic objects or (2) the affordances of digital vision that creates certain kinds of recognizable patterned digital artefacts (see Ellis 2011; Sloan 2011). This is an element of 'down-sampled' representation of a kind of digital past, or perhaps digital passing, in that the kinds of digital glitches, modes and forms that are chosen are very much located historically (Berry 2012a). We might think of these alternative formulations or threads within the new aesthetic as (i) *representations of the digital*, (ii) *mediation by digital processes* and (iii) *digital/computer vision*. In any case, it is clear that so far the main focus of the new aesthetic has been visual patterns, and the wider sensorium needs to be considered in relation to computational processes.

Further, following Charles Sanders Peirce notion of abduction, he also introduces the concept of *musement* to describe the mode of thinking relevant to the aesthetic enjoyment of the abductive as pattern-matching. Peirce defined musement as 'pure play' which is strikingly receptive and leisurely (Salas 2009: 468).

> It is "a lively exercise of one's powers" and yet "has no rules, except this very law of liberty" (6.458). Though musement is leisurely in that it allows the muser to assume different standpoints, it also involves deliberate observation and meditation. "It begins passively enough with drinking in the impression of some nook in one the three universes [a primary universe of sensations or raw experience; a secondary universe of reactions to sensory data; and a tertiary universe of representations or signs used to relate the primary and secondary universes]. But impression soon passes into attentive observation, observation into musing, musing into a lively give-and-take between self and self" (6.459). While in a sense passive and receptive, musement is also that in which "logical analysis can be put to full efficiency" (6.461). We might say that, while "musing" one is both "active" and "contemplative". . . . (Salas 2009: 468, original referencing preserved)

The similarity is striking between Peirce's notion of musement and the Greek concept of *theôria* or contemplation, which according to Aristotle was the highest activity of leisure. Indeed, Peirce distinguishes musement from 'reverie' or 'vacancy and dreaminess' (Salas 2009: 290). This element of playfulness is relevant to a discussion of the aesthetics of computationality, and indeed forms a large part of the new aesthetic that Bridle (2011) and Sterling (2012) describe. It is interesting to note that a properly distanced *musement* is indeed possible towards the *abduction aesthetic* when mediated through the real-time streams made available through Tumblr and other digital asset/object technologies.

In a slightly different register, it is worth looking in some detail at the claims advanced by SR/OOO in relation to the new aesthetic itself (Bogost 2012; Borenstein 2012; Jackson 2012). More specifically, some SR/OOO practitioners critique the new aesthetic in terms of what is considered a misplaced focus on the merely computational and attempt to redefine the new aesthetic in the philosophical problematics of SR/OOO. For me, this is to have the argument the wrong way round. SR/OOO and the new aesthetic must be critically engaged with in relation to computation itself. Indeed, we might say that SR/OOO is standing on its head. This raises the question of what is at stake in accepting the claims of SR/OOO and what are the implications both theoretically and empirically for the new aesthetic more generally. First it is worth exploring what SR/OOO are claiming. Borenstein argues,

> I believe that Sterling is wrong. I believe that the New Aesthetic is actually striving towards a fundamentally new way of imagining the relations between things in the world. To convince you of this, I'll make a case that the New Aesthetic strongly resonates with a recent movement in philosophy called Object-Oriented Ontology and that establishing a closer alliance with OOO might be a way to increase the precision of the New Aesthetic vocabulary and enrich its process by pointing towards new modes of imagining its objects of fascination. (Borenstein 2012)

Here, Borenstein is arguing that the new aesthetic has an SR/OOO predilection or 'resonates' with the claims and descriptions of SR/OOO. In other words, the claim is that the new aesthetics is merely an aesthetic subset of SR/OOO, and as Bogost further argues that the new aesthetic needs to get 'weirder', claiming,

> It's true that computers are a particularly important and influential kind of thing in the world, and indeed I myself have spent most of my career pondering how to use, make, and understand them. But they are just one thing among so many more: airports, sandstone, koalas, climate, toaster pastries, kudzu, the International 505 racing dinghy, the Boeing 787 Dreamliner, the brand name "TaB." Why should a new aesthetic interested only in the relationship between humans and computers, when so many other relationships exist just as much? Why stop with the computer, like Marinetti foolishly did with the race car? (Bogost 2012)

Bogost claims that the new aesthetic is about the 'relationship between humans and computers' and he argues that instead it should be concerned with ontology, in this case the object-oriented relationships between lots of different kinds of objects. Additionally, Jackson identifies, although he also in my mind mistakenly rejects, the importance of 'disorientation' for the new aesthetic,

> The really interesting element of the new aesthetic is that it presents genuinely interesting stuff, but Bridle's delivery strategy is set to "gushing

disorientation." At present, it's the victim of the compulsive insular network it feeds off from. It presents little engagement with the works themselves instead favouring bombardment and distraction. Under these terms, aesthetics only leads to a banal drudgery, where everything melts together into a depthless disco. Any depth to the works themselves are forgotten . . . Memes require instant satisfaction. Art requires depth. (Jackson 2012)

While I think the claim that 'Art requires depth' is a somewhat conservative notion of what art is or should be, it seems to me that disorientation, or what I would call, following Heidegger, *frantic disorientation*, is perhaps an important marker of the specificity of the new aesthetic. Somewhat reminiscent of claims of 'depthlessness' that attended the rise of postmodernism, for example (see Jameson 2006). So in what way would a reading of the new aesthetic through SR/OOO help understand the new aesthetic? The claim is that the new aesthetic points the way to thinking about the relationships between different objects without the mediation of human beings. That is, that we can think in a non-anthropomorphic way, without what Harman calls the 'idea of human access' (Shaviro 2011). As Bogost argues,

Our job is to amplify the black noise of objects to make the resonant frequencies of the stuffs inside them hum in credibly satisfying ways. Our job is to write the speculative fictions of these processes, of their unit operations. Our job is to get our hands dirty with grease, juice, gunpowder, and gypsum. Our job is to go where everyone has gone before, but where few have bothered to linger. (Borenstein 2012)

Bogost (2012) argues that his 'version of object-oriented ontology . . . concerns the experience of objects. What is it like to be a bonobo or a satellite or a pixel?' (Bogost 2012). Putting aside the unlikelihood of discerning 'what it is like to be' something like a pixel – indeed, to me the very question seems to be confusing the fundamental quality of human beings (as *dasein*) able to raise the question of their own being with that of a pixel, which *prime facie* does not (Heidegger 1978). This raises an *anti-correlationist paradox* in the use of human categories to describe 'alien objects' interiority. Not that this method has to be completely unproductive, indeed, Bogost's claims that the 'weird' points to his attempt to do something new or different – however, I would argue, it cannot truly be 'weird' enough, restricted as it is to a descriptive project in which cultural critique is usually dismissed. Indeed, the conservativeness of SR/OOO is apparent when the subject of politics or historicity in relation to philosophy is raised. Added to this, SR/OOO continues the use of human categories even as it is articulating what it considers to be a non-anthropomorphic mode. For example, Borenstein argues, the,

> [new aesthetic] want[s] to know what CCTV means for social networks, what book scanning means for iOS apps, and what face detection means for fashion. And again these objects are not just interesting to each other as a set of constraints and affordances for the objects' human makers but for the hidden inner lives of the objects themselves throughout their existence. (Borenstein 2012)

Does the idea of 'inner lives' even make any sense for iOS apps, CCTV or pixels? Following Heidegger (1978), I would even argue that it doesn't make much sense for humans, let alone SunChips and Doritos. Bogost's attempts to link SR/OOO and new aesthetics by a notion of 'Alien Aesthetics' is similarly problematic, where he argues,

> [t]his Alien Aesthetics would not try to satisfy our human drive for art and design, but to fashion design fictions that speculate about the aesthetic judgments of objects. If computers write manifestos, if Sun Chips make art for Doritos, if bamboo mocks the bad taste of other grasses – what do these things look like? Or for that matter, when toaster pastries convene conferences or write essays about aesthetics, what do they say, and how do they say it? (Jackson 2012)

Again we see the *anti-correlationist paradox* in as much as objects are now considered to make 'aesthetic judgments' of other objects. Patently, 'pastries' do not 'write essays about aesthetics' nor about anything else, indeed, in trying so hard to avoid anthropomorphism ontologically, Bogost appears to allow it in the backdoor through metaphor. Here we might nod towards Heidegger who emphasized the importance of practices in understanding being (for Dasein), and the writing of essays is crucial to the understanding of being a student, for example, not to being a pastry (Heidegger 1978). We are thus left with speculative fictional statements akin to vignettes about objects 'truth' or 'correctness' that nonetheless offer only descriptions of the reified objects disconnected from the social and political context in which they reside. For example, Sun Chips are a product of consumer capitalism and discussing the 'object' and its aesthetic tastes begins to sound like the anthropomorphism of branding statements and marketing campaigns, that is a process of naturalization of the market. SR/OOO is unable, or unwilling, to engage with the way in which objects as objects are produced in a market economy that seeks to hide the social labour that produced them. A reason to be suspicious of its claims to be an explanatory framework for helping to understand the new aesthetic.

The specificity of the new aesthetic, as a comportment and a set of practices, is important because of its implicit recognition of the extent to which digital media has permeated our everyday lives. Indeed, the new aesthetic is a form of 'breakdown' art linked to the conspicuousness of digital technologies. That is both the representation of computation and its representational modes at the level of the screenic. Now I want to drill down further into these issues related to an aesthetics of computation itself by an examination of code aesthetics and related practices.

Code aesthetics

Code aesthetics refers to a number of different notions applied in particular to the creation and practices related to computer code and software. In this section we will briefly examine the main issues related to code and the aesthetic. Indeed, it is useful to consider the nature of code aesthetics in relation to that of the computational more generally (Berry 2011a). Here, the focus is on computer code as an aesthetic moment, and the aesthetic sensibility in the writing of and practices that relate to computer code/ software. This is not to deny that practices related to writing code, such as live coding, are not relevant, indeed they offer interesting scope for examination of their aesthetic and practice-oriented components (see Yuill 2008); however, in this section the aim is to focus on code itself as a textual aesthetic form. These formulations tend to separate the aesthetic from the political, social and economic, and for the sake of brevity this section will reflect that analytic formulation. However, linkages between them are clearly important, and indeed form part of the critique that critical theory introduces into code and new media aesthetic practices (see Cox 2013).

While the importance and relevance of code aesthetic is helpful in under-standing computer code and its related practices, Marino (2006) cautions that, 'to critique code merely for its functionality or aesthetics, is to approach code with only a small portion of our analytic tools'. This is an important re-joinder to efforts that consider code aesthetics outside the practices and context of its production, use and distribution, and also crucially, its political economy.

To some extent, the history of code aesthetics also reflects differing conceptions of the 'online', 'digital', 'virtual' and 'cyberspace', and how *beauty* or an aesthetic *disinterestedness* can be usefully understood in relation to these concepts. This is important because within code and programming culture itself a new form of technical aesthetics has emerged relatively recently. This is linked to a notion of elegance and beauty in both presentation and execution of the code, and relies on both social and community standards of aesthetics, but also often claims an autonomous aesthetic standard which acts as counterfactuals to most code production. In some sense this is reminiscent of aesthetics as the highest possible level of performance, code aesthetics then emphasize their own impossibility, such that 'the proof of the tour de force, the realization of the unrealizable, could be adduced from the most authentic works' (Adorno 2004b: 108).

The growing accessibility and influence on computer code as a representative mode, that is, where it is used to convey some form of semiotic function for code/software, is a growing phenomenon – indeed the new aesthetic and related popular representations of algorithms often rely on code as a signifier for the computational. This includes the reproduction of code-like textual forms, including certain kinds of Ascii art, but more particularly programming code, usually from third-generation programming languages, such as C++, Java and so forth, although other representative forms also exist and are used – such as retro graphic formats and pixelated text. The growing aestheticization of computer code is related to its mediality, particularly moving from CRT-based displays that were constructed through heavily textual interfaces, such as the VT-100/200. Indeed, many of the programmers and hackers of a previous generation remain wedded to a simulated command line aesthetic of white, green or orange on black text – which remains an important and widely recognized visual metonym for the computational.

Increasingly, however, contemporary computer-programming integrated development environments (IDEs) use colour, formatting and other graphical techniques to create an aesthetic of code that gives the text a signification and depth not available in monochrome versions – for example, marking code commentary in green, etc. This increased use of graphics capabilities in the presentation of computer code has correspondingly created new visual forms of programming, such as live coding, like a real-time coding environment for music and visual arts, and visual programming systems that integrate UI and graphic elements into the programming practices. Within the context of an aesthetics of computer code, it is clear that the aesthetic is related to the functional structure of the language, and here I can only gesture towards the increasing reliance on obfuscation in programming language design, and therefore the idea of 'hidden' or 'private' elements of the structure of the code, as opposed to 'available' or 'public' elements and the related aesthetic practices associated with it (see Berry 2011; Dexter 2012).

Increasingly, the writing practices of computer code, combined with reading and understanding, have become deeply inscribed with practices of an aesthetic sensibility. This is sometimes also linked to the Hacker ethic of playfulness and exploratory thinking. The notion of beautiful code is intertwined with both aesthetic and functional characteristics that need to be carefully unpacked to appreciate how this beauty is understood and recognized within the coding communities around which computer code is developed (see Oram and Wilson 2007). These practices are deeply related to what Donald Knuth wrote in the highly influential *Literate Programming* published in 1992, which was described as having a, 'main concern . . . with exposition and excellence of style. . . [the programmer] strives for a program that is comprehensible because its concepts have been introduced . . . [and] nicely reinforce each other' (Black 2002: 131). That is, well-crafted code is reflected in both its form *and* its content as a 'complete' aesthetics of computer code. In some sense then, aesthetically 'beautiful' code avoids what is sometimes referred to as 'messy code', although clearly the boundary construction around what is beautiful and what is not is also interesting to explore. Indeed, examples given by obfuscated code also serve to demonstrate the aesthetic and visual, rather than the merely textual, dimension of code aesthetics (see Berry 2011a: 87–93). In this the code can be said to cross over from the functional into the aesthetic and as such become something to admire as an aesthetic work in its own right but 'there is no denying that even in the principle of construction, in the dissolution of materials and their subordination to an imposed unity, once again something smooth, harmonistic, a quality of pure logicality, is conjured up that seeks to establish itself as ideology' the creation of functionless functioning (Adorno 2004b: 57). A machinic quality of beauty as pure function, representative of the social totality in which code is formed even as 'historical processes and functions are already sedimented in [it] and speak out of [it]' (Adorno 2004b: 112).

This has led to interesting discussions of the relation of code to poetry, and the related aesthetic sensibility shared between them (see Cox et al. 2006). Sharon Hopkins's perl poem 'rush' is a good example of this (see Berry 2011a: 49). Indeed, discussions vary over, for example, the use of camel case, or the contraction of names in code into one word, for example 'ThisIsAFunction', versus the use of underscores, such as 'This_is_a_function' highlights the way in which the formulations of programmers now becomes the material of artists. Additionally, arguments over formatting, indentation, variable names, namespaces and so on are all bound up in the definition of well-constructed computer code. Remarkably, these examples continue to remain an important aspect of contestation over the most aesthetically pleasing code, which is that which has effaced the traces of their production, disguising the human labour that produced it.

In this chapter, I have tried to think about the question raised by aesthetics in relation to computational capitalism drawing from critical theory to think about the *conditions of possibility* for the computational as aesthetic, that is, for the possibility of surfacing the digital through representational, archival and mediational forms. The aesthetics of the computational are then a 'rational refuge for mimesis in a world in which the mimetic impulse is progressively suppressed in classificatory thinking' (Jarvis 1998: 116). More so, as this computational aesthetics claims a dignity rather than a price, even as under late capitalism this claim becomes ever more illusionary, it nonetheless critiques the computational by being an object of the computational which is not fully incorporated into the logics of instrumentalism. Thus the new aesthetic, for example, contributes to a sense of reality, a growing sense or suspicion towards the digital, a disavowal or sense of the limits or even the absolute, because experienced reality beyond everyday life is too difficult for most members of a society to move or understand. A heuristic pattern for everyday life – the *parameterization* of our being-in-the-world, the use of a default (digital) grammar for everyday life, for example, mediated through, say, the 140 characters in Twitter or other social media. The new aesthetic and related computational aesthetics also raise the question of what ways of seeing are possible at all within computational capitalism, and computationality more generally. In the next chapter, I want to look specifically at the problematic this raises in relation to the related question of reason and emancipation in a computational society.

7

Critical praxis and the computational

In this chapter, I look at the implications of the distinction between reason and emancipation for both material and intellectual culture in relation to the digital. Following critical theory, the aim is to develop a notion of software being able to be interpreted as 'a code language for processes taking place in society', but which nonetheless is able to function relatively autonomously. Clearly one of the most important tasks of a critical theory in relation to the digital is to understand what has become an enormous technical system far in excess of that described by the founding members of the Frankfurt School. While they attempted to identify trends and trajectories from the beginnings of the media systems and the culture industry they observed, events have in many cases moved beyond their initial descriptions and analysis. For this reason an urgent task for critical theory is to rethink the new technological forms created by computation, especially the phenomenon of computational devices.

This means a new kind of literacy is required for a new kind of critical theory, including what I call iteracy, and which needs to draw back the screens and interfaces, and develop a deeper critical disposition to the underlying materiality and agency of the computational. This includes the notion of political economy as labour clearly remains an important mediator in computational economies; however, we remain limited in our analysis if we do not follow the lead of the critical theorists in rethinking the relationship between base and superstructure beyond a purely determinate relationship. That is, to appreciate how software is now culture and culture is rapidly becoming softwarized. Borgmann argues:

An important part of genuine world citizenship today is scientific and technological literacy. Here one may hope that an appreciation of the force of technology, nourished by metatechnological practices, would inspire the attention and dedication needed to appropriate the scientific and engineering principles on which the technology rests. Neither the resentful if dutiful, service to the technological machinery that we discharge in labour nor the distracted pleasure of consumption are conducive to the study of technology. But the voluntary discipline . . . and the desire to join the two in order to regain the cosmopolitan franchise may be helpful to the pursuit of scientific and technological education. (1984: 248)

Throughout this book there has been the aim to provide a pathway towards which a critical praxis could be actuated in relation to the computational. The broad contours of such an approach are realized in a commitment to some form of political praxis, critical theorizing and development of a constellation of concepts for thinking about the computal and its inherent contradictions. Added to this is the urgent need for a critical literacy of the digital. As Kellner and Share argue, critical literacy 'gives individuals power over their culture and thus enables people to create their own meanings and identities and to shape and transform the material and social conditions of their culture and society' (Kellner and Share 2005: 381). Lash too argues that this must be 'theoretically infused hands-on work in new media, art, architecture, cultural policy and politics' (Lash 2007: 75). As Horkheimer explained, 'let the sentence that tools are extensions of men's organs be turned around, so that organs are also extensions of men's tools' (Jay 1973: 81). Indeed, computation and its related ontology is a historical condition, and as computation exaggerates the present at the expense of the past, it conforms to Horkheimer and Adorno's claim that this is 'loss of memory as the transcendental condition of science. All reification is forgetting' (Horkheimer and Adorno 2002: 191). The challenge for critical theory is to adjust to the movement of history and contest computation as the 'multiplicity of forms is reduced to position and arrangement, history to fact, things to matter. . . . Formal logic [as] a schema for making the world calculable' (Horkheimer and Adorno 2002: 4).

Part of this approach is to think about how the arrival of computational devices, which on the whole remain opaque to us as *black boxes* in our societies, is beginning to have such profound impacts. It is hardly surprisingly anymore that they do so; indeed, with the greater sophistication of software and hardware, the delegation of extremely complex cognitive activities is a fact of our societies. This indeed offers a unique opportunity for critical theorists as computational devices manifest a possibility of a material site for the analysis of the contradictions of computational and cognitive capitalism. This involves a greater awareness of how power is manifested in technical systems, and how we increasingly find we are mediated and sometimes directly controlled by writings (software) that we can no longer read, and yet which constantly breaks down, fails, glitches and demonstrates the profound stupidity of computation as mere calculation. The increased reliance on computational systems, and the inherent trust placed with them, particularly by what Boltanksi (2011) calls the 'dominant class', offers an important site for critique, but requires a critical praxis that includes their hacking, interrupting and reconfiguration into new pathways and possibilities. Indeed, if critical theory is dedicated to a project of emancipation, then it seems clear that there will be an increasing need for critical theories of software, and critical approaches to the application of rationalization within these systems and their inherent contradictions. Adorno (2005a) wrote in 1951 about the effect of ruthless rationalization on the norms of a society and their communicative interactions:

> If time is money, it seems moral to save time, above all one's own, and such parsimony is excused by consideration for others. One is straightforward. Every sheath interposed between men in their transactions is felt as a disturbance to the functioning of the apparatus, in which they are not only objectively incorporated but with which they proudly identify themselves. That, instead of raising their hats, they greet each other with the hallos of indifference, that, instead of letters, they send each other inter-office communications without address or signature, are random symptoms of a sickness of contact. Estrangement shows itself precisely in the elimination of distance between people. (Adorno 2005a: 41)

The computal in its own way is producing new forms of rationalized communication of estrangement and alienation while paradoxically making it easier than ever to be in constant communication and contact. Today the condition of everyday life is represented by constantly turned down faces glancing at notifications on mobile phones, or distraction from hidden computational devices and wearable technologies. This sense of distraction and its contribution to the heteronomy of the individual raise important questions about our being-in-the-world when we are constantly pulled out of the world. Indeed, this connects to wider questions about how the digital can be reconfigured to contribute to emancipation rather than rationalization. Indeed a crucial part of this has to be moving beyond the commodity layer, the surface of the technology and opening these so-called black boxes, as both technologies and metaphors, that so demand our attention today.

For example, through an analysis of the financial black boxes, placed within the context of a computational society, we can see how in the institution of market exchange antagonism is created and reproduced that could at any time bring organized society to ultimate catastrophe and destroy it. Even as class consciousness remains weak today, it still exists, and particularly in times of financial uncertainty and crisis, such as the 2008–13 financial crisis, the differences between classes become a new site of contestation. Indeed, one of the possible means of such critique is the very disturbing ability of computation to record everything, to create logs and inscriptions that map the very contradictions in the machinery of computation that need to be brought to the surface – and these records are located in databases, computer algorithms and interfaces in addition to documentation. Computation in its classificatory and material effects creates and prescribes categories and classes upon individuals which can be made manifest in the contradictory implementations of what is claimed to be a universal system of rationality. In other words computational domination plays out very differently for the leader of the multinational corporation than it does for the shop-floor worker or teacher. For example, computational systems may be brought into an institution to address the needs of 'austerity' and 'doing more with less' but play out in the creation of prescriptive algorithms whose monitoring functions at differing levels of intensity creates inequalities, conflicts and new forms of solidarity. Indeed, communities of practice can be built around reflexively creating and deconstructing such tools, and the realization that such systems are fragile and open to contestation, change and revision, but also that such systems can create new epistemic knowledges, such as through computational reflexivity, and new structures of power. In other words, computation is intrinsically linked to the question of logistics and the capacity to become organized (Rossiter 2007) and the questions of 'how are we constituted as subjects of our own knowledge? How are we constituted as subjects who exercise or submit to power relations? How are we constituted as moral subjects of our own actions?' (Foucault 1984). The aim then is to explore some of these questions in relation to new circuits of power that are produced within computationality, where moments of conflict occur and how they can form part of a critical praxis of the computational to contribute to a critical interrogation of the present.

Black boxes

In these real-time stream computational ecologies, the notion of the human is one that is radically reconceptualized in contrast to the 'deep attention' of previous ages. Indeed, the user is constantly bombarded with information from multiple data streams, all in real-time, and increasingly needs complementary technology to manage and comprehend this data flow to avoid information overload. Hayles (2007) argues that this creates a need for 'hyper attention'. Additionally, this has an affective dimension as the user is expected to desire the real-time stream, to be in it, to follow it, and to participate in it, and where the user opts out, the technical devices are being developed to manage this too through curation, filtering and notification systems. Of course, this desiring subject is therefore then expected to pay for these streaming experiences, or even, perhaps, for better filtering, curation and notification streams as the raw data flow will be incomprehensible without them (see Berry 2011a: 142–71). Forty years ago this was identified by Simon as information overload; he wrote,

> The critical task is not to generate, store or distribute information but to filter it so that the processing demands on the components of the system, human and mechanical, will not exceed their capacities. A good rule of thumb for a modern information system might be that no new component should be added to the system unless it is an information *compressor* – that is, unless it is designed to receive more information that it transmits. The scarce resource today is not information, but capacity to process it. (Lawrence 1983: 14, original emphasis)

Today streams send huge quantities of information to us, but rather than being compressors, they seek to provide as much detail as possible, for the compression or curation of these streams that make them comprehensible one has to pay for an additional service. Search, discovery and experimentation require computational devices to manage the relationship with the flow of data and allow the user to step into and out of a number of different streams in an intuitive and natural way. This is because the web 'becomes a stream. A real time, flowing, dynamic data stream of information – that we as users and participants can dip in and out of and whether we participate in them or simply observe we are . . . a part of this flow. Stowe Boyd talks about this as the web as flow: "the first glimmers of a web that isn't about pages and browsers"' (Borthwick 2009).

Of course, the user becomes a source of data too, essentially a real-time stream themselves, feeding their own narrative data stream into the cloud via compactants, data which is itself analysed, aggregated and fed back to the user and other users as patterns of data. This real-time computational feedback mechanism may create many new possibilities for computational citizens and services that are able to leverage the masses of data in interesting and useful ways. Indeed, systems are already being designed to auto-curate user-chosen streams, to suggest alternatives and to structure user choices in particular ways (using stream transformers, aggregation and augmentation) such as Google Now, Siri and related notification and contextual computing interfaces. In some senses then this algorithmic process is the real-time construction of a person's possible 'futures' or their 'futurity', the idea, even, that eventually the curation systems will know 'you' better than you know yourself. The teleology of the real-time age is that through technology one can know oneself, both the flaws and the problems, and self-medicate, self-configure or manage to make the future self a better, healthier and a more educated person. This means that the user is 'made' as a part of the system, that is, the user does not ontologically precede the real-time streams, rather the system is a socio-technical network which 'is not connecting identities which are already there, but a network that configures ontologies' (Callon 1998).

This is the computational real-time imaginary envisaged by corporations such as Google that want to tell you what you should be doing next (Jenkins 2010), presenting knowledge as a real-time stream, creating/curating 'augmented humanity'. As Hayles (1999) states:

> Modern humans are capable of more sophisticated cognition than cavemen not because moderns are smarter . . . but because they have constructed smarter environments in which to work. (Hayles 1999: 289)

This *imaginary* of everyday life, a feedback loop within and through streams of data, is predicated on the use of technical devices that allow us to manage and rely on these streaming feeds. Combined with an increasing social dimension to the web, with social media, online messaging and new forms of social interaction, this allows behaviour to be modified in reaction to the streams of data received. However, to facilitate the use of these streams the technologies are currently under construction and open to intervention before they become concretized into specific forms. We should ask questions about how participative we want this stream-based ecology to be, how filtered and shaped do we want it, who should be the curators, and whom can we trust to do this.

Nonetheless, it seems clear that distant reading of streams will become increasingly important. These are skills that at present are neither normal practice for individuals, nor do we see strong system interfaces for managing this mediation yet. This distant reading will be, by definition, somewhat cognitively intense, strengthening the notion of a 'now' and intensifying temporal perception. This is a cognitive style reminiscent of a Husserlian 'comet' subjectivity, with a strong sense of self in the present, but which tails away into history (Berry 2011a: 148). It would also require a self that is strongly coupled to technology, facilitating the possibility of managing a stream-like subjectivity in the first place. Today, memory, history, cognition and self-presentation are all increasingly being mediated through computational devices and it is inevitable that to manage the additional real-time stream data flows new forms of cognitive support software-enabled systems will be called for.

So, more tentatively I would like to suggest an interesting paradox connected with the real-time stream, in that it encourages this comportment towards futurity. That is the real-time streaming technologies that are the hallmark of computationality are geared not towards satisfying immediate desires, but towards the creation of a condition of waiting, of a deferred gratification towards the completed self. This, following Derrida, we might call 'Messianic' (as a structure of experience rather than a religion) (Derrida 1994: 211), connecting the real-time stream to an expectation or an opening towards an entirely ungraspable and unknown other, a 'waiting without horizon of expectation' (Derrida 1994: 211). As Derrida writes:

> Awaiting without horizon of the wait, awaiting what one does not expect yet or any longer, hospitality without reserve, welcoming salutation accorded in advance to the absolute surprise of the arrivant from whom or from which one will not ask anything in return and who or which will not be asked to commit to the domestic contracts of any welcoming power (family, state, nation, territory, native soil or blood, language, culture in general, even humanity), just opening which renounces any right to property, any right in general, messianic opening to what is coming, that is, to the event that cannot be awaited as such, or recognized in advance therefore, to the event as the foreigner itself, to her or to him for whom one must leave an empty place, always, in memory of the hope—and this is the very place of spectrality. (Derrida 1994: 81)

The Messianic refers to a structure of existence that involves waiting. Waiting even in activity, and a ceaseless openness towards a future that can never be circumscribed by the horizons of significance that we inevitably bring to bear upon the possible future. As Tripp (2005) argues, 'the global communications networks, although often invasive and dangerously reductive, also serve as privileged sites of messianic possibility precisely because of their accelerated virtualization'. This is because being connected to the real-time stream and the data provided in the streams is always partial, incomplete and as such the project of the self remains to be completed, to be waited upon. This future quantified self, the realization of the teleological implicit in this computational notion of the 'full' human being, is one that one works towards, spending a lifetime tuning, constructing, reconciling and accounting for. This is the messianic horizon of real-time streaming technologies, an eschatological futurity, a towards-which that sets up the condition for acting today based on the collection of personal data, statistics, actuarial comparisons and self-monitoring. In this, the messianic is situated in a moment of hesitation, and for Walter Benjamin, that moment is one of 'danger' as the past flashes up before disappearing forever. For Derrida, it is a moment of 'haunting' – the spectral other makes its visitation in the disjunction between presence and absence, life and death, matter and spirit, that conditions representation. Indeed, Tripp argues,

> Although the messianic "trembles on the edge" of this event, we cannot anticipate its arrival. Because the arrival is never contingent upon any specific occurrence, the messianic hesitation "does not paralyze any decision, any affirmation, any responsibility. On the contrary, it grants them their elementary condition." The moment of hesitation – the spectral moment – enables us to act as though the impossible might be possible, however limited the opportunities for radical change may appear to be in our everyday experiences. (Tripp 2005)

This futurity raises important questions about the autonomy of the human agent, coupled as it is with the auto-curation of the stream-processing, not just providing information to but actively constructing, directing and even creating the socio-cognitive conditions for the subjectivity of the real-time stream, an *algorithmic humanity*. A subject with a comportment towards *waiting* which forgets as a condition of everyday life and lives, therefore, in a radical present. Indeed, as Derrida suggests, this,

> obliges us more than ever to think the virtualization of space and time, the possibility of virtual events whose movement and speed prohibit us more than ever (more and otherwise than ever, for this is not absolutely and thoroughly new) from opposing presence to its representation, "real time" to "deferred time," effectivity to its simulacrum, the living to the non-living, in short, the living to the living-dead of its ghosts. (Derrida 1994: 212)

Indeed, the consequence of this is the inevitable emergence of a *computational inequality* in that the streams of the rich and powerful will flow faster and deeper, and therefore the more data they will have to think with. The dominant classes 'now' will be more complete, clearer and accurate as their computational systems algorithmically sort their streams automatically. The wider the knowledge that can be bought, the better the access and the computational analysis. This is not a computational divide between the computational haves and the computational have-nots, but the reduction of all knowledge to the result of an algorithm. The postmodern rich won't just think they are better, indeed they won't necessarily be educated to a higher level at all, rather they will just have the better cognitive support technology that allows them to be 'better'. They will have the power to affect the system, to change the algorithms and even write their own code, whereas the dominated will be forced to use partial knowledge, incomplete data and commodified off-the-shelf algorithms which may paradoxically provide a glitch between appearance and reality such that the dominated will understand their condition in the spaces created by this mediation. The dominated may therefore be recognized by the system, whereas the lives of the dominant will be pleasurably and seamlessly mediated, and through recognition may come critical forms of reflexivity and political praxis. Knowledge is here recast to be computable, discrete, connected, in a real-time flow and even shallow – if by shallow we mean that knowledge exists on a plane of immanence rather than hierarchically ordered with transcendental knowledge at the peak.

To build this new computational world order, the existing gatekeepers of knowledge are already restructuring their data, information and media to enable the computational systems to scour the world's knowledge bases to prepare it for this new augmented age.[1] Knowledge and information is said to be the fuel of this new cognitive capitalism. Lyotard clearly identified this postmodern mindset where,

> knowledge becomes a force of production it also becomes both a tool and object of economic and political power. Knowledge . . . is already . . . a major . . . stake in the worldwide competition for power. It is conceivable that nation-states will one day fight for control of information, just as they battled of over territory, and . . . control of access to and exploitation of raw materials and cheap labour. A new field is opened for industrial and commercial strategies on the one hand, and political and military strategies on the other. (Lyotard 1984: 5)

The result of this new circuit of power and knowledge is that knowledge is now connected directly to wealth. Further, the underlying problem is that 'truth' is increasingly tied to expenditure and power, for the pursuit of knowledge is now tied to the use of advanced and, on the whole, expensive technologies. Power is connected to expenditure, for there can be no technology without investment just as there can be no investment without technology. In effect this generates asymmetric access to knowledge, information and data and hence a power differential between those with the money to buy such access and computational power and those that cannot. Governments will have 'top-view' over their societies that citizens and civil society organizations will not, and companies will have 'top-view' over markets that their customers, smaller competitors and perhaps even governments will not.

But further to this, in an era of augmented technology, those who can afford it will have bought the enhanced cognitive capabilities that certain technologies allow. For Lyotard the only way to fight this corporate and military enclosure of knowledge is clear: 'The line to follow for computerization to take . . . is, in principle, quite simple: give the public free access to the memory and databanks' (Lyotard 1984: 67). However, it is also clear that access itself will not be enough, it is not that we live in an information age, rather it is that we live in a *computational* age, and computation costs time and money, something which is unequally distributed throughout the population. Indeed, Lyotard was right in calling for the databanks to be opened, but he might not have realized that they would contain too much information for any single human being to understand without access to the unequally distributed computational technology and know-how. We might therefore paraphrase Lyotard and say that the line is, perhaps, in principle, quite simple: give the public free access to the algorithms and code.

This algorithmically co-constructed humanity, or 'augmented humanity', will require large existing businesses that depend on the economics of scarcity to change to the 'economics of ubiquity', where Google's ex-CEO Schmidt argued, greater distribution means more profits. 'Augmented humanity' will introduce lots of 'healthy debate' about privacy and sharing personal information, and it will be empowering for everybody, not just the elite (Gannes 2010). But it is also a challenge to a cultural elite that is uncomfortable with these changes to the status and distinction acquired by the digitalization of knowledge and learning that previously would have taken years to acquire. Indeed, augmented humanity represents, to some degree, a reconfiguration of the cultural, mediated through the computational in ways that are difficult to foresee.

When thinking about these profound changes introduced by digital technology at a cultural level, it is interesting, then, to see recent arguments being made in terms of discourses over the 'control' of this new computational culture and how computation serves as the gatekeeper to it (see Jarvis 2011; Anderson 2012). On the one side, we have what I call the *moderns*, represented by writers like Carr (2010) and Crawford (2010), and on the other side the *postmodern* camp with writers like Jarvis (2011) and Shirky (2010). So, for example, Jarvis criticizes what he calls the distraction trope, the idea that technology is undermining our ability to think deeply without being sidetracked (see Agger 2009; Freedland 2011). In a similar way to the enlightenment thinkers who pitched the moderns against the old, Jarvis argues, 'isn't really their fear, the old authors, that they are being replaced? Control in culture is shifting' (Jarvis 2011). Indeed, Jarvis attacks 'modern' writers like Carr (2010) and Freedland (2011), who worry about the changes that digital technology introduces into our lives as we are increasingly living non-linear lives. Indeed, this move is indicated as shifting from the modernist subject, unified, coherent, linear, reflexive, to a postmodernist subject, fragmented, incoherent, non-linear and increasingly real-time (see Berry 2011).

Jarvis believes that the moderns' arguments essentially boil down to an attempt to hold back culture and technology so that old elites remain in power. These 'old' elites are not the traditionalists that the original moderns attacked – those traditionalists supported religion, the King and the old hierarchies of status and power. Rather, the moderns are, the bourgeois and the intellectuals tied to privileges of monopoly capitalism. Indeed, Andreessen, the original programmer of the first graphical browser, Mosaic, and now a Silicon Valley entrepreneur, argues, 'the idea of the middle class itself is a myth . . . that experiment has been run and it was a catastrophic failure' (Fernholz and Mims 2012). Indeed, warming to his theme he warned the middle classes that they should 'discourage college students from majoring in English and other humanities' which means that they would have 'a future of shoe sales . . . and encourage them to pick science, technology, engineering, and mathematics instead' (Roose 2012).

For Jarvis, the moderns are the middle class who have benefited from the Humboldtian ideals, the bourgeois who have monopolized the media, the universities and the professional class more generally over the past century based on a humanities education that was a marker of social status, without adequate technical and computing skills. Similar to the German Idealists, like Humboldt, for the moderns,

> culture was the sum of all knowledge that is studied, as well as the cultivation and development of one's character as a result of that study. . . . The modern idea of a university, therefore, allowed it to become the preeminent institution that unified ethnic tradition and statist rationality by the production of an educated cultured individual. (Berry 2011a: 19)

These moderns are the privileged minority who were educated in a national culture and shared in a cultural milieu that they believed was rightfully theirs – they shared what Bourdieu would have called a habitus. This cultural education gave them not only the power of discourse more generally, but also real power, in terms of preparation through elite schools and universities in traditionally humanities education to become dominant class. These are described as the kinds of people that used to read novels like Tolstoy's *War and Peace* (see Carr 2010) – although it is doubtful if they ever did. However, a computational economy and the cognitive loads it generates destabilize previous markers of culture and status, such that older forms of distinction are discarded. As Carr (2008) argues,

> Bruce Friedman, who blogs regularly about the use of computers in medi-cine, also has described how the Internet has altered his mental habits.

> "I now have almost totally lost the ability to read and absorb a longish article on the web or in print," he wrote earlier this year. A pathologist who has long been on the faculty of the University of Michigan Medical School, Friedman elaborated on his comment in a telephone conversation with me. His thinking, he said, has taken on a "staccato" quality, reflecting the way he quickly scans short passages of text from many sources online. "I can't read *War and Peace* anymore," he admitted. "I've lost the ability to do that. Even a blog post of more than three or four paragraphs is too much to absorb. I skim it." (Carr 2008)

Of course, it was a different problem for the working class to have staccato minds dulled by the industrial machine, and to suffer the consequences of the shallowness of thinking bought by mass culture, poor education and limited access to 'high' culture. But these moderns now express their concern that they too may be losing their cognitive powers in a technology-infused society where even the cognitive is now subjected to the processes of capitalism. Indeed, their fears sometimes sound rather like paranoia over a potential loss of the self,

> I can feel it, too. Over the past few years I've had an uncomfortable sense that someone, or something, has been tinkering with my brain, remapping the neural circuitry, reprogramming the memory. My mind isn't going— so far as I can tell—but it's changing. I'm not thinking the way I used to think. I can feel it most strongly when I'm reading. Immersing myself in a book or a lengthy article used to be easy. My mind would get caught up in the narrative or the turns of the argument, and I'd spend hours strolling through long stretches of prose. That's rarely the case anymore. Now my concentration often starts to drift after two or three pages. I get fidgety, lose the thread, begin looking for something else to do. I feel as if I'm always dragging my wayward brain back to the text. The deep reading that used to come naturally has become a struggle. (Carr 2008)

This is identified as a loss being suffered by the 'literary types' (Carr 2008), the cultural elite who previously were able to monopolize the 'deep' thinking in a society. Naturally, these cultural elites also considered themselves the natural leaders of society too. In Britain, we tend to think of Oxbridge-educated politicians like David Cameron, George Osbourne, Nick Clegg and Ed Milliband who monopolize political power – although it is doubtful if we ever thought of them as particularly deep thinkers.[2] But they were certainly educated in the belief that certain kinds of knowledge, usually humanities knowledge, was for 'some humans' an elite that could understand and protect it (Fuller 2010).

In other words, it is not that writers such as Carr are losing their ability to think, rather they, perhaps, no longer earn enough money to buy the right kind of technology to *think with*.

This implies that the new gatekeepers to the centres of knowledge in the information age are given by technologies, cognitive and data-processing algorithms, data visualization tools and high-tech companies. Indeed, thinking itself can be outsourced through cognitive technical devices which will supply the means to understand and process the raw information given by a new politics of access. Provided you have the money to access, and not just access, as we increasingly rely on computational devices to process raw data and information and to mediate others to do physical labour for us, such as with Amazon Mechanical Turk, TaskRabbit or Fancy Hands. Computation thus generates a new proletariat of 'cloud workers', who receive 'no paid holidays, no sick days and no health benefits in this new distributed workforce' (Leonard 2013).

The new barbarians at the gates are increasingly led by techno-libertarians who declare that technology is profoundly disruptive of old powers, status and knowledge. As Schmidt and Cohen argue, 'anyone passionate about economic prosperity, human rights, social justice, education or self-determinaton should consider how connectivity can help us reach these goals and move beyond them' (Schmidt and Cohen 2013: 257). Indeed, this is a restatement of the technological democratization articulated by David Clark (1992) when he famously declared what has become one of the guiding principles of the IETF, 'We reject kings, presidents and voting. We believe in rough consensus and running code' (Hoffman 2010). In other words, putting things within a digital environment and allowing others the access to read, write and republish create new dynamics that undermine hierarchies based purely on old wealth, domination and power, whilst simultaneously instituting new wealth, hierarchy and power – subverting what has been termed elsewhere 'the Cathedral'.

For the postmoderns, the world has already shifted beyond the moderns' control, and this is something that is to be celebrated particularly as the previous hegemony was maintained by an illusion of meritocracy that in many instances served as an ideology for the action of expensive private education, cultural distinction and gatekeeping. Holt (2011) explains,

"No one reads War and Peace," responds Clay Shirky, a digital-media scholar at New York University. "The reading public has increasingly decided that Tolstoy's sacred work isn't actually worth the time it takes to read it." (Woody Allen solved that problem by taking a speed-reading course and then reading War and Peace in one sitting. "It was about Russia," he said afterwards.) The only reason we used to read big long novels before the advent of the internet was because we were living in an information-impoverished environment. Our "pleasure cycles" are now tied to the web, the literary critic Sam Anderson claimed in a 2009 cover story in New York magazine, "In Defense of Distraction". "It's too late," he declared, "to just retreat to a quieter time". (Holt 2011)

The postmoderns, generally educated in technology, business, technology law and the physical sciences, see themselves pitted against an old guard increasingly defending an unsustainable position. For them, knowledge can now be freely mediated through digital technology, and the moderns, as guardians of culture and history, are out-of-date, defunct and obsolete. This is, of course, revolutionary talk, and is reminiscent of the original premise of the social sciences that argued for 'all humans' rather than a privileged subset (see Fuller 2010). Indeed, one could argue that the universalization of their claims to democratic access to knowledge is crucial for their political project. The bulwarks of the modern empire, the university, the state, the large-scale corporation and even the culturally sophisticated educated elite are threatened with being dismantled by a new techno-social apparatus being built by the postmoderns.[3]

However, the arguments of the postmoderns have an important and critical flaw – they are blind to the problems created by economic inequality. The moderns dealt with this political economic problem by educating a minority of the population that would be involved in the social reproduction of knowledge but were crucially committed to the wider 'public good'. The postmoderns, on the other hand, call for the market to right the wrongs of class, status and hierarchy without any countervailing means of correcting for areas where the market produces problems, so-called 'market-failure'.[4] For the moderns, the state can be used as a tool to correct the wrongs of the market and offer solutions through the use of various kinds of intervention, for example, to help prevent inequality, to regenerate an area or to correct lack of investment by the private sector.

Within the terms of the postmodern imaginary, however, the state is itself identified as part of the problem, having been closely entwined with the logic of the moderns. The only solution is transparency and 'openness', a dose of sunlight being applied to all areas of social life. This usually takes the form of private wealth channelled through philanthropy, linked to a calculative instrumental rationality, such as demonstrated by the Gates Foundation.

In this case, 40 superwealthy people want to decide what their money will be used for," Peter Krämer, a Hamburg shipping magnate and philanthropist, told the German magazine *Der Spiegel*. "That runs counter to the democratically legitimate state. In the end, the billionaires are indulging in hobbies that might be in the common good, but are very personal (Bruinius 2010).

Thus, the postmoderns see the world divided starkly between those who work hard and those who do not (usually in hidden areas away from the glare of cleansing technology); for those who work hard will inherit the riches, but for those who do not, a technological black-box solution will be found to solve this problem, usually in the form of league tables, targets, incentive structures and monitoring.

Why is it that the postmoderns think of the digital age as one requiring technical 'black boxes'? This heuristic is widely taken as read in terms of empirical descriptions of technology, the state, the market, everyday life today and so forth, and also in terms of the possibility of a methodology to understand and explore it. Indeed, Galloway (2011) argues,

> Invisibility is not a new concept within political theory [but this] is a specific kind of invisibility, a specific kind of blackness that has begun to permeate cybernetic societies, and further that this blackness is not simply an effect of cybernetic societies but is in fact a necessary precondition for them. . . . The black box: an opaque technological device for which only the inputs and outputs are known. The black bloc: a tactic of anonymization and massification often associated with the direct action wing of the left. Somehow these two things come together near the end of the twentieth century. Is there a reason for this? (Galloway 2011: 239)

This homology is between black boxes and black blocs, where black boxes are the obfuscated technologies that hide what is inside, sometimes productively, sometimes not, in order to simplify systems by hiding complexity or to create abstraction layers. Black blocs, on the other hand, are political strategies or tactics in protests and riots to show oneself as a member of a larger group and to hide or disguise its individual members. Both are methods of obfuscation, and both are practices that are operative within what Galloway calls 'cybernetic societies' and I call computationality. This notion of information hiding, or encapsulation, is also important in object-oriented programming and related technical procedures of creating generative black boxes.

Thus social and political actors become understood through the metaphor of the technical practices of the technologists, and this raises an interesting question over the relationship between invisibility and visibility, or better, what I would call the relationship between means (machinery) and ends (commodity). That is, there is a problem of orientation in computationality when the code(s) are themselves hidden behind an interface or surface which remains eminently readable, but completely inscrutable in its depths. There is also the complementary problem raised in accepting the *surface* demands of a radical group that remains invisible and therefore beyond the possibility of contestation to its so-called 'non-demands' (a political attempt to lay claim to a technical convenience for political convenience). If the black boxing of technology is an urgent problem requiring contestation in postmodern capitalism, I suggest that the 'black blocing' of politics remains equally problematic and in need of opening up. What is fascinating is that on two different levels, the technical and the social, we have a similarity in practices, reflecting instrumental needs in response to technical and political imperatives, respectively.

This raises the notion of an opaque class as a universal class. That a response to the transparency of computational societies is black blocs as the site of resistance within 'cybernetic society' – perhaps the cypherpunk as exemplar. Indeed, it seems more likely that as the state increasingly monitors its citizens, using security services such as the NSA, citizens turn to obfuscation to preserve their anonymity before the state, through cryptography, for example. But perhaps it is also the case that black boxes and black blocs are both symptomatic of computationality and therefore need to be critiqued and opened up and their 'mechanisms' exposed. Indeed there are contradictions presented in, for example, the public use of reason that is obscured and encapsulated within non-transparent forms, or the possibility of obscurity to defend practices of violence, withdrawal and nihilism. Which is not to deny the importance of obscurity in the practice of the private use of reason and away from the surveillance of the state.

In this vein, I want to explore the notion of *availability* in relation to this idea of surface. It is helpful here to think of the way that computationality has affordances that contribute to the possibility of availability in terms of the construction and distribution of a range of commodities. Here I am thinking of a commodity as being available when it can be used as a mere *end*, with the *means* veiled and backgrounded. This is not only in technical devices, of course, and includes the very social labour and material required to produce a device as such. But in the age of the computational, it is interesting to explore how the surface effects of a certain form of computational machinery create the conditions both for the black boxing of technology as such and for thinking about the possibility of political and social action against it. I call this the paradigm of availability following Borgmann (1984: 44). Upon this surface we might read and write whatever we choose, and on the black bloc, we are also offered a surface to which we might read the inscrutable however we might wish – politics itself as consumption.

What is striking about the paradigm of availability, made possible by computationality, is that it radically re-presents the mechanisms and structures of everyday life, themselves reconstructed within the ontology afforded by computationality. This moment of re-presentation is an offering of availability, understood as infinite play and exploitability (interactivity), of a specific commodity form presented by the computational device. Here, I am thinking of the computational device both in terms of its material manifestations and also as a diagram or technical imaginary. That is, it is not only restructuring the mechanisms and structures, but also the very possibility of thinking against them. Here, the notion of the political itself requires reconciliation within the paradigm of availability and is very suggestive in relation to the black bloc itself.

So what is to be done? First and foremost would be a clear critique of both the technical and the political moment of black boxing. It is clear that the surface manifestation of the device, or the politics, is not enough for us to understand and critique what is, at least in terms of this theorization, an ideological manifestation of a computational ontotheology being instantiated in a number of medial moments (technology, politics, social movements, the environment, the state). Second, we need to deconstruct this manifestation of the commodity form as ends without means, in effect an example of commodity fetishism. Lastly, this critique implies the need for a new form of literacy, which I call 'iteracy', that is able to understand and intervene directly in the technological system we inhabit, but also to ensure that black boxing becomes glass boxing, and that political movements such as the black bloc become democratic 'glass blocs'.

Reading the digital

In this section, a method is outlined for digital reading and writing, or *iteracy*, that can form the basis of an approach in critical theory for reading code and opening these black boxes. This approach, which I briefly outline here, uses the pragmata of code, combined with its implicit temporality and goal orientedness to develop an idea of what I call *coping tests*. This notion draws from the concepts developed by Heidegger, as 'coping' being a specific method that takes account of the at-handiness (*zuhandenheit*) of equipment (i.e. entities that are being used). This is useful because it helps us think about the way in which software/code is in some senses a *project* that is not just static text on a screen but a temporal structure that has a past, a processing present and a futural orientation to the completion of a computational task. I want to develop this in contrast to attempts to focus on the code through either a heavily textual, interface/screenic, or a pure functionality-driven approach (which can have idealist implications in some forms) or a heavily mathematized approach.

Testing is a hugely important part of the software lifecycle and links the textual source code to the mechanic software and creates the feedback cycle between the two. This is linked to Boltanski and Thevenot's (2006) discussion of 'tests' – implying that it is crucially the running of these obfuscated code programs that shows that they are code at all (legitimate tests), rather than nonsense. Boltanski (2011) outlines three kinds of test that can be used as a basis of such critique,

> The *truth test* unmasks a universe of signs by exhibiting it in its plenitude and consistency. . . . In and through acts, the *reality test* unmasks the powers concealed in the interiority of beings. . . . The *existential test*, unmasks the incompleteness of reality and even its contingency, by drawing examples from the flux of life that make its bases unstable and challenge it. (Boltanski 2011: 113)

The fact that code objects are often unreadable by humans and yet testable on a number of dimensions is very suggestive. These three ways of approaching a critical testing of software bring to bear another method to complement what we might call the close reading of code, or the distant reading of interface analysis, to engage with the processual nature of algorithms. However, I want to outline a further method of testing drawn from Heideggerian phenomenology. This approach, using the pragmata of code, its materiality and agency to do things, combined with its implicit temporality and goal-orientedness allows us to think about how software works by the notion of *coping tests* that I develop here. For Heidegger, 'coping' is a specific means of experiencing that takes account of the at-handiness (*zuhandenheit*) of equipment that is being used. We 'cope' with objects in the world. Therefore, *coping tests* enable us to observe the *breakdowns* of these objects, they are the moments when, in this case, code objects stop working either partially or completely. So software/code is a happening or a project rather than static text on a screen. The implication being that we can learn a lot about software by deliberately breaking it, glitching it, hacking it and generally crashing its operations (see Alleyne 2011). This is a technique that has a long and respected history, as tinkering with technology, taking it apart and rebuilding it. For software, the fun of running 'coping tests' is exactly to see the extent to which the software under investigation is able to cope with the pressure exerted upon it by the tester. For example, the practice of 'data moshing' is essentially hacking the 'P' and 'I' frames of digitally encoded videos; not only does the effect produce startlingly arresting images and aesthetics, but it also shows how video functions as software. Indeed, as explained on the 'Know Your Meme' website,

> Digital video compression (such as MPEG-4 part 2, h.264, VP8, etc) works by recording the first frame (known as the keyframe) as a complete image, and recording the subsequent frames as only the changes from this first frame. This is done because recording only the changes makes the video easier to compress. By replacing the first frame of a compressed video with another picture, these same changes will be applied to the new image, creating very unusual-looking psychedelic effects. (Brad 2013)

This technique is also surprisingly simple, requiring nothing more than video-editing software, a selection of videos to splice together and experimentation. The glitches and errors thereby introduced show us how our software entertainment systems are structured, and how they cope with graceful failure.

The nature of *coping* that these tests imply and the fact that the mutability of code is constrained through limits placed in terms of the testing and structure of the project orientation (Berry 2011a: 65–6) also allow the researcher to explore where there are restrictions that serve as what Boltanski and Thevenot would call 'legitimate' tests, which themselves are reflexively played with in terms of clever programming that works at the borderline of acceptability for programming practices (hacking is an obvious example of this). Here, it is required that the researcher works and thinks at a number of different levels, of course, from unit testing, application testing, UI testing and system testing more generally in addition to taking account of the context and materialities that serve as conditions of possibility for testing (so this could take the form of a number of approaches, including ethnographies, discursive approaches, etc.).

For critical theory, I think coping tests are an immanent method as an alternative (or in addition to) the close reading of source code or software objects. This can be useful in a humanities perspective for teaching some notions of code through the idea of 'iteracy' for reading code (Berry 2012b) in relation to critical readings of software/code opened up through the categories given by critical theory. But this is also extremely important for contemporary critical researchers and students who require a much firmer grasp of computational principles in order to understand the economy, culture and society which has become softwarized, but also more generally for the digital humanities, where some knowledge of computation is required to undertake research.

One of the most interest aspects of this approach, I think, is that it helps sidestep the problems associated with literary reading of source code, and the problematic of computational thinking *in situ* as a programming practice. Coping tests can be developed within a framework of 'depth' in as much as different kinds of tests can be performed by different research communities, in some senses this is analogous to a *test suite* in programming. For example, one might have UI/UX coping tests, functionality coping tests, API tests, forensic tests (linking to Kirschenbaum's [2008] notion of forensic media) and even archaeological coping tests (drawing from media archaeology, and particularly theorists such as Parikka [2012]) – and here I am thinking both in terms of coping tests written in the present to 'test' the 'past', as it were, and in terms of an interesting history of software testing, which could be reconceptualized through this notion of coping tests, both as test scripts (discursive) and as software programming practice: more generally, social ontologies of testing, testing machines and so forth. We might also think about exploring software epistemologies through the testing of the boundaries of knowledge collected, processed and stored in computational systems.

It is something that I have been thinking about too in relation to the concept of digital *Bildung* (see Berry 2011a). I would like to suggest that iteracy might serve as the range of skills used for understanding computation – as indeed literacy (understanding texts) and numeracy (understanding numbers) do in a similar context. That is, iteracy is specifically the practice or being able to read and write texts and computational processes, rather than the more extensive notion of digital *Bildung* (see Berry 2011a: 20–6). In contrast, digital *Bildung* is the totality of education in the digital university, not as a subject trained in a vocational fashion to perform instrumental labour, nor as a subject skilled in a national literary culture, but rather as a subject that can reconcile the information that society is now producing at increasing rates, and who understands new methods and practices of critical reading (such as code, data visualization, patterns, narrative) and is subject to new methods of pedagogy to facilitate it (Berry 2011a: 168). So digital *Bildung* would include the practices of iteracy and would build on them to facilitate a broader humanistic or critical education. Here, iteracy is defined broadly as communicative competence in reading, writing and executing computer code. This calls for a different kind of relationship in the creation and dissemination of knowledge in the university, perhaps a new form of teaching opposed to the depressingly service-oriented vocationalism that has become increasingly fashionable in university teaching. When we think about the changes wrought by the digital technologies that are increasingly structuring our lives, it is important to remember the warnings that Joseph Weizenbaum gave for the university:

> The function of the university cannot be to simply offer prospective students a catalogue of "skills" from which to choose. For, were that its function, then the university would have to assume that the students who come to it have already become whatever it is they are to become. The university

would then be quite correct in seeing the student as a kind of market basket, to be filled up with goods from among the university's intellectual inventory. It would be correct, in other words, in seeing the student as an object very much like a computer whose storage banks are forever hungry for more "data". But surely that cannot be a proper characterization of what a university is or ought to be about. Surely the university should look upon each of its citizens, students and faculty alike, first of all as human beings in search of — what else to call it? — truth, and hence in search of themselves. Something should constantly be happening to every citizen of the university; each should leave its halls having become something other than she who entered in the morning. The mere teaching of craft cannot fulfill this high function of the university. (Weizenbaum 1984: 278)

Having a grasp of the basic principles of iteracy is crucial for reading code and for undertaking critical theory in the digital age. This is because the ubiquity of computation and the way in which norms and values are delegated into algorithms create an invisible site of power, which also has agentic power. It is also the case that part of the critique of software has to be the ability to unbuild these systems, to take them apart and to provide critical 'readings' of them. Indeed, using something like 'Motion' or 'After Effects' without understanding the basic principles of using and creating loops of visual material, or modern music composition using 'Logic Pro' or 'Pro Tools' without understanding samples, loops of samples, and the aggregation and layering of effects makes the software appear magical rather than a system of interlocking algorithms and interfaces. We now have deeply computational ways of working with media, and those who understand iteracy have an advantage in creating and using these systems and platforms, because of the cognitive maps iteracy provides for circumnavigating complex menuing, object-oriented visual structures, creating looping aggregates and so forth. With the increase in ubiquity of these computer systems in all aspects of life, it is likewise important that citizens have the skills to understand and critique them. Indeed, one way of doing so is to appreciate the aesthetics of computation as it is revealing about practices and structures underlying computation, for example,

Black writes: "to see a line of code as beautiful, one must be able to see why, of all the ways the line could have been written, this way is the most compact, the most effective, and hence the most elegant" (p. 127). Furthering an explicit comparison to the close reading techniques of 20th Century "New Criticism," Black goes on to say that, in this pedagogical tradition, "A program's merit is assessed much the way a poem's would be, in terms of structure, elegance, and formal unity" (p. 131). (Wardrip-Fruin 2009: 34)

Clearly, we have to be careful not to narrow iteracy to only formal programming knowledge. Indeed, I have found it very useful to explain to students that they are 'programming' a computer when they set an alarm on their iPhone or negotiate a menuing system in photoshop. This highlights that it is *black boxes all the way down* for computational systems – this layering within computational technologies we have come across before – but also that we need to be able to potentially open these black boxes all the way down. Iteracy includes the abstract principles of computational thinking, as well as the specifics of learning programming in terms of source code that becomes an 'executable'. This is important in order to highlight the disadvantages that confront individuals who do not have these basic skills for using computational devices. Increasingly, I think 'iteracy' will be as crucial for operating in this computational culture – especially considering the ontologies that are delegated into the devices that surround us take for granted certain computational principles of operation, such as real-time data and media streams – as numeracy and literacy have been.

Iteracy, therefore, also refers to the ability to read, write and understand processes, that is, following Wardrip-Fruin's (2009) notion of 'process descriptions'. To be able to create beautiful processual structures, for example, as found in live coding, but also in more mundane experiences of using technology. So , perhaps, two levels of writing are taking place here: the textual and the processual, which highlights the way in which we can think of these as two forms of digital writing: (1) code/text (deep) and (2) the process/screenic (flat). This is a simplification, as the previous discussion about layers in computational systems demonstrates; however, it is a useful heuristic for thinking about the kinds of things we need to take account of in teaching and researching computational media. This also helps draw attention both to reading code and to reading processes. As Wardrip-Fruin argues,

> there are important reasons that we should not depend on source code for our primary route to information about the operations of the processes of digital works. First, source code is available for only a small proportion of digital works. Second, source code is notoriously difficult to interpret—presenting a significant challenge, often, even to the individual or group responsible for writing it. Third, engaging with the specifics of the source code, while it allows us insight into issues such as individual programming style, is not always an important investment for understanding a work's processes. (Wardrip-Fruin 2009: 36)

While I think Wardrip-Fruin is right in pointing to the difficulty of source-code reading alone as providing a complete means of reading code, I do not think that consequently we can jettison code to focus on process. Indeed, something akin to the hermeneutic circle is needed here, whereby the code is understood not merely through a close reading of the text, but by running it, observing its operation and the processes it institutes, introducing breakpoints and 'print to screen' functions to see inside the code while it is running, such as through the use of these *coping tests*. Programmers who have iteracy by education and habit are able to jump between these perspectives on the code (code as text, code as process, code as whole system), seamlessly backwards and forwards as they develop knowledge and understanding of the code. This is similar to a notion of a 'fusion of horizons' but needs to be supplemented by critical readings that explore how code objects exist in a historical, political and socio-economic context and usually with a certain aim or intention (whether achieved or not).

Iteracy takes its name from the computational structure known as iteration. This is widely used in computer programming as a method of actualizing or implementing and algorithm by repeating a set of instructions. Iteration is a term used in computing to refer to the repetition of a command, code fragment, process, function, etc. Understanding iteration at a micro-level is a crucial skill for the programmer to develop, particularly as it is a method for re-using existing processes (such as in looping structures). Further, iteration itself at a macro-level, combined with constant improvements, is a key way of developing software/code (very much associated with agile programming, for instance). An example of iteration in Ruby code is:

```
5.times do
text "Hello"
end
```

An example of iteration in C++ code is:

```
int loop = 1;
while (loop <= 5)
{
  cout << "Hello #" << loop << endl;
  loop++;
}
```

This instructs the computer to perform the task text 'Hello', or print Hello to the screen, five times in a repetitive loop, or iteration. Here though, I broaden the meaning of iteracy beyond mere looping structures in programming code. What other skills, then, might be associated with this notion of iteracy?[5] I see iteracy as developing the ability to reason critically and communicate using discourse to discuss, critique and study the medium of computer code.[6] Particularly I want to relate this to the notion of a holistic digital education, or digital *Bildung*, more specifically as methods and approaches related to critical inquiry of the computal (Berry 2011a). I do think that iteracy has some heuristic advantages over terms like 'code literacy', 'digital literacy', 'information literacy' and so forth, especially the connotations that iteracy has with iteration, a key part of how code functions are read and written.

Some of the components of iteracy include: (i) *computational thinking*, or being able to devise and understand the way in which computational systems work to be able to read and write the code associated with them. For example abstraction, pipelining, hashing, sorting, etc. (see Wing 2011). (ii) understanding *algorithms*: understanding the specifically algorithmic nature of computational work, for example, recessions, iteration, discretization, etc. (iii), understanding the significance and importance of *data and models* particularly of data, information and knowledge and their relationships to models in computational thinking. (iv) practices in *reading and writing code* which requires new skills to enable the reader/programmer to make sense of and develop code in terms of modularity, data, encapsulation, naming, commentary, loops, recursion, etc. (v) l*earning programming languages* as understanding one or more concrete programming languages enables the student to develop a comparative approach and hones the skills associated with iteracy, for example, procedural, functional, object-oriented languages, etc. (vi) developing skills related to appreciating *code aesthetics*, that is the aesthetic dimension of code, software and algorithms, including notions of 'beautiful code' and 'elegance' as key concepts (see Oram and Wilson 2007), but also the question of the digital and aesthetics in relation to new media art and the new aesthetic. As part of iteracy we therefore have to teach how to program experimentally and learn by hacking within pedagogical contexts rather than coding uncreatively.

Here, *obfuscated code* is a helpful example. Obfuscated code is a computer source code that is functional but very difficult to read. This is not to demonstrate unreadable reading, or even for the spectacular, but rather as a stepping off point to think about the materiality of code through the notion of software testing (see Berry 2011a: 81–4, for a fuller discussion of this). Obfuscated code is a code deliberately written to be unreadable by *humans* but perfectly readable for machines. This can take the form of a number of different approaches, from simply mangling the text (from a human point of view) to using distraction techniques, such as confusing or deliberately mislabelled variables, functions, calls, etc. It can even take the form of aesthetic effects, like drawing obvious patterns, streams and lines in the code, or forming images through the arrangement of the text. It can also be productively used in programming as 'code obfuscation or "information hiding" . . . to make code more modular and abstract and therefore easier to maintain . . . such is the fundamental contradiction: what you see is not what you get. . . . Code is never viewed as it is. Instead code must be compiled, interpreted, parsed, and otherwise driven into hiding by still larger globs of code. Hence the principle of obfuscation' (Galloway 2012: 67–9). Obfuscation and related principles of information hiding such as encapsulation, interfaces and black boxes are all useful means of exploring iteracy and also of applying the method of coping tests in order to determine and understand software functionality. Together, these offer critical-empirical methods for the reading of the digital, which can be developed reflexively to question the how, why, where, when and who of software and subjecting algorithms to critical examination.

One last thought: although I make the link between iteracy and looping/repetition, I think it is probably more accurate to think of iteration not as a circle but as a spiral. That is, that learning builds on previous learning and skills in a virtuous upward spiral that develops competence and capabilities.[7] While here, I have only been able to provide a schematic overview of the development of critical approaches to the digital, and how we might develop a constellation of practices that develop critical theories of the digital, it is clear that it is crucial to begin to think more seriously about the computal in a critical way.

The discussion of political imaginaries that mirror the development of black-boxed computer systems and obfuscation is, in this reading, a worrying development, such as government as a platform, massive comprehensive data collection by government agencies such as the NSA, open access and transparency as ideology, and engineering concepts transferred unproblematically into the political sphere. Additionally, the problem of cognitive capture by corporations through notions of augmented humanity and the computational intervention in pre-consciousness requires urgent critical attention. The important question becomes: how much computation can democracy stand, and what should be the response to it?

If these claims are true that an active citizenry will increasingly need to be a computationally enlightened one, avoiding what we might call the heteronomy of the algorithms for the autonomy of reason, then we must begin teaching the principles of critiquing the computal through notions such as iteracy and digital *Bildung*. This critical spirit is counter to the growing belief that the university is only useful for producing mandarins and workers, and highlights the importance of critical thinking in humanities and social sciences in a digital age (see Berry 2012b). Indeed, I now want to turn to discuss these issues in relation to these concepts in order to draw these strands together and develop a tentative outline of a critical praxis for the digital.

8

Towards a critical theory
of the digital

In this final chapter I want to begin to draw together the constellation of concepts and ideas that have been explored throughout the book. The idea of a
constellation of concepts as a model of thinking comes from Walter Benjamin,
and developed through Adorno. Benjamin who argues that, 'ideas are to
objects as constellations are to stars. This means, in the first place, that [ideas]
are neither their concepts [of objects] nor their laws' (Benjamin 2003: 34).
What Benjamin refers to as concepts, Adorno understands as subsumptive or
classificatory thinking. As discussed earlier, classificatory thinking is 'primarily
concerned with what the object comes under, not what it is in itself' (Jarvis
1998: 178). For Adorno, though, constellations are not timeless, instead they
are a relation between time-bound particulars which must be composed from
the historically actual parts from which they form. As Adorno explains, the
unifying moment of constellations,

> survives without a negation of negation, but also without delivering itself
> to abstraction as a supreme principle. It survives because there is no step-
> by-step progression from the concepts to a more general cover-concept.
> Instead, the concepts enter into a constellation . . . By themselves,
> constellations represent from without what the concept has cut away
> within: the "more" which the concept is equally desirous and incapable
> of being . . . They attain, in thinking, what was necessarily excised from
> thinking. (Adorno 2004a: 162)

To avoid classificatory thinking, and the automated classificatory processes
of computational systems relevant to this book, requires the 'priority of the
object'. That is that 'whilst it is impossible for us to even conceive of a subject
which is not an object, we can very easily conceive of an object which is
not a subject' (Jarvis 1998: 183). In other words, we cannot have access to

any kind of immediate objectivity free of subjectivity and therefore subjective mediation. Indeed, any such approach would be delusive because cognitive 'access' to immediacy is already a mediation of it and therefore the object cannot simply be promoted to the same kind of position of priority which Adorno sees as occupied by the subject in German idealism. As he argues,

> "On that throne the object would be nothing but an ideal" . . . because the decision that the object has priority would be the subject's decision: we would effectively be subjecting ourselves not to the object itself, but to a placeholder for it which we ourselves had installed in its place, deludedly believing it to be a transcendent and independent of our thinking. Nor does Adorno think it possible to guarantee objective knowledge simply by stripping away those elements of cognition considered to be subjective, as though they were an accidental extra. (Jarvis 1998: 183)

Indeed, in a situation whereby SR/OOO condemns the 'correlationism' of much philosophical thought, these are important points. The internalization of computationality, such that its classificatory logic becomes a condition of possibility for everyday life today, needs to be reflexively and critically uncovered. Claims of object orientism or realism, whether in science, technology or philosophy, may be able to put down roots more easily in a culture that is strongly conditioned and shaped by computational categories and classifications. It also suggests the countervailing possibility of critical thought itself which is much harder to practice, teach and understand, when easy technocratic solutions, elegantly presented as a dance of assemblages in engineering models, more easily appear to catch the attention of thinkers and the public.

It is interesting to explore the extent to which computationality is itself also subject to an ideology. If it is indeed the case that computationality represents the incorporation of identity thinking par excellence. And where there is the slightest cognitive dissonance between reality and code, then anticipatory computing can co-opt cognition such that there is a reconciliation of disjuncture. This false unity, structured in part by the hollowing out of human reason and placing it within algorithms, requires only the acceptance of the superior cognitive abilities of the computational devices that mediate the algorithms. Human beings would then only be understood in a minor key, tragically limited in their capacities besides the truth machines of computationality. How then would this be achieved, how could computational processes sustain such a hegemonic hold over the psychic life of the individuals and groups of a computational society?

Perhaps it is achievable through the sheer quantification that computationality makes possible, and which is intoxicating to the human narcissistic urge to collect, store and keep; combined with the other side of the computational coin, that is the ability to 'read' these huge data stores, archives, big data and databases through the mediation of computational visualization. The locked promise of personal histories and stories is held within the frame of the computer, combined with the key of enchanted interfaces, perfect memories and the paradigm of convenience that accompanies the digital. But this is a limited ideological screen, and critically identified through the instabilities, glitches, exceptions and crashes that plague our computational experience. Therefore, we have to keep in mind that individuals within computationality remain 'products of history; they are also the spontaneous and variable points of nexus in processes of exchange and potentially new modes of socialization' (Schecter 2007: 166). Nonetheless, Horkheimer's prophetic words describing a world thrown upside down between 1926 and 1931 seem even more relevant today, when he argues,

> The less stable necessary ideologies are, the more cruel the methods by which they are protected. The degree of zeal and terror with which tottering idols are defended show how far dusk has already advanced. With the development of large-scale industry, the intelligence of the European masses has grown so greatly that the sacred possessions must be protected from it. . . . There is not only the general, systematically engineered brainwashing but the threat of economic ruin, social ostracism, the penitentiary and death to deter reason from attacking the key conceptual techniques of domination. (Horkheimer 1978: 17)

Computational ideologies are protected in computationality by the more subtle apparatuses and more terrible armed guards of drones, algorithms, software and code.[1] Indeed, the pressure placed on persons or organizations involved in megaleaks, such as Edward Snowden, the NSA whistleblower and Wikileaks, demonstrates the dangers of revealing how global power operates under the conditions made possible by computationality. This raises the question of resistance to the growing power of computation in our societies, and the commodity fetishism reinforced by computational devices, for example, through such tactical software/media interventions (see Raley 2009).

Boredom and the gigantic

Bernstein writes that the 'former Age of Anxiety has given way to the Age of Boredom' (Spacks 1995: 3). Today, we attempt to foreclose or avoid boredom, seeking out technologies that enable us to escape the experience of boredom. Whether via entertainment or through the new real-time streaming technologies, such as Twitter, which provide a constant stream of distractions, internet memes, photographs and links, today we live in a world defined by the avoidance of boredom. Indeed, 'idleness and boredom represent glitches in the system, glitches that call for increased and accelerated integration of the bored and potentially bored (the idle) into the institutional networks of time management' (Thiele 1997: 514).

Thus, there is an attempt to consume the boredom away with new gadgets, technologies, devices and distractions, and hence, accelerating levels of consumption become unavoidable. This raises new problems, as Thiele (1997) argues, 'the specter now looms that technological potential alone is capable of sustaining our interest. Once the human condition is experienced as insufficiently up-to-date to hold our attention, philosophy necessarily gives way to engineering' (Thiele 1997: 516). In a similar vein, Adorno conceptualized boredom as the 'eversame' (Adorno 1991: 166; 2004: 95). A product of the culture industry in which 'is the incurable sickness of all entertainment. Amusement congeals into boredom, since, to be amusement, it must cost no effort and therefore moves strictly along the well-worn grooves of association' (Horkheimer and Adorno 2006: 52).

Heidegger also considered boredom, or what he called 'deep boredom', a crucial ontological mood that also enabled the questioning of being through anxiety, but which nonetheless had the danger of invoking nihilism. He wrote,

> The man of today has no more time for anything, and yet, when he has free time, it immediately becomes too long. He must kill long periods of time by whiling them away through pastimes. . . . In this "ennui" nothing appeals to us anymore, everything has as much or as little value as everything else, our existence to the core. Is this possibly our final condition, that a deep boredom, like an insidious fog, creeps to and fro in the bottomless depths of our existence? . . . For the fundamental but hardly noticed mood of deep boredom is probably what drives us into all the time-killing that the strange, the exciting, the bewitching offers us daily in our alienation. (Heidegger 1973: 50–1)

For Heidegger, the fundamental philosophical question of 'why are there beings rather than nothing' becomes forgotten and 'the question is upon us in boredom, when we are equally removed from despair and joy, and everything about us seems so hopelessly commonplace that we no longer care whether anything is or is not' (Heidegger 1987: 1). Instead, he argued that 'anxiety is the mood that brings us "face to face with Nothing itself."' Heidegger contrasts this to profound boredom, which 'draws all things, all men and oneself along with them, together in a queer kind of indifference.

This boredom reveals what-is-in-totality. . . . Yet at the very moment when our moods thus bring us face to face with what-is-in-totality they hide the Nothing we are seeking' (Thiele 1997: 502).

Thus, for Heidegger, the danger of boredom is not that it confronts us with the groundlessness of Being, indeed this, Heidegger argues, is its virtue. Rather, the danger of boredom is that it stifles ontological questioning of this groundlessness in indifference, as explored above within the real-time stream 'Twitter trance'. The question of technology then is a pressing one, more so in our accelerated real-time streaming world of computational devices, computational categories and philosophy as *engineering* (Berry 2011). Indeed, we are confronted with a world of streamed things, lists, tuples and sets, which we have to do more than merely describe if we are to engage with it critically. Heidegger,

> feared that the mood of boredom would be revealed as humanity's final condition, that the water of philosophic life would become too bland for tongues jaded by the taste of constant innovation. Even more, he worried that the technological suppression of all opportunities for the awakening of boredom would destroy the conditions for philosophic thought and undermine the human capacity to discover a home in the world. (Thiele 1997: 517)

Today, 'tongues are jaded' not just by contrivances, but by the constant flow of real-time streams of information and data that rush past us in increasing volumes. As we adapt to flowing stream of data we are increasingly living distracted and 'glitched lives', barely able to keep our heads above the rising rivers of information, or 'rivers of news' (see Media Hackers 2013). Now, it is increasingly more difficult to ask the questions that philosophers have traditionally asked. Indeed, the temptation is, instead, to *list* the things that stream past us in the hope that at some future point our lists may perhaps contribute to a project of understanding, or that these lists and litanies offer an aesthetic or entertaining cathartic release. This, it seems to me, is a particular aesthetic experience of the sense of control that technology offers us in ordering through listing, and which is in another sense, a bureaucratic process of classification or filing.

In the world of glass rectangles that define the computational today, we already see signs of the fragmentation and disconnection that seem to be a hallmark of the computational in everyday life. That is not to say people are less connected, as in an instrumental fashion they have never been more connected in history, and with computational devices able to manage their connections for them, it is probable that these ties between people become hardened and less likely to be accidentally broken. Nonetheless, this world of flitting attention and flighty concentration is one that is not only encouraged by the affordances of our current computational devices, but it is also stabilized by them. This can be witnessed in the horror that greets people who have forgotten their mobile device, thus depriving them of the contacts, friends, email and calendar – their very towards-which. It is also demonstrated in the elevation of a technical imaginary supplied by 'hackers' towards a *doxa*, whereby thinking like a hacker is likened to a revolutionary position, rather than the question being asked about the kind of society that considers its engineers to be a revolutionary class. That is not to say that hackers and programmers more generally do not have important skills and knowledges about the functioning of the technical as such; this is certainly true, but they tend towards naivety in terms of political, economic, sociological, aesthetic and other modes of thought. Instead they tend to collapse alternative ways of seeing into a technocratic, instrumental mode of reasoning. Indeed, as Golumbia (2009) notes,

> It is those in power, and those who align themselves with existing structures of power, who are most often (but not exclusively) served by the advancement of computerization, and who make the fullest use of computers; it is they who endorse most fully the computational rhetoric and the computational beliefs that have become so widespread in our society. (Golumbia 2009: 4)

We should not forget that mass-market personal computational devices have traditionally been sold on a mystique of freedom, liberty and counter-cultural practices in contrast to the centralizing, control and planning discourses that have been used to sell to business. The programming industries, the computer hardware and software companies that increasingly power our economies, are not averse to telling the buyer what she wants to hear in order to move products out of the door. That is not to say that computers have not empowered users, rather 'what is in question is what power it gives what users, how and why . . . it is important to articulate the ideological operations of the computational as they come into being, rather than afterwards' (Golumbia 2009: 13). Today, computers and computational devices are increasingly sold as an entertainment media, they are sold in some sense to combat the boredom created by the excess generated from the computational efficiencies that are changing our economies. It is an ironic twist of computationality that the very tools that have created new spaces by their efficient management of information, time, space and working life should now be deployed to reorganize our non-working time too. More so, that this management of our entertainment and leisure time should involve a degree of surveillance and monitoring that is unprecedented in history, and to which we happily enrol onto with the promise of future, and better, management and entertainment. To assist us, that is, with managing the gigantic quantities of information, media, data, communications and memories, computation makes it possible to store, distribute, process and communicate with others.

We now live in a world where the very size of the real-time stream begins to exceed capacities to understand or make any sense of the sheer flow of data, and Twitter which currently handles 250 million tweets per day, or 1.25 billion per week, is a frightening example of this (Totsis 2011). Ways of thinking about the real-time stream as a totality are needed to help think through the implications of this data-rich world and provide a contribution towards a cognitive map. For this reason, I think that Heidegger's notion of the concept of the 'gigantic' (2012) might prove to be useful. For Heidegger, the gigantic represents a new moment whereby the very impossibility of understanding the extremeness of small and large sizes as calculability becomes itself a change in quality. As Heidegger argues,

> A sign of this event is that everywhere and in the most varied forms and disguises the gigantic is making its appearance. In so doing, it evidences itself simultaneously in the tendency toward the increasingly small. We have only to think of numbers in atomic physics. The gigantic presses forward in a form that actually seems to make it disappear – in the annihilation of great distances by the airplane, in the setting before us of foreign and remote worlds in their everydayness, which is produced at random through radio by a flick of the hand. Yet we think too superficially if we suppose that the gigantic is only the endlessly extended emptiness of the purely quantitative. We think too little if we find that the gigantic, in the form of continual not-ever-having-been-here-yet, originates only in a blind mania for exaggerating and excelling. (Appendix 12) (Heidegger 1977: 135)

And as Livingston (2003) explains, 'at first, the "gigantic" simply meant the unlimited processes of quantification and assumptions of quantifiability that make possible modern technological means of expression and control. But when understood in a broader historical perspective, the ground of the "gigantic" is not just the absence of limits on the process of quantification, but a fundamental aspect or feature of quantity itself' (Livingston 2003: 332–3).

Here, the gigantic is understood as the very possibility of quality being derivational from quantity itself. Thus, the kinds of quantitative possibilities for human existence are measured, calculated, listed, captured, pure data itself as being, 'but as soon as machination is in turn grasped being-historically, the gigantic reveals itself as "something" else. It is no longer the re-presentable objectness of an unlimited quantification but rather quantity as quality. Quality is meant here as the basic character of the quale, of the what, of the ownmost, of be-ing itself' (Heidegger 1999: 94).

The gigantic then becomes the mark of the age of the real-time stream in as much as the gigantic becomes the 'greatness' of this moment. We therefore increasingly use this notion of gigantism as a means of assessing the very importance of things within our everyday experience, not, that is, that the specific value itself has any particular or important meaning, but rather that the sheer impossibility of conceiving of the number (whether large or small) becomes a kind of sublime of unrepresentability. A mere mood or feeling that is associated with the gigantic then becomes something that we routinely consider to be a way to understand meaningful difference. Such that the gigantic becomes a special quality of the quantitative, and 'each historical age is not only great in a distinctive way in contrast to others; it also has, in each instance, its own concept of greatness. But as soon as the gigantic in planning and calculating and adjusting and making secure shifts over out of the quantitative and becomes a special quality, then what is gigantic, and what can seemingly always be calculated completely, becomes, precisely through this, incalculable' (Appendix 13) (Heidegger 1977: 135). The gigantic therefore means:

1   The gigantism of the *slowing down* of history (from the staying away of essential decisions all the way to lack of history) in the semblance of speed and steerability of 'historical' [*historisch*] development and its anticipation.

2   The gigantism of the *publicness* as summation of everything homogeneous in favour of concealing the destruction and undermining of any passion for essential gathering.

3   The gigantism of the claim to *naturalness* in the semblance of what is self-evident and 'logical'; the question-worthiness of being is placed totally outside questioning.

4   The gigantism of the *diminution* of beings in the whole in favour of the semblance of boundless extending of the same by virtue of unconditioned controllability. The single thing that is impossible is the word and representation of 'impossible' (Heidegger 1999: 311; see also Heidegger 2012: 348).

Thus the very fact that we live in a flow of real-time information that exceeds our capacities to understand or follow it – for example, when we have followed enough people such that our stream in Twitter is too fast to understand – is the kind of affect that I think the notion of the gigantic points towards. This is not a feeling of being overwhelmed or being in a situation of losing control, rather, it is a feeling of pure will-to-power, as it were, experiencing the gigantic as a manifestation of oneself. Equally, the flows of data both into and out of one's life then become a marker of one's gigantism, the subjectivity of the stream is constituted by the flow of data through which a moment of curation takes place, but a curation of gigantism, not a reduction as such, but a wholeness or comprehensiveness of coverage. Each of us then becomes his or her own gigantic, in as much as we increasingly generate data flows into and out of the networks of social life mediated through software and code. In the culture of the modern subject who through the logic of representation and computational technologies, 'which seem to overcome the very limits of space and time, the mystery of transcendence can indeed seem to "appear" only through its sheer absence. Such a culture, then, would appear to be a culture of absolute immanence or even "total presence," a culture de-mystified by a subject who, most notably in the technologies of all-consuming light and image, seems to comprehend all' (Carlson 2003).

This is an illusion of total presence in the real-time stream, presented through such real-time streaming interfaces given by Twitter, Facebook (especially through their Ticker) and related technologies (MacMannus 2011). This is a world in which the sheer gigantic incalculability of the calculable becomes an experience beyond the mere technical process or possibility of data collection, transmission and transformation. Indeed, it becomes the very moment when one is caught within the mystery of the sheer unrepresentability, or perhaps better, incomprehensibility of our own streams of data generated and flowing through these new forms of social network. Made manifest, perhaps though digital technology, but also pointing towards the unencoded that remains outside of these networks, as plasma or the *region*, and from which this data is drawn.

Heidegger offers the suggestion that within the gigantic is opened a shadow in the form of a moment of possible transcendentalism, perhaps even a new form of sacred, that points to the possible reconfiguration of previous marginal practices or a reconfiguration of things. This, I want to suggest, opens up new possibilities for a human subjectivity that can undertake the practices of listening and harkening to that which lies behind the rushing sound of the real-time streams and their shadows.

By means of this shadow, the modern world extends itself out into a space withdrawn from representation, and so lends to the incalculable the determinateness peculiar to it, as well as an historical uniqueness. This

shadow also points to something else, which it is denied to us of today
to know. But man will never be able to experience and ponder this that
is denied so long as he dawdles about in the mere negating of the age.
The flight into tradition, out of a combination of humility and presumption,
can bring about nothing in itself other than self-deception and blindness in
relation to the historical moment . . . Man will know, i.e., carefully safeguard
into its truth, that which is incalculable, only in creative questioning and
shaping out of the power of genuine reflection. Reflection transports the
man of the future into that "between" in which he belongs to Being but
remains a stranger amid that which is. (Heidegger 1977: 136)

This computational shadow is suggestive in relation to the notion of
computationality and the need for a critical reflexivity; particularly in relation
to the delightful commodity interfaces of computational technologies and
how these relate to changes in the representation of the means of production
and the machinery that sustains it. That is how changes in the notion of the
commodity and its relation to labour-power are reified in a computational age.
But there is little doubt that there 'is a special relation between the mode
of production and mathematics' (Galloway 2010: 11) and as Galloway has
argued,

> there is something that makes today's mode of production distinct from
> all the others: the prevalence of software. The economy today is not only
> driven by software (symbolic machines), in many cases this economy is
> software, in that it consists of the extraction of value based on the encoding
> and processing of mathematical information. It's not that software is a kind
> of motor underpinning the economy, but that, more and more, software is
> the thing which is directly extracting value. (Galloway 2010: 10)

This is where a new possibility of understanding as response to either as a
set of practices or as direct politicization of this softwarization of the economy
arises. It is not merely an affective response or a mode of appreciation towards
a kind of new media or digital object, although it can include this. Rather, what
I have called iteracy has to be reflexive in practice, critical in its stance and
able to provide signposts towards uncovering the processes of computational
society. Indeed, it is important to avoid a passive approach to the computal,
a *riparian* mode that becomes an all-consuming uncritical boredom (Berry
2011: 144). Rather, and crucially, the constellations of concepts that underlie
and sustain computational capitalism need to be rigorously contested and
the software that makes it possible hacked, disassembled and unbuilt. As
these systems drain us of agency and information, we should seek the means

to erect protective structures that provide spaces, if only temporary, from this all-pervading computationism. As suggested already, for now, *iteratic practices*, like using cryptography, decentralized data systems, distributed logistics and practices and the seizing-up of these systems' operations, might offer some respite but more collective responses will be needed.

Exhaustive media

There is constant talk about the 'fact' that we (or our societies and economies) are exhausted, depleted or in a state of decay (see Wiedemann and Zehle 2012). This notion of decline is a common theme in Western society, for example, Spengler's *The Decline of the West*, and is articulated variously as a decline in morals, lack of respect for law, failing economic or military firepower, relative education levels, threats from ecological crisis and so on. Talk of decline can spur societies into paroxysms of panic, self-criticism and calls for urgent political intervention. That is not to say that claims to *relative* decline are never real as such, indeed, relative measures inevitably shift in respect to generation ageing and change, particularly in relation to other nations. However, the specific decline discourse is interesting for what it reveals about the concerns and interests of each population, and a particular generation within it, whether it be concerns with health, wealth or intellectual ability, and so forth.

The issue of a tendency inherent in a temporal social location, that is, the certain definite modes of behaviour, feeling and thought in what we might call *constantly repeated experience* in a common location in the historical dimension of the social process is what Karl Mannheim called the *generation entelechy* (Mannheim 1952). This is the process of living in a changed world and is a re-evaluation of the inventory and the forgetting of that which is useful and covert and which is not yet won. In other words, the particular stratification of experience in relation to the historical contexts of a specific generation – in both, what we might call, the inner and the outer dimensions of experience. This social process also naturally causes friction between different generation entelechies, such as that between an older and younger generation – there may also be moments of conflict *within* a generation entelechy or what Mannheim called *generation units*, and indeed certain elements of a generation unit may be delegated into computation which becomes prescribed on the next generation.

The relative conditions of possibility, particularly in relation to what we might call the technical milieu for a generation entelechy, contribute towards slower or faster cultural, social and economic change. The quicker the pace of social, technical, economic and cultural change is, the greater the likelihood that a particular generation location group will react to the changed situations by producing their own entelechy. Thus, individual and group experiences act as crystallizing agents in this process, and play out in notions of 'being young', 'freshness', 'cool' or 'with it' in some sense, which acts to position generation entelechies in relation to each other both historically and culturally. Indeed, through critical praxis, such as the unbuilding of reified code objects or revealing the commodity fetishism of algorithmic interfaces, also opens up the possibilities of other ways of doing things, and indeed new ways of being in the world.

Mannheim identifies crucial features of a generation entelechy as (1) new participants in the cultural process are emerging, while (2) former participants in that process are continually disappearing; (3) members of one generation can participate only in a temporally limited section of the historical process; and (4) it is therefore necessary to continually transmit the accumulated cultural heritage; (5) the transition from generation to generation is a continuous process (Mannheim 1952). Indeed, this is a suggestive way of thinking about the movement of culture, but it is important that we do not restrict such agency purely to humans as participants as it is clear that there are other actants, also formed of a generation entelechy, such as code objects, for whom certain assumptions, accumulated cultural heritage and the threat of disappearance are possible. For example, we might consider the code and algorithms still functioning on the British-made Ferranti Argus 500 and 700 computer series which was produced in the early 1980s, and is still used in 2013 for control and data processing in some nuclear power stations in the United Kingdom – it even still boots from 8" floppy disks. This machine is programmed using the CORAL 66 (Computer On-line Real-time Applications Language) programming language based on ALGOL 60 and for these machines it is *still* 1981, lacking any of the features available to modern programmed computers, they nonetheless run as extremely stable systems day-in-day out (Computer History n.d.). Together with their programmers and minders who are also required to work within the technical constraints of the generation entelechy of the early 1980s, certain practices are therefore sedimented in computational devices.

In relation to this general talk of depletion in Europe and the United States, one of the recent decline issues has been, particularly in the United States and United Kingdom context, the worry about the decline of computational ability of young generations. More specifically, it is the lack of *digital literacy* (or what I previously discussed as iteracy) of the new generations. In this specific discourse, the worry is articulated that a new generation is emerging that is not adequately prepared for what appears to be a deeply computational economic and cultural environment. This is usually, although not always, linked to a literal *exhaustion* of the new generation, the implication being a generation that is unprepared, apathetic, illiterate and/or disconnected. Often these claims are located within what Mannheim calls the 'intelligentsia', he writes, 'in every society there are social groups whose special task it is to provide an interpretation of the world for that society. We call these the 'intelligentsia' (Mannheim 1967: 9). It is no surprise, then, that in the instance of digital literacy we see the same strata across society, commenting on and debating the relative merits of computational competences, abilities and literacies at a number of different levels, but particularly in relation to the education of new generations through discussions of school, college and university digital literacies (as previously discussed).

Some of these claims are necessarily the result of a form of generational transference of the older generations' own worries concerning its inadequacies, in this case usually either (1) an inability to use the *correct type* of computational devices/systems; (2) a concern that the young are not using the computers in the *correct manner* that they themselves were taught, for example, using a physical keyboard and mouse; or (3) a dismissal of the new forms of digitality that are seen as trivial, wasteful of time, and hence socially or economically unproductive, a classic example of this is social media. There are a number of themes and levels of analysis that are brought out in these discussions, often, but not limited to the question of moral failings of the new generation, but also to the technical abilities, economic possibilities, such as vocationalism, and also the ways of thinking appropriate to a perceived new environment or economic and technical ecology. This is similar to Foucault's question of a generational *ethos,* as it were, and whether it might be helpful if we,

> envisage modernity rather as an attitude than as a period of history. And by "attitude," I mean a mode of relating to contemporary reality; a voluntary choice made by certain people; in the end, a way of thinking and feeling; a way, too, of acting and behaving that at one and the same time marks a relation of belonging and presents itself as a task. A bit, no doubt, like what the Greeks called an ethos. (Foucault 1984: 39)

Here, I want to take the problem of *exhaustion* of the new generations as a focus, the 'exhausted' literally, as in terms of the Latin *exhaust* as 'drained out'. In other words, to ask the *why, how, who, what* is 'drained out' and *where to,* in our highly computational cultures? That is, to turn the question around and identify exhaustion of the new generations as indeed an important site of concern, but that the *exhaustion* that the new generations are experiencing is not an apathy or lack of energy, but rather a product of the political economy, an ethos that results from being subject to the digital draining data, information and energy into technical systems through specific *drainage points,* operating through and on computational devices, and particularly intimate technologies like mobile phones, tablets and laptops. This is to focus on the extent to which digital media are increasingly becoming *exhaustive media,* and critically interrogate their function, form and content and how they undermine the ability to function as an autonomous being in the Kantian sense of majority.

To put it another way, what would be the 'enlightenment' in relation to the new exhaustive media and the software ecologies of trackers, web bugs, beacons, apps, clouds and streams? If we are to agree with Kant that the enlightenment is the universal, free, public uses of reason (Kant 1991), how do we assure freedom of public reason in the digital age? As Foucault described, for Kant,

> when one is reasoning only in order to use one's reason, when one is reasoning as a reasonable being (and not as a cog in a machine), when one is reasoning as a member of reasonable humanity, then the use of reason must be free and public. Enlightenment is thus not merely the process by which individuals would see their own personal freedom of thought guaranteed. There is Enlightenment when the universal, the free, and the public uses of reason are superimposed on one another. (Foucault 1984: 36–7)

Thus for Kant, to reach our political maturity as human beings we should 'dare to know' or *sapere aude,* that is, 'to have courage to use your own reasoning' (Kant 1991: 54). This remains the challenge for us today, rearticulated by Foucault as thinking in terms of the 'historical ontology of ourselves'. This further enables us to test contemporary reality to find 'change points', and what might the implications be for an investigation of events by which we constitute ourselves as subjects? As Foucault argues,

> I do not know whether we will ever reach mature adulthood. Many things in our experience convince us that the historical event of the Enlightenment did not make us mature adults, and we have not reached that stage yet. However, it seems to me that a meaning can be attributed to that critical interrogation on the present and on ourselves which Kant formulated by reflecting on the Enlightenment. It seems to me that Kant's reflection is even a way of philosophizing that has not been without its importance or effectiveness during the last two centuries. The critical ontology of ourselves has to be considered not, certainly, as a theory, a doctrine, nor even as a permanent body of knowledge that is accumulating; it has to be conceived as an attitude, an ethos, a philosophical life in which the critique of what we are is at one and the same time the historical analysis of the limits that

are imposed on us and an experiment with the possibility of going beyond them. (Foucault 1984: 49)

One way forward might be to begin to map the *exhaustion* of a new generation entelechy in terms of a new computational political economy that is emerging in terms of the ability to *exhaust* us of our thoughts, movements, health, thoughts, life, practices, etc. That is, usefully captured in terms of the term of the art in technical circles of the 'data exhaust' that all users of computational systems create. We might therefore think in terms of the computational imaginaries that are crystallized within particular generation entelechies – and how we might gather a critical purchase on them. In other words the generation entelechy connected to a particular computational *Weltanschauung*, or worldview of computationality (Berry 2011).

We need to move away from a concern with mere competences of a new generation entelechy and widen the focus on the critical and reflexive abilities of a new generation and how they might be actuated. Rather than teach computer programming as a *skill* for a new economy, we need to explore the historical, philosophical, theoretical and critical context for particular kinds of the various forms of digital *praxis*. One way of doing this might be to look at concrete case studies of actual programming sites and projects, in order to understand why and how these forms of activity are related, the context in which they have developed and their trajectories, a research project that has recently begun to be closely associated with critical strands in software studies and digital humanities.

This is a critical means of contributing to the importance of the project of making the invisibility of much of the digital *infrastructures* become visible and available to critique. That is an exploration of the logistics of the computal and its various organizing and classificatory logics. Of course, understanding digital technology is a 'hard' problem for the humanities, liberal arts and social sciences due to the extremely complex forms which contain agentic functions and normative (but often hidden) values. Indeed, we might contemplate the curious problem that as the digital increasingly structures the contemporary world, curiously, it also withdraws and becomes backgrounded (Berry 2011). This enables us to explore how knowledge is transformed when mediated through code and software and to apply critical approaches to big data, visualization, digital methods, digital humanities and so forth. But crucially to also see this in relation to the crystallization of new entelechies around digital technologies – that is we need historical and political critique to understand this new situation.

Thinking about knowledge in this way enables us to explore generational epistemological changes that are made possible by the installation of code/software, for example, in our contemporary instantiation of computational devices, which are increasingly streams, clouds and networks. These computational devices, of course, are not static, nor are they mute, and their interconnections, communications, operation, effects and usage have to be subject to the kind of critical reasoning that both Kant and Foucault called for.

We might consider these transformations in light of what Google calls 'augmented humanity'. Described as a number of moments within the capabilities of contemporary computational systems, such that Google, 'knows roughly who you are, roughly what you care about, roughly who your friends are. . . . Google also knows, to within a foot, roughly where you are. . . . most people don't want Google to answer their questions. . . . They want Google to tell them what they should be doing next' (Eaton 2012b). Translated, this means that Google believes that it knows better than the user what it is that they should be doing, and in many cases even thinking. This is the background to the project of Google Glass and wearable technology that is always available within sight of the new kind of augmented user. Thus, the computational device the user wears or holds contains the means to source the expertise to prescribe action in particular contexts, what we might call 'context consumerism' but which is essentially cognitive co-option. That is, that the user is able to purchase his or her cognitive/memory/expertise capabilities as required on-the-fly. Thus, humanity becomes what we might call, following the development of programming languages such as C++, a new augmented or extended humanity++. Indeed, there are now a number of examples of these developments in relation to, for example, Google Glass, contextual UX, locative technologies, etc. We can also see new developments in brain interfaces that enable direct connection of silicon and brain tissue such that the 'augmentated' technology is quite literally part of the body (Anthony 2013).

Indeed, we might consider the entire technical and media industries in light of what Stiegler (2010a, b) has called the 'programming industries' which are involved in creating institutionalized 'context'. This is data collected from the tacit knowledge of users and their 'data exhaust' and delegated to computer code/software. These algorithms then create 'applied knowledge' and are capable of making 'judgments' in specific use cases. Indeed, today people rarely use raw data – they consume it in processed form, using computers to aggregate or simplify the results. This means that increasingly the 'interface' to computation is 'visualised' through computational/information aesthetics techniques and visualization, a software veil that hides the 'making' of the digital computations involved. Today we see this increasingly being combined with real-time contextual sensors, history and so forth into 'cards' and other push notification systems that create forms of just-in-time memory/cognitive processes and algorithmic interfaces.

These are new forms of invisible interface/ubiquitous computing/ enchanted objects which use context to present user with predictive media and information in real time. The aim, we might say, is to replace forethought by reconfiguring/replacing human 'secondary memory' and thinking with computation. That is, the crucial half-second of pre-conscious decision-forming processes whereby we literally 'make up our own minds' is today subject to the unregulated and aggressive targeting of the programming industry. This temporally located area of the processes of mind we might call the 'enlightenment moment' as it is the fraction of a second that creates the condition of possibility for independent thought and reflexivity itself. Indeed, far from being science-fiction, this is now the site of new technologies in the process of being constructed, current examples including: Google Now, Apple Siri, MindMeld, Tempo, etc. Not to mention the aggressive targeting by advertising companies of this area, but more worryingly of new generation entelechies who are still developing their critical or reflexive skills, such as children and young people. This, of course, raises important questions about whether these targeted computation systems and contextual processes should be regulated in law, especially in relation to the young.

The new imaginaries are already being conceptualized as an 'age of context' within the programming industries (see O'Reilly 2013). Indeed, under this notion all material objects are carriers of signals to be collected and collated into computational systems, even the discarded, the trash, etc. contains RFID chips that can provide data for contextual systems. But more importantly, the phones we carry, the mobile computers and the tablets, now built with a number of computational sensors, such as GPS, compasses, gyroscopes, microphones, cameras, Wi-Fi, radio transmitters and so forth, enable a form of contextual awareness to be technically generated through massive real-time flows of data. For example, in the US Presidential election on 6 November 2012, Twitter recorded 31 million election-related Tweets from users of the streaming – that is 327452 Tweets per minute (TPM) (Twitter 2012) which is then streamed back to its users. In a real-time stream ecology, such as Twitter, the notion of the human is already contested and challenged by a form of 'hyper attention' in contrast to the 'deep attention' of previous ages. Indeed, the user is constantly bombarded with data. This is increasingly understood as a lack within human capabilities which needs to be remedied using yet more technology – real-time streams need visualization, cognitive assistants, push notification, dashboard interfaces and so forth.

This current computational imaginary of an 'age of context' is being built upon the conditions of possibility made feasible by distributed computing, cloud services, smart devices, sensors and new programming practices around mobile technologies. This new paradigm of anticipatory computing stresses the importance of connecting up multiple technologies that provide data from real-time streams and APIs to enable a new kind of intelligence within these technical devices. A good example of this is given by Google's new 'Google Now' product, which attempts to think 'ahead' of the user by providing algorithmic prediction based on past user behaviour, preferences, Google search result history, smart device sensors, geolocation and so forth. As Google explains,

> Google Now gets you just the right information at just the right time. It tells you today's weather before you start your day, how much traffic to expect before you leave for work, when the next train will arrive as you're standing on the platform, or your favorite team's score while they're playing. And the best part? All of this happens automatically. Cards appear throughout the day at the moment you need them. (Google 2012a)

These new technologies form a constellation that creates new products and services, new tastes and desires, and the ability to make an intervention into forethought – to produce the imaginary that Google names 'augmented humanity' (Eaton 2012b). In some senses this follows from the idea that after 'human consciousness has been put under the microscope, [it has been] exposed mercilessly for the poor thing it is: a transitory and fleeting phenomenon' (Thrift 2006: 284). The ideas of augmented humanity and contextual computing are intended to remedy this 'problem' in human cognitive ability. Here the technologists are aware that they need to tread carefully as Eric Schmidt, Google's ex-CEO, revealed 'Google policy is to get right up to the creepy line and not cross it' (Richmond 2010). The 'creepy line' is the point at which the public and politicians think a line has been crossed into surveillance, control and manipulation, by capitalist corporations or the state. Of course, internally, Google's experimentation with these technologies is potentially much more radical and invasive. These new technologies need not be as dangerous as they might seem at first glance, and there is no doubt that the contextual computing paradigm can be extremely useful for users in their busy lives for consuming commodities and services – acting more like a personal assistant than a secret policeman. These technologies are built on complex intertwined webs of software tied together with these new meta-systems which abstract (are built) from the: (1) social layer, such as Twitter and Facebook; (2) ambient data collection layer, using the sensors in mobile devices; (3) web layer, the existing and future web content and technologies; (4) notification layer, enabling reconciliation and unification of real-time streams; and lastly, (5) the app layer, which is predominantly made up of single-function apps,

These various layers are then loosely coupled to interoperate in an unexpected 'delightful' fashion, such as experienced with the conversation interfaces, such as Apple Siri, which have both an element of 'understanding' and contextual information about their user and environment. Critically engaging with this algorithm-enabled age of context is challenging due to the distributed software, material objects, 'enchanted' objects, black-boxed systems and computational 'things' that make it up. The threads that hold these systems together are not well understood as a totality nor even as individual components experienced as they are through new calculative dashboards (e.g. notification interfaces). Indeed, we can already discern new forms of power that are tentatively visible in this new context layer, enabling new political economic actors, and a new form of intensive exploitation, such as that demonstrated by the intensification of the pre-cognitive moment discussed earlier.

I have argued previously that in moments like the new aesthetic, glitches can be critically instructive (Berry 2011, 2012a, b, c), and that *exceptions* and contextual failure are useful to begin mapping these new systems (Berry et al. 2012a, 2013). The black box of these exhaustive systems is spun around us in wireless radio networks and RFID webs – perhaps doubly invisible. We need to critique moments in exhaustive media that are connected to particular forms of what we might call 'exhaustive' governmentality, self-monitoring and life-hacking practices, aesthetic, political, social, economic, etc. but also the way in which they shape generational entelechies. For example, this could be through the creation of an affective relation with real-time streaming ecologies and a messianic mode of media or through the coping tests that disrupt the smooth surfaces of software. Indeed, we might say that the new anticipatory computing paradigm creates a new anticipatory subject, which elsewhere I have called a *riparian citizen* (Berry 2011: 144).

Indeed, it seems to me that it is crucial to understand how computation contributes to new generational entelechies and may function to limit the ability to critically reflect on the historical dimension of the social process. For example, visual rhetorics of the digital – 'new aesthetic', 'pixels', 'sound waves' and so forth – are widely used in interface culture to represent and describe computational agency without a corresponding critical dimension. Indeed, this contributes to a wider discussion of how medial changes create epistemic changes and how critical praxis can be mobilized towards emancipatory knowledge and technologies. For me, this project remains linked to a critical ontology of ourselves as ethos, a critical philosophical life and the historical analysis of imposed limits to reach towards experiments with going beyond current conditions and limits (Foucault 1984).

The possibility of a 'digital' enlightenment ethos needs to be translated into coherent 'labor of diverse inquiries', one of which is the urgent focus on the challenge to thinking represented by the intensification of the programming industries on the 'enlightenment moment' of our pre-thought. This requires new approaches, which could certainly draw on the archaeological and genealogical analysis of practices suggested by Foucault (1984) and also on the logistics and strategic practices associated with shaping both the policies and concrete technologies themselves – perhaps, if not necessarily 'Evil Media' (Fuller and Goffey 2012), then certainly critical software and political praxis. Last, and not least, is the theoretical moment required in developing the conceptual and critical means of defining unique forms of care to things, others and ourselves that are not limited by the framing of computationality.

This book is a contribution to a critical theory of the computal, a continuation of the enlightenment project, which I have termed *iteracy*. These critical technical practices will become crucial to enable us to read and write the digital, the conditions of possibility for a form of critical computational reflexivity, and also to develop the ability to make public use of critical computational reason. To this end, additional critical technical practices and habits in the use of new digital methods and tools are needed, such as antisocial media, hacking, critical *encryption* practices, iteracy, critical digital humanities, and politically engaged computal praxis. This will ensure that we can read and write outside the streams of data collected in the service of computational capitalism and government monitoring and so avoid the shadow of what we might call the *dialectic of computationality*.

Notes

Chapter 1

1 The archiving of software and code and digital media more generally is currently being actively engaged with in fields such as software studies, critical code studies, digital humanities and new media. There is often a temptation to think of the software as a discrete 'object' or package, forgetting that software and code are extremely networked and cannot function when taken away from this software ecology. Here, I am thinking of the platform that supports the software/code, such as the particular hardware, software, operating system, network connections, etc. It is certainly clear that currently emulated environments leave a lot to be desired when interacting with previous software and code. Unlike books which are relatively self-contained objects (Foucault notwithstanding) software/code is not readable in the same manner. Merely storing the software, and here I am thinking particularly about the executable binary, will not be enough to access, read, execute and explore the package. Neither will storing the source code be enough, which requires particular compilers, platforms and processes to reanimate it. In some instances one can imagine that the totality of technical society would need to be stored to adequately reanimate software/code – for example, highly networked software, like zombie botnets, cascading database systems, networked gaming systems, massively parallel virtual worlds, etc. which runs through and across the internet might be an example of this. Perhaps in the future we will have to be content with accepting that the only way to archive some software systems will be to leave them running in a domesticated virtual *scene* captured temporally and looped in eternity. The longer the loop of code/ecology, the better the ability for future historians to explore and understand their use and meaning.

2 Part of a critical project towards the digital will have to involve a means of translating and offering cognitive maps for the comprehension of these gigantic values. At present they remain beyond comprehension and as such are often uncritically accepted or misunderstood.

3 See, for example, Memoto Lifelogging Camera, which is a small wearable camera that takes continual photographs which are automatically uploaded to the cloud. It is claimed to be a tiny, automatic camera and app that gives you a searchable and shareable photographic memory. http://www.memoto.com

4 A great response to this issue is given by Mazières and Kohler (2005) where they attempted to express their irritation of email spamming of their mail

accounts by submitting a paper to the responsible conference with the title 'Get me off your f—g mailing list' consisting solely of ten pages of the repeated phrase 'Get me off your f—g mailing list' together with helpful diagrams. Unfortunately they 'never received official notification of whether the paper was accepted or rejected'. See also Hughes (2010) for a humorous parody of compactant and web-bug data collection.

5 This is very similar to the experience of Thomas Peterffy, an algorithmic trader on Wall Street, who in 1987 was forced by Nasdaq to disconnect a purely digital connection which gave his rapid buy and sell orders to their computer system. Instead, he was told the terms and conditions of a Nasdaq terminal meant that orders had to be typed via the keyboard and screen. As a result he was forced to build a robotic screen reader and keyboard typist that could algorithmically enter data rapidly into the terminal – which although now met the Nasdaq terms and conditions did not exactly enamour him to them (see Steiner 2013: 11–18). Later, of course, Nasdaq was forced to abandon these archaic restrictions and open their data feeds to their clients.

6 Capitalism's uncanny ability to absorb criticism and defuse its opponents is well noted, as indeed the difficulty of positioning such work within such a system (see Jay 1973: xiii). But there is the added difficulty that critical work should always be cognizant of Yeats who reminds us 'The intellect of man is forced to choose between/Perfection of the life or of the work' and as Jay comments, 'when the radical intellectual too closely identifies with popular forces of change in an effort to leave his ivory tower behind, he jeopardizes achieving either perfection. Between the Scylla of unquestioning solidarity and the Charybdis of willful independence, he must carve a middle way or else fail' (Jay 1973: xv).

7 As Liu argues in relation to the importance of taking account of the digital in relation to the literary, 'let me first address the why? question. In general, as I have taken to saying to colleagues suspicious of all the buzz about digital technologies, the stake for literary studies in the digital age is not first of all technological. It is to follow the living language of human thought, hope, love, desire—and hate too—wherever it goes and wherever it has the capacity to be literary, even if the form, style, or grammar of such literariness does not always conform to canonical standards' (Liu 2013). Equally, it seems to me that we are now beyond a knee-jerk technophobia in relation to understanding the digital in relation to the multiple disciplinary traditions within the university.

8 Founded in the early 1990s, the cypherpunk movement has been most active during the 1990s 'cryptowars' and following the 2011 internet spring. The term cypherpunk, derived from (cryptographic) cipher and punk, was added to the Oxford English Dictionary in 2006 (Assange 2012).

9 See uBiome at http://www.ubiome.com and 23andme at https://www.23andme.com

10 For example, Morozov asserts that one should not speak of the 'Internet' because he claims it is not fixed and unified. Unfortunately this betrays a certain lack of understanding of conceptual thinking, indeed a tendency towards the non-noetic and an empiricism that is a hallmark of the very instrumentalism he so disparages in Silicon Valley. Following his logic one

cannot speak of the United States of America, nor of the European Union, nor indeed of the British police force. This admonition is a limitation on thought that cannot be helpful for a critical project to renew thinking.

11 See http://www.newtonproject.sussex.ac.uk/   .

Chapter 2

1 Due to limitations given by space and time I have had to limit the range of critical theory I was able to discuss here. In a later book I intend to examine the digital in relation to the works of Jürgen Habermas, Albrecht Wellmer and Axel Honneth.

2 Morozov suggests, a 'moratorium on using the very term "Internet" and instead going for more precise terminology, like "peer-to-peer networks" or "social networks" or "search engines,"' (Morozov 2013: 44), none of which, to my mind, are any less fraught with multiple interpretations, than the polysemy of 'the internet'.

3 As the novelist and writer Ernst Jünger argued 'the age of technology individuals are no longer concerned with the liberal futurity of progress but possess a new modesty in relation to historical temporality and to the power of the infinite as manifested in the precision and perfection of technological design, distribution and use. As such, for Jünger the twentieth century is the first century "without history", a century that, as Manuel Castells was later to point out, will ultimately reside within a "timeless time" conditioned by the precision of the self-absorbed immediacy of technological activity. As such, the era of technology for Jünger represents the radical forgetting of historical time and it is the job of the thinker to forge a connection between the, eternal, technological present and the ideas and hopes of the ancient historical past in order to make the former authentically thinkable and inhabitable' (Turnbull 2009: 15).

Chapter 3

1 See also the presentation of Taryn Simon and Aaron Swartz's 'Cultural Differences' engine here as a video given in 2012, http://www.vimeo.com/40651117

2 There are examples of 'twitter art' which use Unicode characters to create small ascii-type images in the stream, see, for example: https://www.twitter.com/tw1tt3rart and https://www.twitter.com/search?q=%23twitterart

3 The Library has been collecting materials from the web since it began harvesting congressional and presidential campaign websites in 2000. Today they hold more than 167 terabytes of web-based information, including legal blogs, websites of candidates for national office and websites of Members of Congress (Raymond 2010).

4 Starting 10 October 2010, Twitter began transferring all public tweets to the Library of Congress for archiving. Tweets that are 24 weeks old (6 months) or older will be saved forever, and the user will no longer be able to delete them. By using the hashtag #NoLOC.org, the user will continue to use Twitter like normal, but when the tweet turns 23 weeks old, it is deleted automatically (NoLOC 2011).

5 In contrast to other social networks; Diaspora, for example, is a distributed social networking service, providing a decentralized alternative to social network services like Twitter and Facebook. See also Briar, Crabgrass, Freedombox, Lorea, Secushare, Social Swarm, Thimbl Unhosted, FB Bureau.

6 Two years before the introduction of the ticker in New York City, there was a short-lived attempt to introduce an alternative technology in Paris, called the pantelegraph (Preda 2005). This technology, however, was quickly abandoned and was never used on financial exchanges other than the Paris Bourse (Preda 2005: 777, fn 2).

7 In places like China, the character restriction plays out different as the Chinese script allows quite long message (on Sina Microblog, for example, as Twitter is banned in China). This means that newspapers and corporations are increasingly using Sina Microblog (sometimes referred to as Sina *Weibo*) as a means of distributed communications.

8 'Agencement is a common French word with the senses of either "arrangement", "fitting" or "fixing" and is used in French in as many contexts as those words are used in English: one would speak of the arrangement of parts of a body or machine; one might talk of fixing (fitting or affixing) two or more parts together; and one might use the term for both the act of fixing and the arrangement itself, as in the fixtures and fittings of a building or shop, or the parts of a machine.' (Phillips 2006).

9 'It should be noted here that in the USA and in Britain, at the time of the ticker's invention, several efforts were under way to develop machines for making speech visible. On the one hand, there were attempts at developing technical devices for the deaf, connected to the method of lip-reading. The people involved in these attempts were also involved in the development of better telegraphic devices and tried their hand (though unsuccessfully) at a telegraphic machine fitted for financial transactions. Alexander Graham Bell's father was among those making such efforts' (Preda 2005: 777, fn 8). It would be interesting to have a Twitter to speech 'radio' with an automated text to speech system (see VoiceForge).

10 It is also an interesting observation that in a similar way in which stock tickers, data feeds and financial markets are visualized, there are also many competing Twitter visualization systems, including Visibletweets.com, tweepskey.com, Twitter StreamGraphs, isparade.jp, toriseye.quodis.com, revisit, twistori, MentionMap

11 The term software/code is used to highlight the dyadic structure of software and code (see Berry 2011).

12 See https://www.marketcetera.org for a high-frequency trading system that is released as open source software, meaning the source code is easily accessible for inspection and change.

13 An interesting example of this presentation of computational risk is the
iPhone application ASBOrometer which computes the risk factor of a
particular UK location through the use of government data, see
http://www.asborometer.com/

14 Open source software is source code that is openly developed and
distributed upon the internet (see Berry 2008).

Chapter 4

1 An n-gram is a list of 'n' items from a given sequence of textual materials or
speech. The basic units can be letters, words, syllables, etc. Google n-gram
viewer is a good example of using this technique to search textual corpora:
http://www.books.google.com/ngrams

2 Whether by accident or design Bogost compiles lists of seemingly gendered,
'male', items of interest: gears, machinery, Mexican food, digestive issues
and computer technology. It is also notable that certain items repeat and
certain themes are easy to discern. This may be an ironic move, but it also
reveals the partiality of the list-making method.

Chapter 5

1 Indeed, the constellation is modelled on the human use of language,
Adorno explains, 'language offers no mere system of signs for cognitive
functions. Where it appears essentially as language, where it becomes a
form of representation, it will not define its concepts. It lends objectivity to
them by the relation into which it puts the concepts, centred about a thing.
Language thus serves the intention of the concept to express completely
what it means. By themselves, constellations represent from without what
the concept has cut away within: the "more" which the concept is equally
desirous and incapable of being. By gathering around the object of cognition,
the concepts potentially determine the objects interior. They attain, in
thinking, what as necessarily excised from thinking' (Adorno 2004a: 162).

2 An example of pre-computational collection of data about the self as a
lifestream is represented by Roberts (2004). One of the criticisms that
recur in the peer-review section is that Roberts fails to account for his own
anticipation of his experimentation and previous experimentation colouring
his results. Nonetheless, this kind of self-knowledge through collection is
made both easier, and arguably more rigorous by the collection through
compactants. Especially if the collection is of wide, rather than narrow width,
therefore enabling a post hoc analysis and hypothesis surfacing to occur.
Clearly, compactants also make the collection far easier with mobile devices.

3 Wolfram further writes: 'It's amazing how much it's possible to figure out
by analyzing the various kinds of data I've kept. And in fact, there are many
additional kinds of data I haven't even touched on in this post. I've also

got years of curated medical test data (as well as my not-yet-very-useful complete genome), GPS location tracks, room-by-room motion sensor data, endless corporate records—and much much more. . . . And as I think about it all, I suppose my greatest regret is that I did not start collecting more data earlier. I have some backups of my computer filesystems going back to 1980. And if I look at the 1.7 million files in my current filesystem, there's a kind of archeology one can do, looking at files that haven't been modified for a long time (the earliest is dated 29 June 1980)' (Wolfram 2012).

4 These include HTTP cookies and Locally Stored Objects (LSOs) and document object model storage (DOM Storage).

5 'Cookies are small pieces of text that servers can set and read from a client computer in order to register its "state." They have strictly specified structures and can contain no more than 4 KB of data each. When a user navigates to a particular domain, the domain may call a script to set a cookie on the user's machine. The browser will send this cookie in all subsequent communication between the client and the server until the cookie expires or is reset by the server' (Mittal 2010: 10).

6 Ghostery describes itself on its help page: 'Be a web detective. Ghostery is your window into the invisible web – tags, web bugs, pixels and beacons that are included on web pages in order to get an idea of your online behavior. Ghostery tracks the trackers and gives you a roll-call of the ad networks, behavioral data providers, web publishers, and other companies interested in your activity' (Ghostery 2012a). See also https://www.disconnect.me/

7 Also see examples at: (1) Chartbeat: http://www.static.chartbeat.com/js/ chartbeat.js; (2) Google Analytics: http://www.google-analytics.com/ga.js; (3) Omniture: http://www.o.aolcdn.com/omniunih.js; (4) Advertising.com: http://www.o.aolcdn.com/ads/adsWrapper.js

8 For an example see, http://www.static.chartbeat.com/js/chartbeat.js

9 For example, the page-scraping of data from open access web pages using 'robots' or 'spiders' in order to create user repositories of data through aggregation and data analysis. Interestingly this is the way in which Google collects the majority of the index data it uses for its search results. This is also becoming a digital method in the social sciences and raises particular digital research ethics that have still to be resolved, see https://www. issuecrawler.net/, http://www.socscibot.wlv.ac.uk/, http://www.webatlas.fr/ wp/navicrawler/

10 See these commercial examples of user control software for controlling user public exposure to trackers, web bugs and compactants, although the question is raised as to why you would choose to trust them: https://www. cloudcapture.org/register/ and http://www.abine.com

11 A computer worm is technically similar in design to a virus and is therefore considered to be a sub-class of a virus. Indeed, worms spread from computer to computer, often across networks, but unlike a virus, a worm has the ability to transfer itself without requiring any human action. A worm is able to do this by taking advantage of the file or information transport features, such as the networking setup, on a computer, which it exploits to enable it to travel from computer to computer unaided.

12 One of the ways in which the Stuxnet attack target was identified was through a close reading of the computer code that was disassembled from the worm and the careful analysis of the internal data structures and finite state machine used to structure the attack. Ironically, this was then matched by Ralph Langner with photographs that have been uploaded to the website of the President of Iran, Mahmoud Ahmadinejad, and confirmed the importance of the cascade structure, centrifuge layout and the enriching process by careful analysis of the accidental photographing of background images on computers used by the president, see http://www.president.ir/en/9172 (see Peterson 2012).

13 Offensive Security Research is a term that covers research security work around the intent to attack IT systems, much of it related to finding and publishing zero-day exploits either in the public domain or through various private channels (DeepSec 2012).

14 The timestamp in the file ~wtr4141.tmp indicates that the date of compilation was 03 February 2010 (Matrosov et al. n.d.). Although there is suspicion that there may be three versions of the Stuxnet code in response to its discovery: 'Most curious, there were two major variants of the worm. The earliest versions of it, which appear to have been released in the summer of 2009, were extremely sophisticated in some ways but fairly primitive in others, compared with the newer version, which seems to have first circulated in March 2010. A third variant, containing minor improvements, appeared in April. In Schouwenberg's view, this may mean that the authors thought Stuxnet wasn't moving fast enough, or had not hit its target, so they created a more aggressive delivery mechanism. The authors, he thinks, weighed the risk of discovery against the risk of a mission failure and chose the former' (Gross 2011).

15 Although there are some criticisms that this link may be spurious, for instance Cryptome (2010) argues: It may be that the 'myrtus' string from the recovered Stuxnet file path 'b:\myrtus\src\objfre_w2k_x86\i386\guava.pdb' stands for 'My-RTUs'as in Remote Terminal Unit.

16 After having performed detailed analysis of the Duqu code, Kaspersky Labs stated that they 'are 100% confident that the Duqu Framework was not programmed with Visual C++. It is possible that its authors used an in-house framework to generate intermediary C code, or they used another completely different programming language,' (Evans 2012).

17 Zetter (2012) states that Duqu's specific form of code that allows it to be identified as using: 'object-oriented C to write the event-driven code in DuQu [which] reveals something about the programmers who coded this part of DuQu – they were probably old-school coders. . . . The programming style is uncommon for malware and is more commonly found in professionally-produced commercial software created ten years ago, Raiu says. The techniques make DuQu stand out 'like a gem from the large mass of "dumb" malicious program we normally see'. . . . Kaspersky researchers note' (Zetter 2012).

18 See http://www.quantifiedself.com/

19 Of course some aspects of self-tracking are non-computational, as Hill (2011) describes 'a woman entrepreneur, who wishes to remain anonymous,

drinks her first stream of urine every morning as a "natural form of tracking" in order to remind herself of what she ate and drank the night before. A help desk analyst at a corporate law firm started monitoring his spending after racking up five figures in debt on iTunes and buying CDs. Microsoft researcher Gordon Bell keeps an audio recorder running all day and takes digital photos every 30 seconds – with the idea of outsourcing his memory to a computer. Psychology professor Seth Roberts eats a half stick of butter every day because, he says, it speeds up his ability to do simple math problems by 5%'. However, increasingly the data generated by these activities will inevitably be uploaded to computers systems and subject to computational analysis and even real-time data capture.

20 Some examples of visualization software for this kind of lifestreaming quantification and visualization are shown on these pages from the Quantified Self website: Personal Data Visualization, Jaw-Dropping Infographics for Beginners, A Tour Through the Visualization Zoo, Visual Inspiration.

21 Individuals that supply data into the networks at a large scale have been described as Terabyters. A terabyter is a person who produces more than a terabyte of new information every day (Frey 2010).

22 See http://www.open.sen.se/for a particularly good example of this: 'Make your data history meaningful. Privately store your flows of information and use rich visualizations and mashup tools to understand what's going on' (Sense 2012).

23 Computational actants, drawing the notion of actant from actor-network theory.

24 Of course compactants are not just 'internal' data collection agents. They may also be outside of your data resources and networks probing to get in, this kind of unauthorized access to personal data is on the rise and has been termed the industrialization of data theft (see Fulton 2012). Indeed, Fulton argues that 'scripts, bots, and other non-social means for obtaining access [to data] remains statistically more effective than direct, personal contact – although even these automated means remain astoundingly simple' (Fulton 2012).

25 For example, see Bamford (2012) who writes about the Utah Data Center that is being built for the National Security Agency: It is, in some measure, the realization of the 'total information awareness' programme created during the first term of the Bush administration—an effort that was killed by Congress in 2003 after it caused an outcry over its potential for invading Americans' privacy' (Bamford 2012).

26 What we might call 'outsider code' or 'critical code' is an interesting development in relation to this. A number of websites offer code that data scrapes or screen scrapes information to re-present and analyse it for the user, some examples include the (1) Parltrack software, which is designed to improve the transparency of the EU parliamentary legislative process, http://www.parltrack.euwiki.org/ (2) TheyWorkForYou, which screen scrapes the UK Parliamentary minutes, Hansard, http://www.theyworkforyou.com/

27 See, for example, the Stanford Program on Liberation Technology (Stanford 2012).

Chapter 6

1 The original panel description read: 'Slowly, but increasingly definitively, our technologies and our devices are learning to see, to hear, to place themselves in the world. Phones know their location by GPS. Financial algorithms read the news and feed that knowledge back into the market. Everything has a camera in it. We are becoming acquainted with new ways of seeing: the Gods-eye view of satellites, the Kinect's inside-out sense of the living room, the elevated car-sight of Google Street View, the facial obsessions of CCTV. . . . As a result, these new styles and senses recur in our art, our designs, and our products. The pixelation of low-resolution images, the rough yet distinct edges of 3D printing, the shifting layers of digital maps. In this session, the participants will give examples of these effects, products and artworks, and discuss the ways in which ways of seeing are increasingly transforming ways of making and doing' (SXSW 2012).

2 Here we might consider the growth of computational high-frequency trading and financial systems that are trained and programmed to identify patterns very quickly.

Chapter 7

1 This in part explains the attack on the universities current monopoly on knowledge by both the state and the information techno-capitalists. It also shows why the state is under such pressure to release its own reservoirs of information in the form of the open access movement, with notable examples being the US data.gov and the UK data.gov.uk. For a good example of this see the Cape Town Open Education Declaration.

2 'Consider the social pedigree of the leading lights on both front benches today. Cameron, Clegg and Osborne went to private schools whose fees are more than the average annual wage. More than a third of the current Commons was privately educated, three percentage points up on that elected in 2005, reversing a downward trend over several generations. . . . The Labour leader, Ed Miliband, went to Oxford from affluent north London, graduated in philosophy, politics and economics – or PPE, an apprenticeship scheme for budding pols – and was soon working for Gordon Brown. The defeated David Miliband went to the same Oxford college (Corpus Christi), also did PPE and was soon advising Tony Blair. . . . The shadow chancellor, Ed Balls, is another Oxford man, who also graduated in –yes– PPE and also ended up working for Brown. At Oxford he met his future wife (and current shadow home secretary) Yvette Cooper, which should not be a surprise, because she too was reading PPE' (Neil 2011).

3 If this reminds you of the statements of Julian Assange and Wikileaks, it should. They draw from a similar vein for their critique: 'Its not only in Vietnam where secrecy, malfeasance and unequal access have eaten into the first requirement of foresight ("truth and lots of it").' (Assange 2006).

4 Although a nascent universalization is suggested by the notion of the 'common' as used by movements like the Creative Commons and open source software groups (see Berry 2008).

5 These are offered as a first draft of the kinds of skills iteracy might require. They remain very much a work in progress.

6 There is an interesting question about whether we can read code without any recourse to notions of computation. Personally I do not see any reason why code cannot be read as a self-standing or even historical text. Reading within the horizon of the program itself might be very productive, particularly for large-scale systems that are extremely self-referential and intertextual.

7 Naturally this reminds me of Hegel's notion of History as a spiral. It is also evocative of notions of dialectics as a means of learning and education.

Chapter 8

1 Horkheimer further argues, 'The imperialism of the great European states need not envy the Middle Ages for its stakes. Its symbols are protected by more sophisticated instruments and more fear-inducing guards than the saints of the medieval church. The enemies of the Inquisition turned that dusk into the dawning of a new day. Nor does the dusk of capitalism have to usher in the night of mankind although today it certainly seems to be threatening it' (Horkheimer 1978: 17).

Bibliography

60minutes (2012a) Fmr. CIA head calls Stuxnet virus 'good idea', *60 Minutes*, accessed 04/03/2012, http://www.cbsnews.com/8301-18560_162-57388982/fmr-cia-head-calls-stuxnet-virus-good-idea/

—(2012b) Stuxnet: Computer worm opens new era of warfare, *60 Minutes*, accessed 04/03/2012, http://www.cbsnews.com/8301-18560_162-57390124/stuxnet-computer-worm-opens-new-era-of-warfare/

ActivityStreams (n.d.) Activity Streams, accessed 04/03/2012, http://activitystrea.ms/

ActivityStreamsWG (2011) JSON Activity Streams 1.0, Activity Streams Working Group, accessed 04/03/2012, http://activitystrea.ms/specs/json/1.0/

Adorno, T. (1969) 'Society', in R. Boyers (ed.), *The Legacy of the German Refugee Intellectuals*, New York: Schocken Books.

—(2005a) *Minima Moralia: Reflections on a Damaged Life*, London: Verso.

—(2005b) *The Culture Industry*, London: Routledge.

Adorno, T. W. (1991) 'Free Time', in J. M. Bernstein (ed.), *The Culture Industry*, London: Routledge.

—(2004a) *Negative Dialectics*, London: Routledge.

—(2004b) *Aesthetic Theory*, New York: Continuum.

Agger, M. (2009) Heidegger and the Art of Motorcycle Maintenance, *Slate*, accessed 06/03/2011, http://www.slate.com/id/2218650/

Alexander, C. (1964) *Notes on the Synthesis of Form*, Cambridge, MA: Harvard University Press.

—(1979) *The Timeless Way of Building*, Oxford: Oxford University Press.

Alexander, C., Ishikawa, S. and Silverstein, M. (1977) *A Pattern Language*, Oxford: Oxford University Press.

Algorithmics (2009) Credit Value Adjustment and the Changing Environment for Pricing and Managing Counterparty Risk, retrieved 09/01/2011, http://www.algorithmics.com/EN/media/pdfs/Algo-WP1209-CVASurvey.pdf

Alleyne, B. (2011) We are all hackers now: critical sociological reflections on the hacking phenomenon, under review, pp. 1–32, Goldsmiths Research Online, accessed 01/02/2013, http://eprints.gold.ac.uk/6305/

Anderson, P. (2012) The Force of the Anomaly, *The London Review of Books*, 26 April 2012.

Andreessen, M. (2011) Why Software Is Eating The World, *Wall Street Journal*, 20 August 2011, http://online.wsj.com/article/SB10001424053111903480904576512250915629460.html#articleTabs%3Darticle

Andreson, K. (2011) The Battle for Control—What People Who Worry About the Internet Are Really Worried About, accessed 06/03/2011, http://scholar-lykitchen.sspnet.org/2011/03/02/the-battle-for-control-what-people-who-worry-about-the-internet-are-really-worried-about/?utm_source=feedburner&utm_medium=email&utm_campaign=Feed%3A+ScholarlyKitchen+%28The+Scholarly+Kitchen%29

Anscombe, G. E. M. (1958) 'Modern moral philosophy', *Philosophy*, Vol. 33, pp. 38–40.

Anthony, S. (2013) Brown University creates first wireless, implanted brain-computer interface, *Nature*, accessed 03/03/2013, http://www.extremetech.com/extreme/149879-brown-university-creates-first-wireless-implanted-brain-computer-interface?utm_source=rss&utm_medium=rss&utm_campaign=brown-university-creates-first-wireless-implanted-brain-computer-interface#.UTSlVUbrm4w.hackernews

Antonelli, P. (2011) States of Design 03: Thinkering, *domus*, accessed 28/03/2012, http://www.domusweb.it/en/design/states-of-design-03-thinkering-/

Antonina, K., Barbro, B., Hannu, V., Jarmo, T., and Ari, V. (2003) Prototype-Matching System for Allocating Conference Papers, accessed 31/03/2012, http://www.hicss.hawaii.edu/HICSS36/HICSSpapers/DTDMI06.pdf

AP (2012) Iran says Stuxnet virus infected 16,000 computers, *Associated Press*, accessed 04/03/2012, http://www.foxnews.com/world/2012/02/18/iran-says-stuxnet-virus-infected-16000-computers/

Appleton, B. (2000) Patterns and Software: Essential Concepts and Terminology, accessed 31/03/2012, http://www.cmcrossroads.com/bradapp/docs/patterns-intro.html

Arato, A. and Gebhardt, E. (2005) *The Essential Frankfurt School Reader*, London: Continuum.

Archangel, C. (2012) Working on My Novel, accessed 01/01/2013, http://www.coryarcangel.com/things-i-made/2012-066-working-on-my-novel

Aron, J. (2012) Free apps eat up your phone battery just sending ads, *New Scientist*, accessed 20/03/2012, http://www.newscientist.com/article/mg21328566.400-free-apps-eat-up-your-phone-battery-just-sending-ads.html

Arrington, M. (2007) Quick, Plug The Internet Back In: Major Rackspace Outage, *Techcrunch*, accessed 23/07/2013, http://techcrunch.com/2007/11/12/quick-plug-the-internet-back-in-major-rackspace-outage/

Assange, J. (2006) Of Potholes and Foresight: The Road to Hanoi, *Counterpunch*, accessed 06/03/2011, http://www.counterpunch.org/assange12052006.html

—(2012) *Cypherpunks: Freedom and the Future of the Internet*, London: OR Books.

—(2013) How cryptography is a key weapon in the fight against empire states, *The Guardian*, accessed 09/07/2013, http://www.guardian.co.uk/commentisfree/2013/jul/09/cryptography-weapon-fight-empire-states-julian-assange

Ayman (2010) How many characters do you tweet?, accessed 13/02/2011, http://www.ayman-naaman.net/2010/04/21/how-many-characters-do-you-tweet/

Baker, J. (2012) European Watchdog Pushes for Do Not Track Protocol, accessed 10/03/2012, http://www.pcworld.com/businesscenter/article/251373/european_watchdog_pushes_for_do_not_track_protocol.html

Bamford, J. (2012) The NSA Is Building the Country's Biggest Spy Center (Watch What You Say), *Wired*, accessed 19/03/2012, http://www.wired.com/threatlevel/2012/03/ff_nsadatacenter/all/1

Barnett, E. (2010) Twitter building 'interest graph' to target users, *The Telegraph*, accessed 13/02/2011, http://www.telegraph.co.uk/technology/twitter/8016062/ Twitter-building-interest-graph-to-target-users.html

Bassett, C. (2007) *The Arc and the Machine: Narrative and New Media*, Manchester: Manchester University Press.

Bateson, G. (1979) *Mind and Nature: A Necessary Unity, (Advances in Systems Theory, Complexity, and the Human Sciences)*, Hampton Press, accessed 31/03/2012, http://www.oikos.org/mind&nature.htm

BBC (2012a) iPhone apps Path and Hipster offer address-book apology, *BBC*, accessed 28/03/2012, http://www.bbc.co.uk/news/technology-16962129

—(2012b) Backlash over email and web monitoring plan, accessed 02/04/2012, http://www.bbc.co.uk/news/uk-politics-17580906

Beaulieu, A. and de Rijcke, S. (2012) Network Realism, accessed 20/05/2012, http://networkrealism.wordpress.com/

Beck, R. (n.d.) The CDS market: A primer including computational remarks on 'Default Probabilities online', retrieved 09/01/2011, http://www.dbresearch. com/PROD/DBR_INTERNET_EN-PROD/PROD0000000000185396.pdf

Beecher, F. (2010) UI Guidelines for Skeuomorphic Multi-Touch Interfaces, accessed 29/03/2012, http://userexperience.evantageconsulting.com/2010/11/ ui-guidelines-for-skeuomorphic-multi-touch-interfaces/

Benjamin, W. (2003) *The Origin of German Tragic Drama*, London: Verso.

Benkler, Y. (2007) *The Wealth of Networks*, USA: Yale University Press.

Bernstein, M. S., Little, G., Miller, R. C., Hartman, B., Ackerman, M. S., Karger, D. R., Crowell, D., and Panovich, K. (2010) Soylent: A Word Processor with a Crowd Inside, accessed 04/05/2012, http://groups.csail.mit.edu/uid/ other-pubs/soylent.pdf

Berry, D. M. (2008) *Copy, Rip, Burn: The Politics of Copyleft and Open Source*, London: Pluto Press.

—(2011a) *The Philosophy of Software: Code and Mediation in the Digital Age*, London: Palgrave Macmillan.

—(2011b) 'The Computational Turn: Thinking about the Digital Humanities', *Culture Machine*, Special Issue on The Digital Humanities and Beyond, Vol. 12, accessed 12/09/2011, http://www.culturemachine.net/index.php/cm/article/ view/440/470

—(2012a) Computational Thinking: Some thoughts about Abduction, *Stunlaw*, 05/04/2012, http://stunlaw.blogspot.co.uk/2012/03/computational-thinking- some-thoughts.html

—(2012b) *Understanding Digital Humanities*, London: Palgrave.

—(2012c) Thinking Software: Realtime Streams and Knowledge in the Digital Age, UnlikeUs 2012, accessed 29/03/2012, http://vimeo.com/39256099

—(2012d) 'The Social Epistemologies of Software', *Social Epistemology: A Journal of Knowledge, Culture and Policy*, Vol. 26, No. 3–4, pp. 379–98.

—(2012e) 'The Relevance of Understanding Code to International Political Economy', *International Politics*, Vol. 49, No. 2, pp. 277–96.

—(2013) 'Against Remediation', in G. Lovink and M. Rasch (eds), *Unlike Us: Social Media Monopolies and Their Alternatives*, Amsterdam: Institute for Network Cultures.

Berry, D. M. and Moss, G. (2006) 'The Politics of the Libre Commons', *First Monday*, Vol. 11, No. 9, September 2006.

Berry, D. M., Dartel, M. v., Dieter, M., Kasprzak, M. Muller, N., O'Reilly, R., and Vicente, J. L. (2012) *New Aesthetic, New Anxieties*, Amsterdam: V2.

Bhaskar, R., Frank, C., Høyer, K. G., Naess, P. and Parker, J. (2010) *Interdisciplinarity and Climate Change: Transforming Knowledge and Practice for Our Global Future*, London: Routledge.

Biederman, I. (1987) 'Recognition-by-Components: A Theory of Human Image Understanding', *Psychological Review*, Vol. 94, No. 2, pp. 115–47, accessed 31/03/2012, http://www.cim.mcgill.ca/~siddiqi/COMP-558-2012/rbc.pdf

Bishop, C. (2012) Digital Divide, *Artforum*, September 2012, accessed 08/07/2013, http://hybridge.files.wordpress.com/2011/02/bishop-digital-divide-artforum-sep-2012.pdf

Black, M. J. (2002) *The Art of Code*, PhD dissertation, University of Pennsylvania.

Blake, T. (2012) Review: Lettre À Tristan Garcia, accessed 03/03/2013, http://terenceblake.wordpress.com/2013/02/27/harman-as-post-badiousian-epigone-review-of-mehdi-belhaj-kacems-lettre-a-tristan-garcia/

Bogoslaw, D. (2007) Big Traders Dive Into Dark Pools, Business Week, 3 October 2010, retrieved from http://www.businessweek.com/investor/content/oct2007/pi2007102_394204.htm

Bogost, I. (2008) 'The Phenomenology of Videogames', in S. Günzel, M. Liebe and D. Mersch (eds), *Conference Proceedings of the Philosophy of Computer Games 2008*, Potsdam: University Press, pp. 22–43, accessed 18/04/2012, http://pub.ub.uni-potsdam.de/volltexte/2008/2454/

—(2009a) What is Object-Oriented Ontology? A Definition for Ordinary Folk, accessed 20/05/2012, http://www.bogost.com/blog/what_is_objectoriented_ontolog.shtml

—(2009b) Object-Oriented P*, accessed 23/05/2012, http://www.bogost.com/blog/objectoriented_p.shtml

—(2011) Writing Book People Want to Read: Or How to Stake Vampire Publishing, accessed 23/05/2012, http://www.bogost.com/blog/writing_books_people_want_to_r.shtml

—(2012a) *Alien Phenomenology: or What It's Like to Be a Thing*, Minnesota University Press.

—(2012b) The New Aesthetic Needs to Get Weirder, *The Atlantic*, accessed 18/04/2012, http://www.theatlantic.com/technology/archive/2012/04/the-new-aesthetic-needs-to-get-weirder/255838/

Boltanski, L. (2011) *On Critique: A Sociology of Emancipation*, London: Polity.

Boltanski, L. and Thévenot, L. (2006) *On Justification: Economies of Worth*, Oxford: Princeton University Press.

Booksprints (2013) BookSprints.net, accessed 23/06/2013, http://www.booksprints.net

Borenstein, G. (2012) What Its Like to Be a 21C Thing?, *Creators Project*, accessed 07/04/2012, http://www.thecreatorsproject.com/blog/in-response-to-bruce-sterlings-essay-on-the-new-aesthetic#4

Borgmann, A. (1984) *Technology and the Character of Contemporary Life: A Philosophical Inquiry*, London: University of Chicago Press.

Borthwick, J. (2009) Distribution . . . now, accessed 12/09/2011, http://www.borthwick.com/weblog/2009/05/13/699/

—(2013) Betaworks Shareholder Letter 2012, accessed 10/02/2013, http://betaworks.com/shareholder/2012/index.html

Brad (2013) Datamoshing, accessed 03/03/2013, http://knowyourmeme.com/memes/datamoshing

Bridle, J. (2011a) Waving at the Machines, *Web Directions*, accessed 05/04/2012, http://www.webdirections.org/resources/james-bridle-waving-at-the-machines/

—(2011b) Regarding the library with envious eyes, Booktwo.org, accessed 05/04/2012, http://booktwo.org/notebook/books-computational-value/

—(2012a) The New Aesthetic, accessed 05/04/2012, http://new-aesthetic.tumblr.com/

—(2012b) #sxaesthetic, accessed 06/04/2012, http://booktwo.org/notebook/sxaesthetic/

Brown, W., Malveau, R., McCormick, H. and Mowbray, T. (1998) AntiPatterns, accessed 31/03/2012, http://www.antipatterns.com/

Bruinius, H. (2010) Can Warren Buffett and Bill Gates save the world?, *Christian Science Monitor*, accessed 06/03/2011, http://www.csmonitor.com/Business/Guide-to-Giving/2010/1120/Can-Warren-Buffett-and-Bill-Gates-save-the-world

Bryant, L. (2011) *The Democracy of Objects*, Ann Arbor: Open Humanities Press.

—(2012) The Materiality of SR/OOO: Why Has It Proliferated?, accessed 22/08/2012, http://larvalsubjects.wordpress.com/2012/06/03/the-materiality-of-srooo-why-has-it-proliferated/

Bryant, L., Srnicek, N., and Harman, G. (2011) *The Speculative Turn: Continental Materialism and Realism*, Melbourne: Re.Press.

Bucher, T. (2012) Want to be on the top? Algorithmic power and the threat of invisibility on Facebook, *New Media and Society*, Vol. 14, No. 7, pp. 1164–80, Online Print, accessed 22/04/2012, http://nms.sagepub.com/content/early/2012/04/04/1461444812440159.abstract

Callon, M. (1998) 'Introduction: Embeddedness of Economic Markets in Economics', in M. Callon (ed.), *The Laws of the Markets*, Oxford: Blackwell Publishers, pp. 1–57.

Canabarro, E. and Duffie, D. (2004) 'Measuring and Marking Counterparty Risk', in L. Tilman (ed.), *ALM of Financial Institutions*, Institutional Investor Books.

Carlson, T. (2003) 'Locating the Mystical Subject', in M. Kessler and C. Sheppard (eds), *Mystics*, Chicago: University of Chicago Press, accessed 02/12/2011, http://www.soc.ucsb.edu/projects/ct3/docs/LocatingtheMysticalSubject.doc.

Carr, N. (2008) Is Google Making Us Stupid? What the Internet is doing to our brains, *The Atlantic Magazine*, July/August 2008, accessed 06/03/2011, http://www.theatlantic.com/magazine/archive/2008/07/is-google-making-us-stupid/6868/

—(2010) *The Shallows: How the Internet is Changing the Way We Think, Read and Remember*, London: Atlantic Books.

—(2012) E-reading after the e-reader, accessed 02/02/2013, http://www.roughtype.com/?p=2245

Castells, M. (2000) *The Rise of the Network Society*, London: Blackwell.

Catt, R. D. (2012) Why the New Aesthetic isn't about 8bit retro, the Robot Readable World, computer vision and pirates, accessed 08/04/2012, http://revdancatt.com/2012/04/07/why-the-new-aesthetic-isnt-about-8bit-retro-the-robot-readable-world-computer-vision-and-pirates/

CBSNews (2010) Iran Confirms Stuxnet Worm Halted Centrifuges, *CBSNews*, accessed 04/03/2012, http://www.cbsnews.com/stories/2010/11/29/world/main7100197.shtml

Charlesworth, J. J. (2012) We are the droids we're looking for: the New Aesthetic and its friendly critics, accessed 25/05/2012, http://blog.jjcharlesworth.com/2012/05/07/we-are-the-droids-were-looking-for-the-new-aesthetic-and-its-friendly-critics/

Cherry, S. (2010) How Stuxnet Is Rewriting the Cyberterrorism Playbook, *IEEE Spectrum: Inside Technology*, accessed 04/03/2012, http://spectrum.ieee.org/podcast/telecom/security/how-stuxnet-is-rewriting-the-cyberterrorism-playbook

Chopra, S. and Dexter, S. (2008) *Decoding Liberation: The Promise of Free and Open Source Software*, USA: Routledge.

Chun, W. H. K. (2006) *Control and Freedom: Power and Paranoia in the Age of Fiber Optics*, Cambridge, MA: MIT Press.

—(2011) *Programmed Visions: Software and Memory*, Cambridge, MA: MIT Press.

Clark, D. (1992) A Cloudy Crystal Ball – Visions of the Future, Presentation given at the 24th Internet Engineering Task Force, accessed 06/03/2011, http://ietf.org/proceedings/prior29/IETF24.pdf

Cole, L., Austin, D., and Cole, L. (2004) Visual Object Recognition using Template Matching, accessed 31/03/2012, http://www.araa.asn.au/acra/acra2004/papers/cole.pdf

Computer History (n.d.) Ferranti Argus 700, accessed 07/07/2013, http://www.computinghistory.org.uk/det/16225/Ferranti-Argus-700/

Cope, A. S. (2012) Study for Roger, 2012, accessed 07/04/2012, http://www.aaronland.info/weblog/2012/03/13/godhelpus/#sxaesthetic

Copyfarleft (n.d.) Copyfarleft, retrieved 1/06/2010, http://p2pfoundation.net/Copyfarleft

Cox, G. (2013) *Speaking Code: Coding as Aesthetic and Political Expression*, Cambridge, MA: MIT Press.

Cox, G., McLean, A., and Ward, A. (2006) 'The Aesthetics of Generative Code' accessed 20/06/2012, http://generative.net/papers/aesthetics/

Cranor, L. F. and McDonald, A. M. (2008) The Cost of Reading Privacy Policies. *I/S: A Journal of Law and Policy for the Information Society*, 2008 Privacy Year in Review issue, accessed 26/03/2012, http://lorrie.cranor.org/pubs/readingPolicyCost-authorDraft.pdf

Crawford, M. (2010) *The Case for Working with Your Hands: or Why Office Work is Bad for Us and Fixing Things Feels Good*, London: Viking.

Cryptome (2010) Stuxnet Myrtus or MyRTUs?, accessed 04/03/2012, http://cryptome.org/0002/myrtus-v-myRTUs.htm

Davies, N. (2013) MI5 feared GCHQ went 'too far' over phone and internet monitoring, *The Guardian*, accessed 22/06/2013, http://www.guardian.co.uk/uk/2013/jun/23/mi5-feared-gchq-went-too-far

Davies, R. (2012) SXSW, the new aesthetic and writing, accessed 07/04/2012, http://russelldavies.typepad.com/planning/2012/03/sxsw-the-new-aesthetic-and-writing.html

DeepSec (2012) Thoughts about Offensive Security Research, *DeepSec*, accessed 24/03/2012, http://blog.deepsec.net/?p=792

Deleuze, G. and Guattari, F. (2003) *A Thousand Plateaus*, London: Continuum.

Derrida, J. (1994) *Specters of Marx: The State of the Debt, the Work of Mourning, & the New International*, trans. Peggy Kamuf, London: Routledge.

Deuze, M., Blank, P., and Speers, L. (2012) 'A Life Lived in Media', *Digital Humanities Quarterly*, Vol. 6, No. 1, accessed 29/02/2012, http://digitalhumanities.org/dhq/vol/6/1/000110/000110.html

Dewey, R. A. (2011) Top-down and Bottom-up Processing http://www.intropsych.com/ch07_cognition/top-down_and_bottom-up_processing.html

Dexter, S. (2012) 'The Esthetics of Hidden Things', in D. M. Berry (ed.), *Understanding Digital Humanities*, London: Palgrave, pp. 127–44.

Dixon, D. (2012) 'Analysis Tool or Design Methodology? Is there an epistemological basis for patterns?', in D. M. Berry (ed.), *Understanding Digital Humanities*, London: Palgrave.

Dobias, J. (2010) 'Privacy Effects of Web Bugs Amplified by Web 2.0', in S. Fischer-Hübner, P. Duquenoy, M. Hansen, R. Leenes, and G. Zhang (eds), *Privacy and Identity Management for Life*, London: Springer.

Douglass, J. (2007) Joining the Software Studies Initiative at UCSD, accessed 16/09/2011, http://writerresponsetheory.org/wordpress/2007/12/04/joining-the-software-studies-initiative-at-ucsd/

Dreyfus, H. L. (1997) Highway Bridges and Feasts: Heidegger and Borgmann on How to Affirm Technology, accessed 27/02/2012, http://www.focusing.org/apm_papers/dreyfus.html

—(2001) *Being-in-the-world: A Commentary on Heidegger's Being and Time, Division I*, Cambridge, MA: MIT Press.

Dreyfus, H. L. and Radinow, P. (1982) *Michel Foucault: Beyond Structuralism and Hermeneutics*, Chicago: The University of Chicago Press.

Eaton, K. (2012a) How One Second Could Cost Amazon $1.6 Billion In Sales, Fast Company, *Fast Company*, accessed 24/03/2012, http://www.fastcompany.com/1825005/impatient-america-needs-faster-intertubes

—(2012b) The Future According to Schmidt: 'Augmented Humanity,' Integrated into Google, *Fast Company*, 25 January 2011, http://www.fastcompany.com/1720703/future-according-schmidt- augmented-humanity-integrated-google

Economist (2012) Counting every moment, *The Economist*, accessed 02/03/2012, http://www.economist.com/node/21548493

—(2013) The rise of smart beta, *The Economist*, accessed 07/07/2013, http://www.economist.com/news/finance-and-economics/21580518-terrible-name-interesting-trend-rise-smart-beta

Edley Jr, C. (2009) Building a new UC – in cyberspace, *Los Angeles Times*, accessed 20/04/2011, http://articles.latimes.com/2009/jul/01/opinion/oe-edley1

EFF (1999) The Web Bug FAQ, accessed 02/03/2012, http://w2.eff.org/Privacy/Marketing/

Efrati, A. (2011) 'Like' Button Follows Web Users, *Wall Street Journal*, accessed 02/03/2012, http://online.wsj.com/article/SB10001424052748704428150457632 9441432995616.html

Eldridge, M. (n.d.) Clarifying the Process of Abduction and Understanding 'Inductive' Generalization, accessed 31/03/2012, http://www.philosophy.uncc.edu/mleldrid/SAAP/USC/TP26.html

Ellis, E. (2011) The New Aesthetic, accessed 05/04/2012, http://www.warrenellis.com/?p=12811

Ensmenger, N. L. (2010) *Computer Boys Take Over*, Cambridge, MA: MIT Press.

Evans, S. (2012) Duqu Trojan used 'unknown' programming language: Kaspersky, CBR Software Malware, accessed 09/03/2012, http://malware.cbronline.com/news/duqu-trojan-used-unknown-programming-language-kaspersky-070312

Evers, J. (2006) How HP bugged e-mail, accessed 02/03/2012, http://news.cnet.com/How-HP-bugged-e-mail/2100-1029_3-6121048.html

Exinfoam (2012) Hello, QR, accessed 18/04/2012, http://exinfoam.wordpress.com/2012/04/13/hello-qr/

Eyal, N. (2012) How to Manufacture Desire, TechCrunch, accessed 05/03/2012, http://techcrunch.com/2012/03/04/how-to-manufacture-desire/

Facebook (2012) Data Use Policy, accessed 02/03/2012, http://www.facebook.com/about/privacy/

Feenberg, A. (2004) *Heidegger and Marcuse: The Catastrophe and Redemption of History*, London: Routledge.

Fernandez, P. (2012) The New Aesthetic: A Response, accessed 18/04/2012, http://plummerfernandez.tumblr.com/post/21026026010/new-aesthetic

Fernholz, T. and Mims, C. (2012) Eight things Marc Andreessen said to Quartz that made us sit up and listen, *Quartz*, accessed 12/07/2013, http://qz.com/36368/eight-things-marc-andreessen-said-to-quartz-that-made-us-sit-up-and-listen/

Film Policy Review Panel (2012) A Future for British Film: It begins with the audience . . . , accessed 17/01/2012, http://www.culture.gov.uk/images/publications/DCMS_film_policy_review_report-2012.pdf

Foucault, M. (1984) 'What is Enlightenment?', in P. Rabinow (ed.), *The Foucault Reader*, New York: Pantheon Books, pp. 32–50.

—(2010) *The Birth of Biopolitics: Lectures at the Collège de France, 1978-1979*, Basingstoke: Palgrave Macmillan.

Fowler, M. (2013) Our Apology, accessed 03/03/2013, http://www.solidgoldbomb.com/pages/our-apology

Frankfurt Institute (1972) *Aspects of Sociology*, Boston: Beacon Press.

Freedland, J. (2011) We owe the internet for changing the world. Now let's learn how to turn off, *The Guardian*, accessed 06/03/2011, http://www.guardian.co.uk/commentisfree/2011/feb/22/internet-learn-to-turn-off

Freeman, E. T. (1997) The Lifestreams Software Architecture, Ph.D. Dissertation, Yale University Department of Computer Science, May 1997, accessed 02/03/2012, http://www.cs.yale.edu/homes/freeman/dissertation/etf.pdf

—(2000) Welcome to the Yale Lifestreams homepage!, accessed 02/03/2012, http://cs-www.cs.yale.edu/homes/freeman/lifestreams.html

Freeman, H. (2012) Open thread: iPad and iPhone art, *The Guardian*, accessed 05/04/2012, http://www.guardian.co.uk/artanddesign/2012/jan/17/art-hockney

Freestyle-Chess (2010) The concept and history of Freestyle Chess, accessed 02/12/2012, http://freestyle-chess.webs.com

Frey, T. (2010) The Coming of the Terabyters, accessed 01/04/2012, http://www.futuristspeaker.com/2010/07/the-coming-of-the-terabyters/

Fried, I. (2006) Dunn grilled by Congress, accessed 02/03/2012, http://news.cnet.com/Dunn-grilled-by-Congress/2100-1014_3-6120625.html

Fuller, M. (2005) *Media Ecologies: Materialist Energies in Art and Technoculture*, Cambridge, MA: MIT Press.

Fuller, M. and Goffey, A. (2012) *Evil Media*, Cambridge, MA: MIT Press.

Fuller, S. (2010) 'Humanity: The Always Ready – or Never to be – Object of the Social Sciences?', in J. W. Bonwel (ed.), *The Social Sciences and Democracy*, London: Palgrave Macmillan.

—(2011) *Humanity 2.0: What it Means to be Human Past, Present and Future*, London: Palgrave.

Fulton, S. M. (2012) The Industrialization of Data Theft: Verizon's Staggering New Data, *ReadWrite Enterprise*, accessed 26/03/2012, http://www. readwriteweb.com/enterprise/2012/03/the-industrialization-of-data.php?utm_ source=feedburner&utm_medium=feed&utm_campaign=Feed%3A+readwr iteweb+%28ReadWriteWeb%29

Galloway, A. (2010) Quentin Meillassoux, or The Great Outdoors, in *French Theory Today – An Introduction to Possible Futures*, Brooklyn: Public School New York.

Galloway, A. R. (2006) *Protocol: How Control Exists After Decentralization*, Cambridge, MA: MIT Press.

—(2011) 'Black Box, Black Bloc', in B. Nyes (ed.), *Communization and its Discontents: Contestation, Critique, and Contemporary Struggles*, New York: Minor Compositions.

—(2012) *The Interface Effect*, Cambridge: Polity.

—(2013) The Poverty of Philosophy: Realism and Postfordism, forthcoming in *Critical Inquiry*.

Galloway, A. and Thacker, E. (2007) *The Exploit: A Theory of Networks*, USA: Minnesota University Press.

Gannes, L. (2010) Eric Schmidt: Welcome to 'Age of Augmented Humanity', *The New York Times*, accessed 06/03/2011, http://www.nytimes.com/external/ gigaom/2010/09/07/07gigaom-eric-schmidt-welcome-to-age-of-augmented-humanity-28143.html

Garber, M. (2012) Americans Love Google! Americans Hate Google!, *The Atlantic*, accessed 02/03/2012, http://m.theatlantic.com/technology/ archive/2012/03/americans-love-google-americans-hate-google/254253/

Gelernter, D. (1994) The cyber-road not taken, *The Washington Post*, April 1994.

—(2010) Time to start taking the Internet seriously, *Edge*, accessed 23/02/2012, http://www.edge.org/3rd_culture/gelernter10/gelernter10_index.html

Ghostery (2010) The Many Data Hats a Company can Wear, accessed 02/03/2012, http://purplebox.ghostery.com/?p=948639073

—(2011) Ghostrank Planetary System, accessed 02/03/2012, http://purplebox. ghostery.com/?p=1016021670

—(2012a) About Ghostery, accessed 02/03/2012, http://www.ghostery.com/about

—(2012b) About ChartBeat, accessed 02/03/2012, http://www.ghostery.com/ apps/chartbeat

Goetz, T. (2011) Harnessing the Power of Feedback Loops, *Wired*, accessed 12/09/2011, http://www.wired.com/magazine/2011/06/ff_feedbackloop/

Gold, M. K. (2012) *Debates in the Digital Humanities*, Minneapolis: University of Minnesota Press.

Golumbia, D. (2009) *The Cultural Logic of Computation*, Harvard: Harvard University Press.

—(2012) berry on object-oriented ontology, accessed 03/03/2013, http://www. uncomputing.org/?p=133

Goodale, G. (2012) Jedi knights of online privacy strike back at data-mining empires, *The Christian Science Monitor*, accessed 20/03/2012, http://www.csmonitor.com/Innovation/2012/0314/Jedi-knights-of-online-privacy-strike-back-at-data-mining-empires

Google (2012a) Google Now, *Google*, http://www.google.com/landing/now/

—(2012b) Privacy Policy, accessed 02/03/2012, http://www.google.com/policies/privacy/

Gostev, A. (2012) Stuxnet/Duqu: The Evolution of Drivers, SecureList, accessed 02/03/2012, https://www.securelist.com/en/analysis/204792208/Stuxnet_Duqu_The_Evolution_of_Drivers

Grant, C. (2010) David Hockney's instant iPad art, *BBC*, accessed 05/04/2012, http://www.bbc.co.uk/news/technology-11666162

Greenberg, A. (2012) Meet The Hackers Who Sell Spies The Tools To Crack Your PC (And Get Paid Six-Figure Fees), *Forbes Magazine*, accessed 24/03/2012, http://www.forbes.com/sites/andygreenberg/2012/03/21/meet-the-hackers-who-sell-spies-the-tools-to-crack-your-pc-and-get-paid-six-figure-fees/

Greenwald, G., MacAskill, E., and Poitras, L. (2013) Edward Snowden: the whistleblower behind the NSA surveillance revelations, *The Guardian*, accessed 22/06/2013, http://www.guardian.co.uk/world/2013/jun/09/edward-snowden-nsa-whistleblower-surveillance

Gregory, J. (2009a) The Role of Counterparty Risk in the Credit Crisis, accessed 08/12/2010, http://oftraining.com/files/creditrisksummit_09.pdf

—(2009b) *Counterparty Credit Risk: The New Challenge for Global Financial Markets*, London: John Wiley.

Gross, M. J. (2011) A Declaration of Cyber-War, *Vanity Fair*, accessed 02/03/2012, http://www.vanityfair.com/culture/features/2011/04/stuxnet-201104

Grusin, R. (2012) The 'new aesthetic' is just the latest name for remediation, all dressed up with nowhere to go, accessed 18/04/2012, https://twitter.com/#!/rgrusin/status/192622844860047361

Guardian (2012) Amazon acts to halt sales of 'Keep Calm and Rape' T-shirts, *The Guardian*, accessed 03/03/2013, http://www.guardian.co.uk/technology/2013/mar/02/amazon-withdraws-rape-slogan-shirt

—(2013) Amazon acts to halt sales of 'Keep Calm and Rape' T-shirts, *The Guardian*, accessed 13/10/2013, http://www.theguardian.com/technology/2013/mar/02/amazon-withdraws-rape-slogan-shirt

Gyford, P. (2011) One of today's futures, accessed 05/04/2012, http://www.gyford.com/phil/writing/2011/05/26/new-aesthetic.php

Haines, T. (2011) How long does Twitter keep tweets?, Quora, accessed 13/02/2011, http://www.quora.com/How-long-does-Twitter-keep-tweets

Halsbury (1951) Letter from The Earl of Halsbury to Strachey, 9 November 1951, Bodleian Archives, A. 39, MS.Eng.Misc.b.251.

Harman, G. (2002) Tool-being: Heidegger and the Metaphysics of Objects, Chicago: Open Court Publishing Co.

—(2009a) Technology, objects and things in Heidegger, *Cambridge Journal of Economics*, doi:10.1093/cje/bep021

—(2009b) what correlationism reminds me of, accessed 23/05/2012, http://doctorzamalek2.wordpress.com/2009/11/08/what-correlationism-reminds-me-of/

—(2012) on philosophical movements that develop on the internet, accessed 23/08/2012, http://doctorzamalek2.wordpress.com/2012/06/03/on-philosophical-movements-that-develop-on-the-internet/

—(2013) a few more thoughts on the previous post, accessed 03/03/2013, http://doctorzamalek2.wordpress.com/2013/03/03/a-few-more-thoughts-on-the-previous-post/

Harraway, D. J. (2007) *When Species Meet*, Minneapolis, MN: University of Minnesota Press.

Harvey, A. (2011) OpenCV Face Detection: Visualized, accessed 08/04/2012, http://vimeo.com/12774628

—(2012) CV Dazzle, Camouflage from Computer Vision, accessed 05/04/2012, http://cvdazzle.com/

Hastac (2013) 'Amplified Marginalia': Social Reading, Listening, and Writing, Hastac, accessed 07/07/2013, http://hastac.org/forums/amplified-marginalia

Hayles, N. K. (1999) *How We Became Posthuman: Virtual Bodies in Cybernetics, Literature and Informatics*, Chicago: University of Chicago Press

—(2004) 'Print Is Flat, Code Is Deep: The Importance of Media-Specific Analysis', *Poetics Today*, Vol. 25, No. 1, pp. 67–90.

—(2007) 'Hyper and Deep Attention: The Generational Divide in Cognitive Modes', *Profession*, Vol. 13, pp. 187–99.

—(2012) *How We Think: Digital Media and Contemporary Technogenesis*, Chicago: Chicago University Press.

Heidegger, M. (1966) 'Only a God Can Save Us': The Spiegel Interview, accessed 23/06/2013, http://www.ditext.com/heidegger/interview.html

—(1973) 'Messkirch's Seventh Centennial', *Listening*, Vol. 8, pp. 50–1.

—(1977 [1938]) 'The Age of the World Picture', in M. Heidegger (ed.), *The Question Concerning Technology and other Essays*, New York: Harper Perennial, pp. 115–54.

—(1977) *The Question Concerning Technology and other Essays*, London: Harper & Row.

—(1978) *Being and Time*, London: Wiley-Blackwell.

—(1987) *An Introduction to Metaphysics*, New Haven: Yale University Press.

—(1995) *Basic Questions of Philosophy: Selected 'Problems' of 'Logic'*, London: John Wiley & Sons.

—(1999) *Contributions to Philosophy (From Enowning)*, Indiana: Indiana University Press.

—(2001) *Poetry, Language, Thought*, New York: Perennial Classics.

—(2012) *Contributions to Philosophy (of the Event)*, Indiana: Indiana University Press.

Heires, K. (2009) Real-Time Racing, *Risk Professional*, August 2009, pp. 33–7.

Held, D. (1997) *Introduction to Critical Theory: Horkheimer to Habermas*, London: Polity.

Hickman, L. (2013) How algorithms rule the world, *The Guardian*, accessed 02/07/2013, http://www.guardian.co.uk/science/2013/jul/01/how-algorithms-rule-world-nsa

Hill, K. (2011) Adventures in Self-Surveillance, aka The Quantified Self, aka Extreme Navel-Gazing, *Forbes*, accessed 01/04/2012, http://www.forbes.com/sites/kashmirhill/2011/04/07/adventures-in-self-surveillance-aka-the-quantified-self-aka-extreme-navel-gazing/

Hoffman, P. (2010) The Tao of IETF: A Novice's Guide to the Internet Engineering Task Force, accessed 06/03/2011, http://www.ietf.org/tao.html

Holmwood, J. (2013) Neo-liberalism: a problem of social science and for society, *Making Science Public Blog*, accessed 23/06/2013, http://blogs.nottingham.ac.uk/makingsciencepublic/2013/05/29/neo-liberalism-a-problem-of-social-science-and-for-society/

Holt, J. (2011) Smarter, Happier, More Productive, *The London Review of Books*, Vol. 33, No. 5, accessed 06/03/2011, http://www.lrb.co.uk/v33/n05/jim-holt/smarter-happier-more-productive

Hopkins, N. (2011) 'New Stuxnet' worm targets companies in Europe, *The Guardian*, http://www.guardian.co.uk/technology/2011/oct/19/stuxnet-worm-europe-duqu

Horkheimer, M. (1972) *Critical Theory: Selected Essays*, New York: Continuum.

—(1978) *Dawn & Decline*, London: Seabury Press.

—(1993) The Present Situation of Social Philosophy and the Tasks of an Institute for Social Research, accessed 07/07/2013, http://www.marxists.org/reference/archive/horkheimer/1931/present-situation.htm

—(2004) *Eclipse of Reason*, New York: Continuum.

Horkheimer, M. and Adorno, T. W. (2002) *The Dialectics of Enlightenment: Philosophical Fragments*, Stanford, CA: Stanford University Press.

—(2006) 'The Culture Industry: Enlightenment as Mass Deception', in M. G. Durham and D. Kellner (eds), *Media and Cultural Studies: Keyworks*, Oxford: Blackwell Publishing.

HTCwire (2010) Algorithmic Terrorism on Wall Street, retrieved 06/08/2010, http://www.hpcwire.com/blogs/Algorithmic-Terrorism-on-Wall-Street-100079719.html

Hubspot (2009) State of the Twittersphere, June 2009, accessed 13/02/2011, http://blog.hubspot.com/Portals/249/sotwitter09.pdf

Huff, J. (2012) Beyond the Surface: 15 Years of Desktop Aesthetics, *Rhizome*, accessed 05/04/2012, http://rhizome.org/editorial/2012/mar/14/beyond-surface-15-years-desktop-aesthetics/

Hughes, L. (2010) Santa's Privacy Policy, *McSweeneys*, accessed 13/02/2012, http://www.mcsweeneys.net/articles/santas-privacy-policy

Humphries, M. (2010) Bill Gates: Forget university, the web is the future for education, accessed 20/04/2011, http://www.geek.com/articles/news/bill-gates-forget-university-the-web-is-the-future-for-education-2010087/

Hutchins, E. (1996) *Cognition in the Wild*, Cambridge, MA: MIT Press.

Hyde, L. (2006) *The Gift: How the Creative Spirit Transforms the World*, London: Canongate.

ICO (2012) New PECR rules – what do they mean for me? – ICO, accessed 01/04/2012, http://www.ico.gov.uk/news/current_topics/new_pecr_rules.aspx

Irani, L. and Silberman, M. S. (2013) Turkopticon: Interrupting Worker Invisibility in Amazon Mechanical Turk, accessed 10/07/2013, http://www.ics.uci.edu/~lirani/Irani-Silberman-Turkopticon-camready.pdf

Israel, S. (2012) Age of Context: Really Smart Mobile Devices, *Forbes*, 5 September 2012, http://www.forbes.com/sites/shelisrael/2012/09/05/age-of-context-really-smart-mobile-devices/

ITU (2012) Measuring the Information Society, accessed 01/01/2013, http://www.itu.int/ITU-D/ict/publications/idi/material/2012/MIS2012-ExecSum-E.pdf

Jackson, R. (2011) Why we should be Discrete in Public – Encapsulation and the Private lives of Objects, accessed 04/06/2012, http://robertjackson.info/index/wp-content/uploads/2011/01/Aarhus-presentation.pdf

—(2012) The Banality of The New Aesthetic, *Furtherfield*, accessed 18/04/2012, http://www.furtherfield.org/features/banality-new-aesthetic

Jameson, F. (2006) 'Postmodernism or the Cultural Logic of Late Capitalism', in D. Kellner and M. G. Durham (eds), *Media and Cultural Studies Keywords*, London: Blackwell.

Jarvis, J. (2011) The distraction trope, accessed 06/03/2011, http://www.buzzmachine.com/2011/02/24/the-distraction-trope/

Jarvis, S. (1998) *Adorno: A Critical Introduction*, Cambridge: Polity.

—(2009) 'The Truth in Verse? Adorno, Wordsworth, Prosody', in D. Cunningham and N. Mapp (eds), *Adorno and Literature*, New York: Continuum.

Jay, M. (1973) *The Dialectical Imagination: A History of the Frankfurt School and the Institute of Social Research, 1923-1950*, New York: Little Brown.

Jenkins, H. W. (2010) 'Google and the Search for the Future', *The Wall Street Journal*, 14 August 2010, retrieved from http://on.wsj.com/aippTz

Jones, M. (2011) Sensor-Venacular, Berg, access 05/04/2012, http://berglondon.com/blog/2011/05/13/sensor-vernacular/

Jorion, P. and Zhang, G. (2009) 'Credit Contagion from Counterparty Risk', *The Journal of Finance*, Vol. 64, No. 5, pp. 2053–87.

JPEG (2012) JPEG Homepage, accessed 31/03/2012, http://www.jpeg.org/jpeg/index.html

Kaganskiy, J. (2012) In Response To Bruce Sterling's 'Essay On The New Aesthetic', *Creators Project*, accessed 07/04/2012, http://www.thecreatorsproject.com/blog/in-response-to-bruce-sterlings-essay-on-the-new-aesthetic

Kalakota, R. (2011) Big Data Infographic and Gartner 2012 Top 10 Strategic Tech Trends, accessed 05/05/2012, http://practicalanalytics.wordpress.com/2011/11/11/big-data-infographic-and-gartner-2012-top-10-strategic-tech-trends/

Kampfner, J. (2012) The fight for control of the internet has become critical, *The Guardian*, accessed 26/08/2012, http://www.guardian.co.uk/commentisfree/2012/aug/22/fight-control-internet-become-critical

Kant, I. (1991) 'An Answer to the Question: What is Enlightenment?', in *Kant: Political Writings*, Cambridge: Cambridge University Press.

—(1998) *Critique of Pure Reason*, Cambridge: Cambridge University Press.

Kasparov, G. (2010) The Chess Master and the Computer, *The New York Review of Books*, accessed 02/12/2012, http://www.nybooks.com/articles/archives/2010/feb/11/the-chess-master-and-the-computer/

Kellner, D. and Share, J. (2005) 'Toward Critical Media Literacy: Core concepts, debates, organizations, and policy', *Discourse: studies in the cultural politics of education*, Vol. 26, No. 3, pp. 369–86.

Kennish, B. (2011) Tracking the Trackers: How Our Browsing History is Leaking into the Cloud, *Youtube*, accessed 26/03/2012, http://www.youtube.com/watch?v=BK_E3Bjpe0E

Kimbell, L. (2013) 'The Object Strikes Back: An interview with Graham Harman', *Design and Culture*, Vol. 5, No. 1, accessed 03/03/2013, http://www.lucykimbell.com/stuff/Kimbell_Harmaninterview_final_public_2013.pdf

Kirschenbaum, M. G. (2008) *Mechanisms: New Media and the Forensic Imagination*, Cambridge, MA: MIT Press.

Kitchin, R. (2011) 'The Programmable City', *Environment and Planning B: Planning and Design*, Vol. 38, pp. 945–51

Kitchin, R. and Dodge, M. (2011) *Code/Space: Software and the Everyday*, Cambridge, MA: MIT Press.

Kittler, F. (1997) *Literature, Media, Information Systems*, London: Routledge.

—(1999) *Gramophone, Film, Typewriter*, Stanford, CA: Stanford University Press.

Kopstein, K. (2013) DARPA's 1.8 gigapixel drone camera is a high-res Fourth Amendment lawsuit waiting to happen, *The Verge*, accessed 03/03/2013, http://www.theverge.com/2013/2/1/3940898/darpa-gigapixel-drone-surveillance-camera-revealed

Kruszelnicki, K. (2011) Stuxnet opens cracks in Iran nuclear program, accessed 02/03/2012, http://www.abc.net.au/science/articles/2011/10/26/3348123.htm

Langley, P. (2008) 'Sub-prime mortgage lending: a cultural economy', *Economy and Society*, Vol. 37, No. 4, pp. 469–94.

Langner, R. (2011) Ralph Langner: Cracking Stuxnet, a 21st-century cyber weapon, accessed 02/03/2012, http://www.youtube.com/watch?feature=player_embedded&v=CS01Hmjv1pQ

Lash, S. (2002) *Critique of Information*, London: Sage.

—(2007) 'Power after Hegemony, Cultural Studies in Mutation?', *Theory, Culture & Society*, Vol. 24, No. 3, pp. 55–78.

Lash, S. and Lury, C. (2007) *Global Cultural Industry: The Mediation of Things*, London: Polity.

Latour, B. (2005) *Reassembling the Social: An Introduction to Actor-Network-Theory*, Oxford: Oxford University Press.

Lawrence, S. H. (1983) Centralization and Decentralization: The Compunications Connection, Programme on Information Resources Programme, Center for Information Policy Research, Cambridge, MA: Harvard University.

Lea, D. (1977) Christopher Alexander: An Introduction for Object-Oriented Designers, accessed 31/03/2012, http://g.oswego.edu/dl/ca/ca/ca.html

—(1997) Christopher Alexander: An Introduction for Object-Oriented Designers, accessed 31/03/2012, http://g.oswego.edu/dl/ca/ca/ca.html

Leonard, A. (2013) The Internet's destroying work—and turning the old middle-class into the new proletariat, *Salon*, accessed 12/07/2013, http://www.salon.com/2013/07/12/the_new_proletariat_workers_of_the_cloud/

Lessig, L. (1999) *Code and Other Laws of Cyberspace*, New York: Basic Books.

—(2005) *Free Culture: The Nature and Future of Creativity*, London: Penguin.

Levine, R., Locke, C., Searls, D., and Weinberger, D. (2001) *The Cluetrain Manifesto: The End of Business as Usual*, USA: Perseus Publishing.

Lippman, W. (1997) *Public Opinion*, London: Simon & Schuster.

Liu, A. (2004) *The Laws of Cool: Knowledge Work and the Culture of Information*, Chicago: University Of Chicago Press.

—(2011) Alan Liu: The State of the Digital Humanities: A Report and a Critique, accessed 23/06/2013, http://www.sms.cam.ac.uk/media/1173142 [video]

—(2013) 'From Reading to Social Computing', in K. Price and R. Siemens (eds), *Literary Studies in the Digital Age: An Evolving Anthology*, New York: MLA P/MLA Commons, accessed 11/02/2013, http://DLSAnthology.commons.mla.org>.

Livingston, P. (2003) 'Thinking and Being: Heidegger and Wittgenstein on Machination and Lived-Experience', *Inquiry*, Vol. 46, pp. 324–45.

Love, D. (2012) Here's The Information Facebook Gathers On You As You Browse The Web, *Business Insider*, accessed 02/03/2012, http://www.businessinsider.com/facebook-tracking-2011-11

Lukács, G. (1971) *History and Class Consciousness*, Berlin: Merlin Press.

Lyotard, J. F. (1984) *The Postmodern Condition: A Report on Knowledge*, Manchester: Manchester University Press.

Mac, R. (2012) Move Over Siri, Alohar Wants To Learn Everything About You, *Forbes*, accessed 01/04/2012, http://www.forbes.com/sites/ryanmac/2012/03/23/move-over-siri-alohar-wants-to-learn-everything-about-you/

MacKenzie, D. and Wacjman, J. (1999) *The Social Shaping of Technology*, London: Open University Press.

MacManus, R. (2011) The Pros & Cons of Frictionless Sharing, *ReadWriteWeb*, accessed 02/12/2011, http://www.readwriteweb.com/archives/frictionless_sharing_pros_cons.php

Madrigal, A. (2012) I'm Being Followed: How Google—and 104 Other Companies—Are Tracking Me on the Web, *The Atlantic*, accessed 02/03/2012, http://m.theatlantic.com/technology/archive/2012/02/im-being-followed-how-google-and-104-other-companies-are-tracking-me-on-the-web/253758/

—(2013) DARPA's 1.8 Gigapixel Drone Camera Could See You Waving At It From 15,000 Feet, *The Atlantic*, accessed 03/03/2013, http://www.theatlantic.com/technology/archive/2013/02/darpas-18-gigapixel-drone-camera-could-see-you-waving-at-it-from-15-000-feet/272796/

Malik, C. (2009) Religion Gets in the Way of Batik Copyrighting, *JakartaGlobe*, retrieved 01/09/2010, http://thejakartaglobe.com/national/religion-gets-in-the-way-of-batik-copyrighting/317672

MAME (2012) Multiple Arcade Machine Emulator, http://mamedev.org/

Mannheim, K. (1952) 'The Problem of Generations', in P. Kecskemeti (ed.), *Karl Mannheim: Essays*, London: Routledge, pp. 276–322, accessed 15/02/2013, http://www.history.ucsb.edu/faculty/marcuse/classes/201/articles/27MannheimGenerations.pdf

—(1967) *Ideology and Utopia*, London: Harvest.

Manovich, L. (2001) *The Language of New Media*, Cambridge: MIT Press.

—(2008) Software Takes Command, accessed 16/09/2011, early pdf draft, http://lab.softwarestudies.com/2008/11/softbook.html

—(2013) *Software Takes Command*, Cambridge, MA: MIT Press.

Marcuse, H. (1978) *The Essential Frankfurt School Reader*, New York: Continuum.

Marino, M. C. (2006) Critical Code Studies, Electronic Book Review, accessed 16/09/2011, http://www.electronicbookreview.com/thread/electropoetics/codology

—(2011) Who has a good alternative to 'literacy', marcmarino, Twitter, 15/09/2011, accessed 16/09/2011, https://twitter.com/markcmarino/status/114448471813144578

Markoff, J. and Sanger, D. S. (2010) In a Computer Worm, a Possible Biblical Clue, *The New York Times*, accessed 04/03/2012, http://www.nytimes.com/2010/09/30/world/middleeast/30worm.html?_r=1

Marx, K. (1990) *Capital: Critique of Political Economy Volume 1*, London: Penguin.

Matrosov, A., Rodionov, E., Harley, D., and Malcho, J. (n.d.) Stuxnet Under the Microscope, accessed 04/03/2012, http://go.eset.com/us/resources/white-papers/Stuxnet_Under_the_Microscope.pdf

Mazières, D. and Kohler, E. (2005) Get me off your f——g mailing list. Submitted to the 9th World Multi-Conference on Systemics, Cybernetics, and Informatics, Orlando, FL, July 2005, accessed 20/11/2012, http://www.scs.stanford.edu/~dm/home/papers/remove.pdf

McNeil, J. (2012) The New Aesthetic: Seeing Like Digital Devices at SXSW 2012, accessed 07/04/2012, http://joannemcneil.com/index.php?/talks-and-such/new-aesthetic-at-sxsw-2012/

Media Hackers (2013) River of News, accessed 26/06/2013, http://tabs.mediahackers.org

Meillassoux, Q. (2009) *After Finitude: An Essay on the Necessity of Contingency*, London: Continuum.

Menkman, R. (2010) Glitch Studies Manifesto, accessed 20/05/2012, http://rosa-menkman.blogspot.com/2010/02/glitch-studies-manifesto.html

Microsoft (2012) Organizing Patterns, accessed 01/04/2012, http://msdn.microsoft.com/en-us/library/ff647589.aspx

Milian, M. (2011) Making it harder for ads to track you online, *CNN*, accessed 04/03/2012, http://edition.cnn.com/2011/TECH/web/06/21/ad.tracking/

Miller, R. (2007) Truck Crash Knocks Rackspace Offline, *Data Centre Knowledge*, accessed 23/06/2013, http://www.datacenterknowledge.com/archives/2007/11/13/truck-crash-knocks-rackspace-offline/

Mitcham, C. (1998) 'The Importance of Philosophy to Engineering', *Teorema*, Vol. XVII, No. 3, pp. 27–47.

Mittal, S. (2010) User Privacy and the Evolution of Third-party Tracking Mechanisms on the World Wide Web, Thesis, accessed 04/03/2012, http://www.stanford.edu/~sonalm/Mittal_Thesis.pdf

Mmpc2 (2010) The Stuxnet Sting, accessed 04/03/2012, http://blogs.technet.com/b/mmpc/archive/2010/07/16/the-stuxnet-sting.aspx

Moler, C. (2004) Numerical Computing with MATLAB, accessed 31/03/2012, http://www.mathworks.se/moler/chapters.html

Moretti, F. (2007) *Graphs, Maps, Trees: Abstract Models for a Literary History*, London: Verso.

Morgan, M. (n.d.) Feature Analysis, accessed 31/03/2012, http://www.staff.city.ac.uk/~morgan/FeatureAnalysis.pdf

Morozov, E. (2012a) Afterword to the Paperback Edition, *The Net Delusion*, accessed 24/03/2012, http://www.scribd.com/doc/85936832/Afterword-TND

—(2012b) Google Should Not Choose Right and Wrong, accessed 20/12/2012, http://evgenymorozov.tumblr.com/post/38636421217/my-ft-oped-on-google-and-algorithmic-nudging

—(2013) *To Save Everything Click Here: The Folly of Technological Solutionism*, New York: PublicAffairs.

Morton, T. (2011) Here Comes Everything: The Promise of Object-Oriented Ontology, *Qui Parle*, accessed 25/05/2012, http://ucdavis.academia.edu/TimMorton/Papers/971122/Here_Comes_Everything_The_Promise_of_Object-Oriented_Ontology

Naraine, R. (2012a) 0-day exploit middlemen are cowboys, ticking bomb, ZDNet, accessed 24/03/2012, http://www.zdnet.com/blog/security/0-day-exploit-middlemen-are-cowboys-ticking-bomb/10294

—(2012b) Offensive security research community helping bad guys, ZDNet, accessed 24/03/2012, http://www.zdnet.com/blog/security/offensive-security-research-community-helping-bad-guys/10228

Neil, A. (2011) The fall of the meritocracy, *The Spectator*, accessed 06/03/2011, http://www.spectator.co.uk/essays/6650303/part_3/the-fall-of-the-meritocracy.thtml

NoLOC (2011) #NoLOC.org: Keep Your Tweets From Being Archived Forever, accessed 13/02/2011, http://noloc.org/

NYFA (2012) An Xiao on Twitter as an Artistic Medium, accessed 03/01/2013, http://www.nyfa.org/nyfa_current_detail.asp?id=17&fid=1&curid=757

NYU (2011a) Business & Political Economy (BPE) program, accessed 20/04/2011, http://www.stern.nyu.edu/UC/ProspectiveStudent/Academics/PoliticalProgram/index.htm

—(2011b) Global Liberal Studies Program, accessed 20/04/2011, http://www.nyu.edu/admissions/undergraduate-admissions/academic-programs/global-liberal-studies-program.html

O'Connor, B. (2013) *Adorno*, London: Routledge.

O'Reilly, T. (2013) Context Aware Programming, *O'Reilly Radar*, accessed 07/07/2013, http://radar.oreilly.com/2013/07/context-aware-programming.html

Oettinger, A. G. and Legates, J. C. (1977) '"Compunications": a policy agenda', *Telecommunications Policy*, Vol. 1, No. 5, pp. 431–3.

Online Learning Task Force (2011) Collaborate to compete: Seizing the opportunity of online learning for UK higher education, *HEFCE*, accessed 20/04/2011, http://www.hefce.ac.uk/pubs/hefce/2011/11_01/11_01.pdf

Oram, A. and Wilson, G. (2007) *Beautiful Code*, London: O'Reilly.

Outhwaite, R. W. (1975) *Understanding Social Life: The Method Called Verstehen*, London: George Allen and Unwin Ltd.

—(2012) *Critical Theory and Contemporary Europe*, New York: Continuum.

Owens, T. (2012) The New Aesthetic and the Artifactual Digital Object, accessed 18/04/2012, http://www.trevorowens.org/2012/04/the-new-aesthetic-and-the-artifactual-digital-object/

Parikka, J. (2010) *Insect Media: An Archaeology of Animals and Technology*, Minneapolis: University of Minnesota Press

—(2012) *What is Media Archaeology?*, London: Polity.

Parikka, J. and Huhtamo, E. (2011) *Media Archaeology: Approaches, Applications, and Implications*, Berkeley: University of California Press

Parisi, L. and Portanova, J. (2012) Soft thought (in architecture and choreography), *Computational Culture*, accessed 08/04/2012, http://computationalculture.net/article/soft-thought

Pathak, A., Hu, Y. C., and Zhang, M. (2012) Where is the energy spent inside my App? Fine Grained Energy Accounting on Smartphones with Eprof, accessed 20/03/2012, http://research.microsoft.com/en-us/people/mzh/eurosys-2012.pdf

Peirce, C. S. (1958) *The Collected Works of Charles Sanders Peirce*, Cambridge, MA: Harvard University Press.

—(1988) 'Pragmatism as the Logic of Abduction', in C. S. Peirce (ed.), *The Essential Peirce: Selected Philosophical Writings, 1893–1913*, Bloomington: Indiana University Press.

Peterson, D. G. (2012) Langner's Stuxnet Deep Dive S4 Video, accessed 04/03/2012, http://www.digitalbond.com/2012/01/31/langners-stuxnet-deep-dive-s4-video/

Pew (2012) Search Engine Use 2012, accessed 09/03/2012, http://pewinternet. org/Reports/2012/Search-Engine-Use-2012/Summary-of-findings.aspx

Phillips, J. (2006) Deleuze and Guattari, accessed 13/02/2011, http://courses.nus. edu.sg/course/elljwp/deleuzeandguattari.htm

Pinterest (2012) Pinterest, accessed 05/04/2012, http://pinterest.com/

Poitras, L., Rosenbach, M., Schmid, F., Stark, H., and Stock, J. (2013) How the NSA Targets Germany and Europe, *Spiegel*, accessed 02/07/2013, http://www. spiegel.de/international/world/secret-documents-nsa-targeted-germany-and-eu-buildings-a-908609.html

Poster, M. (1996) *The Second Media Age*, London: Polity.

Preda, A. (2005) 'Socio-Technical Agency in Financial Markets: The Case of the Stock Ticker', *Social Studies of Science*, October 2006, Vol. 36, No. 5, pp. 753–82.

Quinton, L. (2005) RDF Direct Schedule Revealed, accessed 13/02/2011, http:// db.riskwaters.com/public/showPage.html?page=427560

Radlab (2009) Recovery-oriented computing, accessed 23/06/2013, http://radlab. cs.berkeley.edu/about

Raine, L. and Duggan, M. (2012) E-book Reading Jumps; Print Book Reading Declines, *Pew Internet and American Life*, accessed 27/12/2012, http:// libraries.pewinternet.org/2012/12/27/e-book-reading-jumps-print-book-reading-declines/

Raley, R. (2009) *Tactical Media*, Minneapolis: University of Minnesota Press.

—(2013) 'Dataveillance and Countervailance', in L. Gitelman (ed.), *'Raw Data' Is an Oxymoron*, Cambridge, MA: MIT Press.

Raymond, M. (2010) How Tweet It Is!: Library Acquires Entire Twitter Archive, accessed 13/02/2011, http://blogs.loc.gov/loc/2010/04/how-tweet-it-is-library-acquires-entire-twitter-archive/

Rhizome (2012) Prosthetic Knowledge Picks: The Algorists, accessed 06/07/2012, http://rhizome.org/editorial/2012/jul/5/prosthetic-knowledge-picks-algorists/

Richmond, S. (2010) Eric Schmidt: Google Gets Close to 'the Creepy Line', *The Telegraph*, 5 October 2010, http://blogs.telegraph.co.uk/technology/ shanerichmond/100005766/eric-schmidt-getting-close-to-the-creepy-line/

Rieland, R. (2012) So What Do We Do With All This Data?, *The Smithsonian*, accessed 04/03/2012, http://blogs.smithsonianmag.com/ideas/2012/01/so-what-do-we-do-with-all-this-data/

Robbins, J. (2007) Failure Happens: An SLA is just a contract & Data Centers are single points of failure too, *O'Reilly Radar*, accessed 23/06/2013, http://radar. oreilly.com/2007/11/failure-happens-an-sla-is-just.html

Roberts, B. F., Lemus, A. M., D'Argenio, M., and Relyea, D. H. (2012) Methods and Systems for Presenting an Advertisement Associated with an Ambient Action of a User, US Patent 2012/0304206, accessed 20/12/2012, http://info. publicintelligence.net/Verizon-DVR-Patent.pdf

Roberts, J. (2004) 'The dialectic of enlightenment', in F. Rush (ed.), *The Cambridge Companion to Critical Theory*, Cambridge: Cambridge University Press.

Roberts, S. (2004) 'Self-experimentation as a source of new ideas: Examples about sleep, mood, health, and weight', *Behavioral and Brain Sciences*, Vol. 27, pp. 227–62, accessed 21/03/2012, http://escholarship.org/uc/item/2xc2h866#page-1

Roose, K. (2012) Marc Andreessen Denies the Existence of the Middle Class, *New York Magazine*, accessed 06/07/2013, http://nymag.com/daily/intelligencer/2012/12/marc-andreessen-and-the-middle-class.html

Rossiter, N. (2007) *Organized Networks: Media Theory, Creative Labour, New Institutions*, Amsterdam: Institute of Network Cultures NAi Publishers.

Rush, F. (2004) 'Conceptual foundations of early Critical Theory', in F. Rush (ed.), *The Cambridge Companion to Critical Theory*, Cambridge: Cambridge University Press.

Rybczynski, W. (2009) Do You See a Pattern?, *Slate*, accessed 31/03/2012, http://www.slate.com/articles/arts/architecture/2009/12/do_you_see_a_pattern.html

Salas, E. (2009) 'Abduction and the Origin of 'Musement': Peirce's 'Neglected Argument' for the Reality of God', *International Philosophical Quarterly*, Vol. 49, No. 4, Issue 196, pp. 459–71.

Scalar (2013) The Alliance for Networking Visual Culture, accessed 23/06/2013, http://scalar.usc.edu

Schecter, D. (2007) *The History of the Left from Marx to the Present: Theoretical Perspectives*, London: Continuum.

—(2010) *The Critique of Instrumental Reason from Weber to Habermas*, New York: Continuum.

Schmidt, E. and Cohen, J. (2013) *The New Digital Age: Reshaping the Future of People, Nations and Business*, London: John Murray.

Schofield, M. (2013) Memories of Stasi color Germans' view of U.S. surveillance programs, *McClatchy*, accessed 02/07/2013, http://www.mcclatchydc.com/2013/06/26/195045/memories-of-stasi-color-germans.html

Schott, B. (2009) Twittergraphy, *The New York Times*, accessed 13/02/2011, http://www.nytimes.com/2009/08/03/opinion/03schott.html?_r=1

Schumpeter (2011) The Higher Education Bubble, *The Economist*, accessed 20/04/2011, http://www.economist.com/blogs/schumpeter/2011/04/higher-education_bubble_0

Schurz, G. (2008) 'Patterns of Abduction', *Synthese*, Vol. 164, No. 2, pp. 201–34.

Schwartz, M. (2013) 'Like a Mosquito', *London Review of Books*, 4 July 2013, Vol. 35, No. 13.

Searls, D. (2013) Android as a life management platform, accessed 04/02/2013, http://blogs.law.harvard.edu/doc/2013/01/06/android-as-a-life-management-platform/

Sense (2012) Feel. Act. Make sense, accessed 04/03/2012, http://open.sen.se/

Servin, J. (2010) David Hockney's Fresh Flowers, *Vogue*, accessed 28/03/2012, http://www.vogue.com/culture/article/david-hockneys-fresh-flowers/

Shaffer, M. (2011) Back to the Future with Peter Thiel, *National Review Online*, accessed 20/04/2011, http://www.nationalreview.com/articles/257531/back-future-peter-thiel-interview?page=3

Shanken, E. A. (2012) Investigatory art: Real-time systems and network culture, accessed 07/07/2013, http://www.necsus-ejms.org/investigatory-art-real-time-systems-and-network-culture/

Shaviro, S. (2011) 'The Actual Volcano: Whitehead, Harman and the Problem of Relations', in L. Bryant, N. Srnicek, and G. Harman (eds), *The Speculative Turn: Continental Materialism and Realism*, Melbourne: Re.Press.

Shirky, C. (2010) *Cognitive Surplus: Creativity and Generosity in a Connected Age*, London: Allen Lane.

Shunmugam, V. (2010) Financial markets regulation: The tipping point, retrieved from http://www.voxeu.org/index.php?q=node/5056

Simon, T. and Swartz, A. (2012a) Cultural Differences, accessed 02/12/2012, http://difference.theinfo.org/

—(2012b) Image Atlas, accessed 14/05/2013, http://www.newmuseum.org/exhibitions/view/taryn-simon-cultural-differences

Sloan, R. (2011) The New Aesthetic, accessed 05/04/2012, http://snarkmarket.com/2011/6913

Smith, R. (2007) In Galleries, a Nervy Opening Volley, *The New York Times*, accessed 06/07/2013, http://www.nytimes.com/2007/11/30/arts/design/30newm.html?pagewanted=all&_r=0

Söderberg, J. (2013) Means of production, *Le Monde Diplomatique*, accessed 02/07/2013, http://mondediplo.com/2013/03/10makers

Spacks, P. M. (1995) *Boredom: The Literary History of a State of Mind*, Chicago: University of Chicago Press.

Spiegel (2013) Snowden Claims: NSA Ties Put German Intelligence in Tight Spot, *Spiegel*, accessed 08/07/2013, http://www.spiegel.de/international/world/whistleblower-snowden-claims-german-intelligence-in-bed-with-nsa-a-909904.html

Stampoulis, T. (2010) Bank of Japan Workshop - Credit Value Adjustment Trends, retrieved 09/01/2011, http://www.boj.or.jp/en/type/release/adhoc10/data/fsc1006a3.pdf

Stanford (2012) Program on Liberation Technology, accessed 02/02/2012, http://liberationtechnology.stanford.edu/

Steiner, C. (2013) *Automate This: How Algorithms Came To Rule Our World*, London: Penguin.

Sterling, B. (2012a) An Essay on the New Aesthetic, *Wired*, accessed 05/04/2012, http://www.wired.com/beyond_the_beyond/2012/04/an-essay-on-the-new-aesthetic/

—(2012b) The Industrial Internet according to General Electric, *Wired*, accessed 01/12/2012, http://www.wired.com/beyond_the_beyond/2012/11/the-industrial-internet-according-to-general-electric/

Stiegler, B. (2010a) *Taking Care of Youth and the Generations*, London: Polity.

—(2010b) *For a New Critique of Political Economy*, Cambridge: Polity Press.

—(2011) *The Decadence of Industrial Democracies*, London: Polity.

—(n.d.) Anamnesis and Hypomnesis, accessed 06/05/2012, http://arsindustrialis.org/anamnesis-and-hypomnesis

SXSW (2012) The New Aesthetic: Seeing Like Digital Devices, *SXSW*, accessed 07/04/2012, http://schedule.sxsw.com/2012/events/event_IAP11102

Terrett, B. (2012) SXSW, the new aesthetic and commercial visual culture, accessed 07/04/2012, http://noisydecentgraphics.typepad.com/design/2012/03/sxsw-the-new-aesthetic-and-commercial-visual-culture.html

Thaler, R. H. and Sunstein, C. R. (2009) *Nudge: Improving Decisions About Health, Wealth and Happiness*, London: Penguin.

Thiele, L. P. (1997) 'Postmodernity and the Routinization of Novelty- Heidegger on Boredom and Technology', *Polity*, Vol. 29, No. 4 (Summer 1997), pp. 489–517.

Thomson, A. (2006) *Adorno: A Guide for the Perplexed*, London: Continuum.

Thomson, I. (2009) 'Understanding Technology Ontotheologically, or: The Danger and the Promise of Heidegger, an American Perspective, In Jan-Kyrre Berg Olsen, Evan Selinger, and Søren Riis (eds), *New Waves in the Philosophy of Technology*. New York: Palgrave Macmillan, pp. 146–66.

—(2011) Heidegger's Aesthetics, *Stanford Encyclopaedia of Philosophy*, accessed 05/04/2012, http://stanford.library.usyd.edu.au/archives/sum2011/entries/heidegger-aesthetics/

Thrift, N. (2006) 'Re-inventing Invention: New Tendencies in Capitalist Commodification', *Economy and Society*, Vol. 35, No. 2 (May 2006), p. 284.

Totsis, A. (2011) Twitter Is At 250 Million Tweets Per Day, iOS 5 Integration Made Signups Increase 3x, *TechCrunch*, accessed 02/12/2011, http://techcrunch.com/2011/10/17/twitter-is-at-250-million-tweets-per-day/

Tripp, S. (2005) From Utopianism to Weak Messianism: Electronic Culture's Spectral Moment, *Electronic Book Review*, accessed 12/09/2011, http://www.electronicbookreview.com/thread/technocapitalism/dot-edu

Tsukayama, H. (2012) FTC releases final privacy report, says 'Do Not Track' mechanism may be available by end of year, *Washington Post*, accessed 28/03/2012, http://www.washingtonpost.com/business/technology/ftc-releases-final-privacy-report-says-do-not-track-mechanism-may-be-available-by-end-of-year/2012/03/26/gIQAzi23bS_story.html

Tugend, A. (2012) Bad Habits? My Future Self Will Deal With That, accessed 04/03/2012, http://www.nytimes.com/2012/02/25/business/another-theory-on-why-bad-habits-are-hard-to-break-shortcuts.html?_r=3&pagewanted=all

Turnbull, N. (2009) 'Heidegger and Jünger on the 'significance of the century': technology as a theme in conservative thought', *Writing Technologies*, Vol. 2, No. 2, pp. 9–34.

Twitter (2010) Tweet Preservation, accessed 14/01/2013, https://blog.twitter.com/2010/tweet-preservation

—(2012) Search 'newaesthetic', Twitter, accessed 18/04/2012, self-updating, https://twitter.com/#!/search/newaesthetic

Ullman, E. (2011) *The Soul of a New Machine*, London: Little, Brown.

Valentino-Devries, J. and Gorman, S. (2013) Secret Court's Redefinition of 'Relevant' Empowered Vast NSA Data-Gathering, *Wall Street Journal*, accessed 09/07/2013, http://online.wsj.com/article_email/SB10001424127887323873904578571893758853344-lMyQjAxMTAzMDAwODEwNDgyWj.html

W3C (2012) Tracking Protection Working Group, accessed 14/03/2012, http://www.w3.org/2011/tracking-protection/

Waldrip-Fruin (2009) *Expressive Processing: Digital Fictions, Computer Games, and Software Studies*, London: MIT Press.

Wauters, R. (2012) 427 Million Europeans are Now Online, 37% Uses More than One Device: IAB, *The Next Web*, 31 May 2012, http://thenextweb.com/eu/2012/05/31/427-million-europeans-are-now-online-37-uses-more-than-one-device-iab/

Weber, S. (2005) *The Success of Open Source*, Boston: Harvard University Press.

Weiner, L. R. (1994) *Digital Woes*, New York: Addison Wesley.

Weiser, M. (1991) The Computer for the 21st Century, *Scientific American*, accessed 18/04/2011, http://nano.xerox.com/hypertext/weiser/SciAmDraft3.html

Weizenbaum, J. (1984) *Computer Power and Human Reason: From Judgement to Calculation*, London: Penguin Books.

Wellman, B., Quan-Haase, A., Boase, J., Chen, W., Hampton, K., Isla de Diaz, I., and Miyata, K. (2003) 'The Social Affordances of the Internet for Networked Individualism', *Journal of Computer-Mediated Communication*, Vol. 8, No. 3 (April 2003), accessed 25/04/08, http://jcmc.indiana.edu/vol8/issue3/wellman.html

Wiedemann, C. and Zehle, S. (2012) *Depletion Design: A Glossary of Network Ecologies*, Amsterdam: Institute for Network Cultures.

Wiener, N. (1960) 'Some Moral and Technical Consequences of Automaton', *Science*, Vol. 131, No. 3410 (6 May 1960), pp. 1355–58.

Wiggershaus, R. (1994) *The Frankfurt School: Its History, Theory and Political Significance*, London: Polity Press.

—(1995) *The Frankfurt School: Its History, Theory and Political Significance*, London: Polity Press.

Williford, J. (2011) Graphing Culture, *Humanities Magazine*, March/April 2011, accessed 16/09/2011, http://www.neh.gov/news/humanities/2011-03/Graphing.html

Wing, J. (2011) Research Notebook: Computational Thinking—What and Why?, accessed 16/09/2011, http://link.cs.cmu.edu/article.php?a=600

Winograd, T. and Flores, F. (1987) *Understanding Computers and Cognition: A New Foundation for Design*, London: Addison Wesley.

Wolfram, S. (2012) The Personal Analytics of My Life, accessed 09/03/2012, http://blog.stephenwolfram.com/2012/03/the-personal-analytics-of-my-life/

Yarrow, J. (2011) CHART OF THE DAY: Here's How Much a Unique Visitor is Worth, *Business Insider*, accessed 02/03/2012, http://www.businessinsider.com/chart-of-the-day-revenue-per-unique-visitor-2011-1

Yuill, S. (2008) All Problems of Notation Will be Solved by the Masses: Free Open Form Performance, Free/Libre Open Source Software, and Distributive Practice, accessed 07/05/2013, http://www.lipparosa.org/essays/problemsofnotation.pdf

Zax, D. (2011) You Can't Keep Your Secrets From Twitter, *Fast Company*, accessed 28/03/2011, http://www.fastcompany.com/1769217/there-are-no-secrets-from-twitter

Zetter, K. (2010) Blockbuster Worm Aimed for Infrastructure, But No Proof Iran Nukes Were Target, *Wired*, accessed 02/03/2012, http://www.wired.com/threatlevel/2010/09/stuxnet/

—(2011) Report Strengthens Suspicions That Stuxnet Sabotaged Iran's Nuclear Plant, *Wired*, accessed 02/03/2012, http://www.wired.com/ threatlevel/2010/12/isis-report-on-stuxnet/
—(2012) DuQu Mystery Language Solved With the Help of Crowdsourcing, *Wired*, accessed 19/03/2012, http://www.wired.com/threatlevel/2012/03/duqu-mystery-language-solved
Zhu, S. H. and Pykhtin, M. (2007) A Guide to Modeling Counterparty Credit Risk, *GARP Risk Review*, July/August 2007, retrieved 21/01/2011, http://ssrn.com/ abstract=1032522

Index

Lightning Source UK Ltd.
Milton Keynes UK
UKOW06f0515291015

261584UK00009B/201/P